W9-ADK-033

ILLINOIS CENTRAL COLLEGE   2

A12901 484629

WITHDRAWN

Age Discrimination in the American Workplace

Age Discrimination in the American Workplace

Old at a Young Age

RAYMOND F. GREGORY

WITHDRAWN

I. C. C. LIBRARY

RUTGERS UNIVERSITY PRESS
New Brunswick, New Jersey, and London

KF
3465
.G74
2001

Library of Congress Cataloging-in-Publication Data

Gregory, Raymond, F., 1927–
    Age discrimination in the American workplace : old at a young age /
Raymond F. Gregory.
        p. cm.
    Includes bibliographical references and index.
    ISBN 0–8135–2906–9 (cloth : alk. paper)
    1. Age discrimination in employment—Law and legislation—United States. I. Title.

KF3465 .G74 2001
344.7301'394'09—dc21

                                                                00–062538

British Cataloging-in-Publication data for this book is available from the British Library.

Copyright © 2001 by Raymond F. Gregory
All rights reserved
No part of this book may be reproduced or utilized in any form or by any means, electronic or mechanical, or by any information storage or retrieval system, without written permission from the publisher. Please contact Rutgers University Press, 100 Joyce Kilmer Avenue, Piscataway, NJ 08854–8099. The only exception to this prohibition is "fair use" as defined by U.S. copyright law.

Manufactured in the United States of America

For
Mary,
Raymond, Pamela, George,
John, Dawn,
Emma, Alanna, George II,
and all future additions

Contents

Age Discrimination in the American Workplace

Introduction

The Older Worker in Today's Workplace

Discrimination against middle-aged and older workers has long been a common practice of American business firms. Nearly all middle-aged and older workers, at some time during their work careers, will suffer the consequences of an age-biased employment-related action. Although the law bars age discrimination in the workplace, middle-aged and older workers are nevertheless subjected to adverse employment decisions motivated by false, stereotypical notions concerning the physical and mental abilities of older workers. As a consequence, these workers are routinely ushered into earlier than planned retirements, are denied promotions or terminated, or are otherwise adversely affected by decisions based on their age.

In recent years, worker opposition to these discriminatory practices has engendered an explosion of litigation in the federal and state courts, but the full extent of worker opposition to employer age discriminatory conduct is just beginning to unfold. The baby-boomer generation now accounts for more than seventy million workers in the U.S. workplace, or just under 50 percent of the entire workforce. A substantial portion of this generation already has passed the age that provides them with the protections of the federal laws against acts of age discrimination. By the year 2006, the entire baby-boomer generation will fall within those protections. A vast army of workers stands ready to contest employer acts of age discrimination.

It appears likely that the baby-boomer-generation workers may be more disposed than their predecessors to oppose age discriminatory conduct. This generation of workers is the best educated in history, and, typically, the better-educated workers resolve to remain on the job longer, deferring retirement for as long as possible. But the business world favors early retirement over extended workplace participation. Thus, the stage is set for a massive collision of interests—the interests of an expanding group of older workers to remain in the workforce and the interests of their employers to replace them with younger, lower-paid workers.

As worker opposition to age-biased conduct develops, all Americans must remain fully alert to the legal rights of our older citizens, if for no other reason than that each of us, if we live to middle or old age, will eventually find ourselves in circumstances requiring the protection of the laws barring age discrimination. But U.S. workers are generally unaware of the rights afforded them by the federal and state age discrimination laws. Indeed, the average American worker knows little if anything about age discrimination. Until the worker actually experiences an age-biased act, age discrimination remains a non-issue for him. But even when he is subjected to acts of age bias, the worker may fail to recognize his employer's conduct to be unlawful or may remain oblivious to the legal protections afforded him against acts of age discrimination.

Typically, an older worker subjected to a workplace decision materially affecting her employment status fails to attribute her employer's conduct to age bias. But if, over time, her job status continues to be undermined, eventually, age discrimination will cross her mind. Then, for the first time, she considers the possibility that her advancing age has been a factor in the decisions adversely affecting her employment status. But every decision adverse to an older worker, even if eminently unfair, is not necessarily age motivated. Age discrimination and unfair treatment are distinct. But how may the worker make that distinction?

Before running off to a lawyer, the worker commonly wrestles with the problem while consulting with fellow workers, friends, and family members. Unfortunately, they are unlikely to be very helpful, since they also lack any specific knowledge of the laws protecting workers against age discrimination. They may attribute an illicit motive to conduct that in reality is merely unfair, or they may label conduct unfair when, in fact, it is unlawful. The worker, therefore, requires another source of information. He needs to know the types of employer conduct that the courts have declared to be discriminatory. He needs to know how other workers have responded to and dealt with age-biased conduct. He needs to know under what circumstances other older workers have charged their employers with age discrimination, and when those charges have been proven to be valid and when they have not. Until now, workers in those circumstances could not find an extended treatment of age discrimination written for them rather than for lawyers and other legal experts. This book fills that void.

Law students acquire knowledge of the law through the casebook method; they learn by reading reported court cases. This book uses a modification of the casebook method. The reader is presented with various real situations selected to provide a broad, general picture of how age discrimination appears in the workplace. By reviewing these case summaries, a worker should gain an understanding of the basic concepts underlying the law of age discrimination and acquire some facility in identifying age discriminatory conduct. The reader will then be equipped to determine when it is time to consult a lawyer and, in addition, will be prepared to assist his or her lawyer in developing a solid legal case for presentation in court.

This book has been written primarily for the layperson, not the lawyer. Every attempt has been made to eliminate technical language and legal jargon and to preclude immersion in legal intricacies and technical data having less than general application to age discriminatory conduct. In discussion of those areas of the law where some technical knowledge of the law of age discrimination is required, such as those related to the methods used by lawyers to prove age discriminatory conduct, emphasis has been placed on the general applicability of the law, without regard to exceptions to the law. The broad picture takes precedence over details that may be relevant to only a limited number of instances.

Throughout the book, the word "worker" has generally been used instead of "employee" to avoid the confusion that might result from the words "employer" and "employee" appearing too often or too close together. The reader should understand "worker" to refer to the entry-level worker, unskilled worker, skilled and professional worker, CEO, and any other worker of every sort and type.

Many age discrimination cases are settled before trial—some even during trial—and the defendant-employer usually demands that the terms of the settlement remain confidential to the parties and not be disclosed. Employers also frequently require the plaintiff-worker and his or her attorney to agree not to discuss the case with others or to later disparage the employer. Rather than submit my clients to the risk of being charged with violating these settlement provisions, I have resorted in some of the cases related in the book to using fictitious names for my client and the employer.

The Age Discrimination in Employment Act, enacted by Congress in 1967, was intended to eradicate age discrimination from the American workplace. Congress's intent has not been fulfilled. The law has accomplished much, but age discrimination remains a scourge in the workplace. Ultimately, age discrimination will be eradicated only if American workers steadfastly challenge their employers' acts of age discrimination. This book has been written to encourage workers to commit themselves to undertaking that challenge.

1 | Age Discrimination and the Arrival of the Baby-Boomer Generation at Middle Age

Employers commonly make decisions affecting older workers that assume these workers are no longer capable of performing adequately. Older workers are thus subjected to adverse employment decisions, motivated by false and stereotypical notions relating to age, without regard to the actual state of their physical or mental capabilities.

Older workers confront employment problems of two sorts. One older worker may experience difficulties in performing job responsibilities because of actual deterioration in physical or mental ability. Another may work for an employer who assumes the worker has suffered physical or mental deterioration even if, in fact, this is not the case. Employers readily assume that physical and mental deterioration occurs concurrently with advancing age, in view of the fact that it is far less expensive to act on that assumption than it is to test the general capability and work proficiency of each of their older workers.

Age closes doors. It severely limits the range of employment options available to the older worker. An older worker may reach the highest point in her career and feel she has more to offer her employer than at any previous time in her life and yet find that her age presents a formidable barrier to any further advancement. The position to which she may aspire will more likely be awarded to a much younger person lacking the experience and, probably, the enthusiasm and dedication of the older worker. The younger worker has only her youth to recommend her, but that will prove more than sufficient. She will be awarded the promotion, while the older woman will remain in her present position. A year later the older worker may be downsized or forced into retirement on some pretext. Her chances then of finding another position are practically nil, and she will remain in retirement, like it or not.

Until the 1950s, age bias occurring in the workplace was not a matter addressed by the laws of most states, and it was not until 1967 that Congress recognized that *ageism* was outdated and irreconcilable with civilized society and American cultural values. In that year, Congress passed and President Lyndon B. Johnson signed into law the Age Discrimination in Employment Act (ADEA).[1] Simply stated, the new law encouraged Americans to refrain from the adverse treatment of older workers—then defined as workers falling into the age group forty to sixty-five—and made it unlawful for an employer to permit a worker's age to influence employment decisions.

In enacting the ADEA, Congress and the president reacted to rampant age discrimination in the workplace, then perceived as a national disgrace. The *Congressional Record* reflects the view prevalent at the time that employer insistence upon compulsory retirement of older workers—the opposition to which was one of the driving forces behind enactment of the statute—was simply outdated and inconsistent with the viewpoint of Americans in general:

> The view that a man or a woman is so old at 65 as to warrant compulsory retirement from industry stems from an era before the turn of the century and comes to us from a period when life expectancy was about half of the life expectancy of Americans . . . at the present time. . . . In fact,

today they are not as old at 65 in thought, action, physical and mental ability as men and women . . . were at the
age of 40 in the 1880s. Yet, for some reason or other, we
Americans have adhered to this view of 65 being the proper
age for retirement notwithstanding the fact that this concept is today as outdated and outmoded as are flint-lock
muskets and candle dips of the 18th century.[2]

Congress intended the ADEA to end compulsory retirement
and eradicate other age-related acts affecting the employment
relationship. The ADEA has failed to fulfill this role, since to
this day discrimination against older workers remains a national
disgrace. The methods used to discriminate have changed; the
results have not. Downsizing and early retirement plans eliminate older workers from the workplace with the same dispatch
as coerced retirements and massive layoffs formerly accomplished.

Reemployment is not a likely prospect for the older worker
who has been downsized or forced into early retirement. Any
unemployed person attempting reentry into the labor market
does so from a weakened position, because the stigma of dismissal, whatever the circumstances, remains a negative force
militating against a return to the workplace. Surmounting this
obstacle, however, is far more difficult for the older worker. Today, a man in his fifties who loses his job faces lifestyle changes
of calamitous proportions. For a woman, the calamity may occur when she reaches her late forties, and sometimes even earlier. The older the terminated worker, the more likely he or she
will remain unemployed, and thus the discharge of an older
worker is fittingly described as the "industrial equivalent of capi-
tal punishment."[3] The fate of the terminated older worker is
so well documented that one wonders how an employer, in good
conscience, can terminate an older worker without first fully
exploring every conceivable alternative to dismissal.

Morally, it has been argued, the longer a worker remains
with an employer, the greater the loyalty owed to that worker
by the employer. As a worker grows older, with each passing

year he becomes less employable elsewhere. Therefore, as the term of the employment relationship lengthens, the employer's moral commitment to the worker increases. As Willie Loman says in *Death of a Salesman,* "You can't eat the orange and throw away the peel—a man is not a piece of fruit." Under the law, however, the employer is not bound to any such commitment. Rather, the employment-at-will doctrine allows the employer to fire an employee regardless of length of service without violating the law.

The general acceptance of the employment-at-will doctrine in this country places the United States virtually alone among Western industrialized nations in failing to provide workers with protection against unjust discharge. A classic statement of the doctrine was made by the Tennessee Supreme Court more than one hundred years ago in an 1884 decision: "All may dismiss their employees at will, be they few or many, for good cause, for no cause, or even for cause morally wrong, without being thereby guilty of legal wrong."[4]

Most Americans believe it is morally indefensible for an employer to fire a long-term older worker without reason. Consequently, most states have adopted some legislative and judicially created limitations to the employment-at-will doctrine, but nevertheless to this day the doctrine is generally applicable across the country. Unless you work in Montana—whose statute prohibits employers from discharging employees without good cause[5]—the law of the state in which you work will afford you little or no protection against your employer if you are fired, even if you have done nothing to warrant dismissal.

Except for union and civil service employees, "wrongful discharge" has little or no meaning for the worker. Nearly all union-management collective bargaining agreements and state and municipal civil service laws and rules prohibit dismissal of an employee without good cause. However, if you are not a union, state, or municipal employee, and you do not have a contract of employment for a specified period of time, your employer may fire you at any time for a good reason, a bad reason, or no reason at all, and you generally have no recourse against your employer unless your discharge constitutes a discriminatory act under federal or state law.

Regardless of the circumstances, dismissed workers rarely admit that their terminations are justifiable, and they frequently seek legal remedies for what they perceive to be unlawful acts on the part of their employers. They soon learn, however, that the employment-at-will doctrine does not provide them with a legal remedy. They then turn to the discrimination statutes, and here, some workers find a source for hope. If a worker is able to prove that his discharge was based upon or motivated by his race, color, sex, national origin, religion, disability, or age, he may recover monetary damages or attain other forms of relief against his employer. He may even be able to force his employer to rehire him. But probably fewer than one in ten of those dismissed are able to garner evidence of discrimination sufficient to file a claim against his or her employer. Nonetheless, in the past twenty years, federal and state courts, the Equal Employment Opportunity Commission (EEOC), and various state fair-employment-practices agencies have been inundated with employment discrimination cases. Between 1970 and 1989, the number of filings of employment discrimination cases in the federal courts increased almost 2,200 percent, while all other types of cases rose 125 percent. Not least among these job discrimination cases were those advancing allegations of age discrimination. While the number of race, sex, and other discrimination cases is not expected to rise significantly in the near term, a massive increase in age cases appears to be on the horizon.

As our population grows older—as it is now doing—the incidence of acts of age discrimination inevitably will rise. More than eighty million Americans now living were born during the two decades following World War II. The baby-boomer generation, far more numerous than any generation either preceding or following it, will be the largest constituent of a population growing increasingly older over the next twenty-five to thirty years.[6] The oldest baby boomers—those who turned fifty in 1996—will be fifty-five in 2001 and sixty-five in 2011.

Even before the boomer generation reached middle age, the populace was growing older. By 1983, the number of Americans over sixty-five exceeded all the teenagers in the country, and it is estimated that by 2025, Americans over sixty-five will outnumber teenagers by a two-to-one margin.[7] Emphasis on better health care, diet, and lifestyle has increased life expectancy from age forty-nine in 1900 to age seventy-six today. Americans now reaching their sixty-fifth birthday can reasonably expect to live into their eighties. The number of Americans age seventy-five and older has also grown swiftly, from ten million in 1980 to nearly fifteen million in 1998.[8]

In 1995, just over 12 percent of the population was sixty-five or over. In that same year, nearly 19 percent of the people living in Florida were included in that age group, the highest senior citizen ratio in the country. By 2025, the sixty-five and over group will constitute more than 18 percent, not just of Florida's residents, but of the entire nation. As expressed by Peter G. Peterson, former secretary of commerce, by 2025 "America, in effect, will become a nation of Floridas."[9]

Boomer generation workers now number more than seventy million, or 49 percent of the entire workforce. In 2006, the youngest boomers will turn forty, and all boomers then will be protected by the age discrimination prohibitions of the ADEA. With the mere passage of time, the potential increase in the number of ADEA claimants is enormous.

Because boomers tend to view themselves as young, they, more likely than their predecessors, will react aggressively to perceived acts of age discrimination. As the baby boomers pass into middle age and grow more aware of the pernicious role of age in workplace decisions, the number of age discrimination claims will escalate and the courts will be inundated by a deluge of these claims. Unless U.S. employers dramatically alter their perception and treatment of older workers in the workplace, a crisis of unequaled proportions will confront our court system.

Yet another phenomenon will add to this crisis. At present, the proportion of men age sixty-five and older who remain in the labor force in Europe varies from 3 to 5 percent, but in Japan the rate is 37 percent.[10] Currently in this country, nearly 20 percent of male college graduates over sixty-five continue to work, while less than 10 percent of workers that age without a high school diploma remain in the workforce.[11] The better educated—those more likely to have professional, technical, and managerial positions—find their work more meaningful and enjoyable and thus have less reason or desire to accept retirement. Members of the boomer generation, one of the best educated in history, are more likely to want to remain longer in the workforce.

The rate of participation of older women in the workplace has already risen, steadily increasing since the mid-1980s. Seventy-four percent of female workers in age group forty-five to fifty-four remained on the job in 1995, and by 2005, it is projected that those remaining in the workforce will increase to 80 percent. Similarly, 49 percent of female workers in age group fifty-five to sixty-four were still working in 1995, and this figure is expected to grow to 56 percent by 2005.[12] As better-educated female boomers move into these age brackets, the participation of older women in the workplace will increase even more. It is likely that members of the age sixty-five and over group, both male and female, also will wish to extend their work lives, greatly adding to the number of potential age discrimination claimants.

Americans can effectively deal with the forthcoming litigation crisis by reducing the incidence of acts of age discrimination in the workplace, but the nation's experience with the ADEA over the past thirty-five years portends that this probably will not occur. Employer acceptance of the concept of continued employment for workers over the age of sixty-five would greatly contribute to the resolution of another problem currently confronting the American public—the looming bankruptcy of the Social Security system. As noted, in 1995, more than 12 percent of the population was sixty-five or older. By 2030, this group will comprise more than 20 percent of the population. Between 1995 and 2030, the twenty-five to sixty-four population group will decrease from just under 52 percent to approximately

47 percent of the total population.[13] Thus, if Americans continue to retire at age sixty-five, the ratio of the potential number of workers in the labor force—those contributing to the system through payroll deductions—to those in retirement will gradually decrease and, if the trend is permitted to continue, will bankrupt the Social Security system. But the Social Security system is keyed to retirement; to receive benefits, a worker must leave the job. Obviously, retirement at age sixty-five is no longer an acceptable social policy. In order to maintain Social Security benefits at their present levels, the system must be amended to encourage longer labor force participation. In fact, Congress already has acted to solve the problem, at least in part, by gradually raising the normal retirement age, beginning in 2003, until it reaches age sixty-seven in 2027. In addition, beginning January 1, 2000, the annual earnings limitation was eliminated. Workers between ages sixty-five and seventy are no longer subject to a reduction of Social Security benefits because their earnings exceed specified levels.

Longer participation in the workforce is clearly conceivable as more Americans reach postnormal retirement ages—their late sixties and seventies—still in good health. But the trend has been in the opposite direction because the business world clearly favors early retirement over longer workplace participation. Until now, the growth in the older population has been accompanied by a decline in workforce participation resulting from a general tendency to retire earlier rather than later. Nearly 84 percent of American workers retire before they reach sixty-five. The median retirement age is sixty-one.[14] Only 16 percent of male workers work past age sixty-five and a mere 8 percent past seventy.[15]

In 1990, the Commonwealth Fund conducted a study that found that nearly two million retirees were willing to return to work and were physically and mentally capable of returning. Fifty-seven percent of those retirees, however, had made no attempt to return to the workplace because they believed no suitable jobs were available for them or that the business world perceived them as "too old."[16]

Although the booming economy of the late 1990s resulted in a substantially reduced unemployment rate and the creation of labor shortages in some areas, employer attitudes toward the retention of older workers appear not to have materially changed. Without a basic change in attitude, employer perceptions pertaining to age will continue to plague those of our older population who wish to continue working.

Workplace decisions based on age clearly are discriminatory and unlawful. Until now, little information about age discrimination has been generally available for the public, and most workers are unaware of their legal rights when they receive a notice of dismissal. They have no answers for the questions that occur to them at that time. What is age discrimination? Are employers who resort to exerting subtle pressures upon older workers to retire guilty of age discrimination? When are early-retirement plans discriminatory? Are the laws barring age discrimination effective? How are they enforced?

Those are some of the subjects to be explored in the remainder of this book. In chapter 2, we will examine the role of age stereotypes in employment decisions affecting older workers. Chapters 3, 4, and 5 will be devoted to a review of age discrimination in reductions-in-force and early-retirement plans, and chapters 6 and 7 to the ways older workers have been discriminated against at various stages of working life, from hiring through dismissal. Employer retaliation against workers claiming age discrimination is the subject of chapter 8, and discrimination against older women is the topic of discussion in chapter 9. Various issues that surface in the litigation of an age discrimination suit will be analyzed in chapters 10 through 13, and the roles played in these proceedings by the courts, the EEOC, arbitrators, attorneys, and older workers are considered in chapters 14 through 18. Recommendations for changes in the ADEA and its enforcement are discussed in chapter 19, and, finally, prospects for the future are considered in the conclusion.

For more than thirty-five years, I have been engaged as an attorney in advising and assisting victims of discrimination in the workplace. In the years immediately following the enactment of the ADEA in 1967, older workers appeared reluctant to file age claims, but eventually, growing numbers of older workers have sought legal recourse for what they perceive as age bias. Many of my clients have been dismissed in corporate downsizings, and others have been coerced into accepting early retirement packages. Still others have been fired for reasons bordering on the absurd.

Typically, the period immediately following a job loss by an older worker is one of grief, denial, and depression. The older worker's loss of self-esteem and self-identity frequently is far more devastating than the economic strain resulting from the loss of his or her job. More often than not, my older clients have been unable to find alternative employment, and thus a dismissal at that stage of life quickly evolved into a life-shattering event, affecting not only the dismissed worker but also his or her entire family. My clients have attested to the pain of the older worker who confronts the prospect of never working again. The stories of some of those clients and of other workers are related in this book. Their stories graphically illustrate the obstacles and anguish facing older workers who confront their employers and take a stand against acts of age discrimination.

Just about every worker, at one time or another, has been or will be affected by an employment decision made on the basis of his or her age. Age discrimination in the workplace is nearly universal. Acts of age discrimination, however, are generally quite subtle and difficult to detect. Since workers are often unaware that age bias has been a moving force in their lives, many discriminatory acts have not been addressed in a legal forum. Recent surveys confirm that the number of older workers suffering age discrimination far exceeds the number who actually file claims against their employers.[17]

Workers' lawsuits have successfully addressed the more extreme forms of age discrimination, but lawsuits involving more subtle and less apparent forms have not fared as well in the courts. Regardless of its form, age discrimination must be vigorously contested if the laws barring age bias in the workplace are to be properly enforced.

Ignorance of the law and a general feeling of futility about becoming involved in complex legal proceedings undoubtedly contribute to older workers' reluctance to challenge acts of age discrimination. Employers, of course, are well aware of this attitude. Thus, workers themselves inadvertently encourage discriminatory practices. Until older workers become committed to opposing age discrimination in all its forms, it will remain prevalent in the workplace.

2 | Age Stereotypes and Employment Discrimination

The first legislative action outlawing age discrimination in the workplace was undertaken in Colorado in 1903. Over the next fifty years, a few states followed suit, such as Massachusetts in 1937, but it was not until the 1950s and 1960s that a broad-based movement developed in state legislatures to afford these protections to older workers. In 1958, age was added to the New York statute barring discrimination in employment, and similar statutes were adopted in Connecticut and Wisconsin (1959), in California, Ohio, and Washington (1961), in New Jersey (1962), and in Michigan and Indiana (1965).[1] With the 1997 enactment of an age statute in Alabama, every state now offers protection against workplace discrimination to the older worker.

Enactment of federal legislation barring age discrimination lagged behind because initially these protections lacked broad public support. It has been suggested that other programs for the elderly, such as Social Security, Medicare, and Medicaid, offered little cause for controversy and invited little public opposition because these laws also benefited the children of the elderly, who might otherwise be forced to assume the burden of their parents' retirement and medical costs. Laws barring age

discrimination less directly benefit the young. In fact, on occasion younger workers are affected adversely, as statutory protections against age discrimination may result in more jobs held
by older workers and, in turn, fewer jobs available for their
younger colleagues.[2]

Title VII of the Civil Rights Act of 1964—the first major
step undertaken on the federal level to bar employers from discriminating against their employees—prohibits discrimination
in the workplace based upon race, color, religion, sex, or national origin.[3] When the legislation was first proposed, Congress
had also included age in the bill's protections, but it was later
excluded. The final version of the legislation, however, directed
the secretary of labor to "make a full and complete study" of
the factors underlying age discrimination in employment and
its consequences to older workers and to the economy.

One year later, Secretary of Labor W. Willard Wirtz submitted his report to Congress, setting forth five basic conclusions:

1. Many employers adopt specific age limits upon those they
   will employ.
2. These age limitations markedly affect the rights and opportunities of older workers.
3. Although age discrimination rarely is based on the sort of
   animus that motivates racial, national origin, or religious
   discrimination, it is based upon stereotypical assumptions
   of the abilities of the aged, unsupported by objective facts.
4. The evidence available at the time showed that the arbitrary
   removal of older workers from the workplace was generally
   unfounded, and that, overall, the performance of the older
   worker was at least as good as that of the younger worker.
5. Age discrimination is profoundly harmful in that it deprives
   the national economy of the productive labor of millions
   of workers and substantially increases the costs of both unemployment insurance and Social Security benefits, and it
   inflicts economic and psychological injury upon workers
   deprived of the opportunity to engage in productive and sat-
   isfying occupations.[4]

Wirtz's study focused primarily on the common employer practice of setting age limits in the hiring process. Previous studies had shown that approximately 50 percent of all job openings were closed to applicants over age fifty-five, and even workers as young as forty-five were barred from 25 percent of those positions.[5] Thus, the original impetus for the enactment of a federal statute barring age discrimination in employment emerged from discriminatory hiring practices prevalent in the business world rather than from discriminatory terminations or retirements of older workers.

A congressional committee studying the problem of age bias in the workplace later concurred in Wirtz's findings, affirming his conclusions that employers generally operated under false assumptions regarding the effects of aging in older workers, that these assumptions led to the common usage of age barriers in the hiring process and, consequently, that a disproportionate number of older workers were among the unemployed. Testimony before the committee described age discrimination as "inhuman," "unjust," and "cruel," and at the root of the high national unemployment rates.[6]

Congress then drafted and adopted the Age Discrimination in Employment Act, and President Johnson signed the law on December 16, 1967, to become effective June 12, 1968. The newly adopted ADEA joined Title VII of the Civil Rights Act of 1964 in Congress's continuing effort to eradicate discrimination in the workplace. Both laws reflect, as the Supreme Court later noted, "societal condemnation of invidious bias in employment decisions."[7]

The preamble to the ADEA emphasizes the individual as well as the social costs of age discrimination in employment. The act confirmed the secretary of labor's findings that employers had commonly established age limits for the hiring and retention of employees, regardless of their potential for job performance, and that older workers found themselves materially disadvantaged in preserving their employment status and, more particularly, in regaining employment after having been displaced. The act was intended to promote employment opportunities for older workers by requiring employer decisions affecting job status to be based upon the capability of the individual worker rather than upon his or her age.

The language Congress used in the ADEA to define unlawful age discrimination is simple and direct:

> It shall be unlawful for an employer—
> (1) to fail to hire or to discharge any individual or otherwise discriminate against any individual with respect to his compensation, terms, conditions, or privileges of employment, because of such individual's age;
> (2) to limit, segregate, or classify its employees in any way which would deprive or tend to deprive any individual of employment opportunities or otherwise adversely affect his status as an employee, because of such individual's age; or
> (3) to reduce the wage rate of any employee in order to comply with this [Act].[8]

The ADEA makes it illegal for an employer to refuse to hire, fire, or take any other adverse action against a worker because of his or her age.

While barring employers from engaging in unlawful acts of age discrimination, Congress also made certain that the ADEA permitted them to use neutral criteria, not directly dependent on age, in employment decisions affecting older workers.[9] Regardless of age, a worker may always be dismissed for inadequate or poor job performance. Even decisions based on age may be justified where age is a bona fide occupational qualification, such as in positions affecting public safety. Airline pilots, the police, and firefighters fall into that category.

Since 1967, Congress has amended the ADEA on several occasions, each amendment expanding the scope of the act while reaffirming the basic goal of retaining older people in the labor force. The original act did not apply to the federal government or to the states or their political subdivisions. In 1973, a Senate committee declared that these gaps in coverage were serious as "there is . . . evidence that, like the corporate world, government managers also create an environment where young is sometimes better than old."[10] Congress recognized another serious gap in ADEA coverage in that the act failed to bar age discriminatory acts of employers having fewer than twenty-five employees. In 1974, Congress eliminated the first gap by extending coverage of the law to federal, state, and local governments and partly filled the second gap by excluding from the law's coverage only those employers with fewer than twenty workers.

As originally proposed, the law was designed to bar discrimination against workers age forty-five to sixty-five. Before enactment of the law, Congress changed the lower limit to forty, since the evidence submitted to it tended to show that forty was the age at which discrimination began to be observable. The upper age limit, however, was not changed. Therefore, as originally enacted, the statute benefited the middle-aged but not the aged. Workers over sixty-five were not protected by the act and could still be forced into retirement. Consequently, even after enactment of the legislation, mandatory retirement remained a common occurrence for workers over sixty-five.

Public opinion polls, however, had shown for some time that the mandatory retirement of sixty-five-year-olds was not popular, as most of the populace felt that workers capable of continued performance on the job should not be forced into retirement.[11] Accordingly, in 1978, Congress raised the ADEA's upper age limit to seventy. In 1986, however, Congress decided that forced retirement at age seventy was no more defensible than forced retirement at age sixty-five. Moreover, it recognized that mandatory retirement at any age was detrimental to the Social Security system and that the retention of experienced and highly skilled workers in the labor force benefited the national economy. At that point, the upper age limit was deleted from the law, and the long history of legally sanctioned mandatory retirement came to an end.

Through these amendments, Congress converted the ADEA from a statute affording age bias protection for the middle-aged to a statute providing protections for the aged worker as well. A worker age seventy-five still capable of performing his job functions cannot be fired or forced into retirement merely because of his age. The amendments outlawing mandatory retirement also reflect a shift in national priorities, from emphasizing the hiring of older workers to preserving job security for workers forty and over.

Since 1967, the ADEA has developed into a significant factor in the American workplace and, concurrently, has become a major source of litigation in the federal courts.[12]   In courts throughout the country, the ADEA quickly dominated and surpassed previously adopted state statutes barring age discrimination. For age complainants, the ADEA has become the law of choice. Whether the law has performed as the lawmakers originally intended is a matter that will be examined later at some length. First, we must consider the arena in which the law is applied—the workplace—and the effects of age bias suffered by older workers.

The Wirtz report defined age discrimination as the rejection of an older worker on account of assumptions about the effect of age on the worker's ability to perform *"when there is in fact no basis for these assumptions"* (my emphasis).[13] Age discrimination, therefore, is based on false assumptions or, to put it more bluntly, on ignorance. In most instances, age does not set off one group against another. Age discrimination is not seated in aversion, hatred, or intolerance of the older worker. In that regard, it differs from discrimination on account of race, sex, or national origin. Further, the basis of age discrimination is not a discreet and immutable characteristic of the person. A person born black remains a black; a person born a woman remains a woman; and a person born Hispanic remains Hispanic. Race, sex, and national origin are settled at birth. But we all age, and thus age discrimination is based on a relative rather than an unchanging characteristic of the worker.

Age discrimination—again, different from all other forms of unlawful employment discrimination—is based on inaccurate data. While emotion, prejudice, or hatred generally underlie race, national origin, and (sometimes) sex discrimination, the sources of age discrimination are inaccurate, stereotypical conceptions of the abilities of older workers in general. Unjustified views of the diminished abilities of older workers coalesce or merge into stereotypical beliefs that form the basis for employer decisions affecting older workers.

Many of the negative stereotypes attributed to older workers appear to have developed before World War II, at a time when industry attempted to improve production efficiency. An increase in the speed of work was thought to increase stress in the worker, and this led to the assumption that worker productivity inevitably declined with age. Gaining wide acceptance, this assumption was used to justify age limitations on hiring, mass dismissals of middle-aged workers, and mandatory retirement of older workers.

Stereotypical preconceptions that have persisted over the years consign to all older workers of a particular age the physical and mental characteristics perceived to be those of the average worker of that age. Age-stereotypical thinking fails to distinguish between the physical and mental capabilities of an individual older worker and those viewed as common among members of the same age group. The fundamental philosophical underpinning of the ADEA requires acceptance of the principle that the process of psychological and physiological degeneration caused by aging varies from individual to individual, and as a consequence, age stereotyping in the workplace has no basis in fact, is pernicious, and must be rejected.

Since the enactment of the ADEA, the Supreme Court in its decisions relating to age discrimination has repeatedly affirmed that "it is the very essence of age discrimination for an older employee to be fired because the employer believes that productivity and competence decline with age."[14]

Federal court of appeals judge Richard A. Posner has written: "To some, age stereotyping is every bit as vicious as racial stereotyping. The concern is that if everybody is believed to age, this might be thought to imply that every old person is less competent intellectually than an otherwise similar young person. That would indeed be false."[15] False though it may be, such thinking still pervades the workplace.

Stereotypical thinking is the child of "ageism," a term generally credited to Dr. Robert Butler, counted among the country's most influential gerontologists and a pioneering authority on aging. Ageism leads to a wholly distorted view of the aged. According to Butler, an ageist's typical perceptions of the elderly include the following:

> An older person thinks and moves slowly. He does not think as he used to or as creatively. He is bound to himself and can no longer change or grow. He can learn neither well nor swiftly and even if he could, he would not wish to. Tied to his personal traditions and growing conservatism, he dislikes innovations and is not disposed to new ideas. Not only can he not move forward, he often moves backward. He enters a second childhood, caught up in increasing egocentricity and demanding more from his environment than he is willing to give to it. Sometimes he becomes an intensification of himself, a caricature of a lifelong personality. He becomes irritable and cantankerous, yet shallow and enfeebled. He lives in the past, he is behind the times. He is aimless and wandering of mind, reminiscing and garrulous. Indeed, he is a study in decline, the picture of mental and physical failure. He has lost and cannot replace friends, spouse, job, status, power, influence, income. He is often stricken by diseases which, in turn, restrict his movement, his enjoyment of food, the pleasures of well being. He has lost his desire and capacity for sex. His body shrinks, and so too does the flow of blood to his brain. His mind does not utilize oxygen and sugar at the same rate as formerly. Feeble, uninteresting, he awaits his death, a burden to society, to his family, and to himself.[16]

An employer with this view of the elderly and of his older workers is undoubtedly surrounded by youthful employees.

Employer bias against older workers emerges from these ageist concepts. Employers discriminating against older workers are motivated by assumptions as to the worker's utility to the company, and too often these assumptions misconstrue the relationship of advancing age to the capability of the worker. Negative employer perceptions of aging are expressed in these common stereotypes:

1. Older workers are stubborn, inflexible, resistant to change, and less likely to accept new technology.
2. Older workers are less productive than younger workers.
3. Older workers are less adaptable, and as they are slow learners, they find it more difficult to learn new skills.
4. Older workers are more difficult to retrain if their skills become obsolete.
5. The cost of employee benefits for the older workers are greater than those for the younger workers.
6. Older people are eager to retire at the earliest opportunity. They have an eye to retirement and merely want to ride out what remains of their careers.
7. Because their remaining tenure with the company will probably be short, it is economically unreasonable to invest in training older workers in new technologies and processes.

Along with stereotypical assumptions of the work capabilities of the older worker, some employers tend to accept inflated suppositions regarding the benefits of employing younger workers. For these employers, strength and vitality are concomitant only with youth. They believe that young workers are fresh, eager, highly motivated, and trainable, and that they arrive upon the work scene without preconceived notions and thus can readily be persuaded to accept direction. All too frequently, stereotypes and suppositions of this sort lead to employment decisions favoring the younger worker over the older. But is there any basis in fact to support these decisions?

Little evidence exists to support age stereotypes. The Commonwealth Fund report referred to earlier revealed no correlation between age and ability to perform, except in those jobs demanding strenuous physical labor.[17] Older workers consistently receive high ratings regarding job skills, loyalty, reliability, and lack of turnover and absenteeism. Other studies show that older workers who are continually challenged by their jobs demonstrate little or no decline in interest or motivation, that older workers are not resistant to change, and that they accept new technologies. Generally, the performance of older workers is at least as good as and sometimes better than that of younger workers.

The Wirtz report previously referred to found that 70 percent of those employers who set age limits for hiring did so without having any data to support a need for age limits. A recent AARP study disclosed that management decisions are often based on wholly subjective impressions regarding the cost of employing the older worker rather than on age-related cost studies.[18] In fact, the general claim that the costs of older workers' benefits are always greater than those for younger workers is simply not true. Given the disinclination of employers to investigate the facts or to reexamine the accuracy of their assumptions about older workers, it is not surprising that workplace decisions continue to be based on false data. Decisions based on factual data rather than on false suppositions would create an entirely different workplace in terms of workers' ages.

An early study showed that although a worker's job performance will eventually be affected by age, variations in performance among individuals actually increase with age, and thus age becomes a poorer predictor of performance as a person grows older.[19] Moreover, physiological and cognitive changes tend to occur at different times within the same individual, and the degree and rate of aging vary among individuals without regard to chronological age. As a group, the elderly appear to be more heterogeneous than homogeneous. In addition, people start to age from different levels of capability. Federal court of appeals judge Richard A. Posner, quoted earlier, has observed: "A 75-year-old who had outstanding capabilities when he was 30, and has aged slowly, not only may be immensely more capable than a 75-year-old who was mediocre at 30 and has aged rapidly, he may also . . . be more capable than a mediocre 30-year-old."[20] Gerontologists generally agree that most aspects of job performance vary significantly from individual to individual, without any strong correlation with age. Moreover, an individual's positive or negative image of aging may itself cause an increase or decrease in capability.

Although the older worker may experience a decline in capacity to perform some job functions, individual assessment of his capacity is required, since the worker still may be able to perform satisfactorily in his particular position. Thus, even where a lessening in capability in an older worker is noted, the employer is required to determine whether those particular capabilities are necessary for that worker's job responsibilities. Indeed, the Supreme Court has emphasized that the ADEA *commands* an employer to evaluate older workers individually, based on particular capability and not on age.[21] Employers who rely on individual assessment of employee capability banish stereotypes from their workplace.

Because ageism assumes the mental and physical deterioration of the older worker, it also is fixed upon age sixty-five as the normal age of retirement. Consequently, in this mindset, age sixty-five stands as a marker establishing the time when it becomes *necessary* for the older worker to depart from the workplace. As noted, this concept was clearly rejected with congressional amendments to the ADEA. In any event, age sixty-five is an artificial milestone, having no relevancy to the aging process, a milestone that was arbitrarily selected in Germany in 1889 when the first national retirement system was established. Our own Social Security Act also adopted age sixty-five as the age of retirement, but only as a result of a compromise. At the time, a retirement age of sixty would have made the program too costly and a retirement age of seventy would have eliminated almost everyone from the system's benefits, in view of the fact that life expectancy then stood at age sixty-two. As more Americans now reach their sixties, seventies, and eighties in good physical and mental health, age sixty-five, viewed as "the normal age for retirement," is an anomaly, a symbol of the past.

From one perspective, age discrimination is more insidious than discrimination by reason of race, national origin, or sex. People are more conscious of these latter biases but often are unaware of their age bias. Age stereotypes persist because people tend not to examine the basis for these stereotypes and also give disproportionate weight to any data they believe tend to support them. In this view, since we all eventually wear down, the perception that the elderly are all sick, weak, and less quick of mind is justified.

We also tend to correlate status with age—too old to get married; too young to die—and we rely upon age to pinpoint a person's attitude, behavior, and interests. Stereotyping may also be a product of the fear of aging, a fear that may muddle our views of the aged. A 1975 survey conducted by Louis Harris and Associates for the National Council on Aging found that a great majority of Americans agreed that most people over sixty-five are not physically active, are not open-minded or adaptable, and are not useful members of their communities.[22] Unfortunately, we bring these perceptions to the workplace and apply them to all workers over sixty-five.

Workers over the age of sixty-five, however, reject this view. A 1990 U.S. Department of Health and Human Services study showed that 80 percent of workers between ages sixty-five and sixty-eight reported they were not limited in the amount or kind of work they performed, and even among workers in age group sixty-nine to seventy-four, 78 percent stated they were not disadvantaged by their ages.[23]

In some respects, the responsibility for eliminating age stereotypes from the workplace is a task for younger workers, particularly those in supervisory positions. Since the younger worker himself will age, it seems a matter of self-interest to purge age bias from the work site before he also becomes vulnerable to stereotypical thinking. Regrettably, young supervisors all too frequently permit immediate company concerns to prevail, and if the employer's financial statement bottom line can be enhanced by reducing payroll through the elimination of high salaries of some of the older workers, the bottom line often takes precedence over the duty to exclude age bias from workplace decisions. Young workers, moreover, find it difficult to conceive of themselves as growing old, and thus they fail to empathize

with the older worker. Then, too, with current trends emphasizing job mobility, the younger worker does not think in terms
of remaining employed by the same employer until he reaches
middle age, and hence he is not motivated by his own interests to remove age bias from his current workplace.

Robert Butler, the renowned gerontologist quoted earlier,
believes that systematic stereotyping of the elderly allows the
younger generation to see older people as different from themselves and to "subtly cease to identify with their elders as human beings."[24] This indeed constitutes a serious charge, but
older workers may also contribute to the problem.

The "not me" or "I'm the exception" syndrome leads the
older supervisor to disassociate herself from age stereotypes she
uses to typecast her subordinates of the same age. Most CEOs
are over forty and should be aware of the capabilities of older
workers in general and be less likely to hold inaccurate stereotypes. My own clients have advised me, however, that frequently
this is just not the case. The older CEO is just as likely as his
younger colleagues to assume that an older employee who has
not moved beyond midlevel management has a performance
problem related to age.

The perception of a supervisor, whether young or old, may
lower the expectations of the older worker and thus adversely
affect his motivation. If older workers are expected to be inflexible and less productive, they actually may become so. The stereotype then becomes self-fulfilling. Older workers also tend
to perpetuate age stereotypes by accepting rather than challenging them. If older workers acquiesce to being stereotyped, they
themselves create negative assessments that only strengthen and
protract the use of stereotypes.

Stereotypical thinking also creates vicious cycles that culminate in the perpetuation of age stereotypes. A supervisor who
favors younger subordinates gives a younger worker a new and
challenging assignment. Through the assignment, the younger
worker enhances her skills and knowledge and thus becomes
a more valued employee. A fellow older worker, on the other
hand, is denied the opportunity to advance in skill and knowl-

edge and then is perceived as less motivated and hence less productive. Barred from new and challenging assignments, the older worker, in fact, becomes less interested in the job. Lowered expectations lead to decreased effort. The older worker who accedes to this script succeeds only in giving credence to the age stereotypes that initiated the process. As Robert Butler has observed, "People can convince themselves to act according to stereotype—to think of themselves as unproductive, decrepit, and passive."[25] Thus they themselves perpetuate the stereotypes.

Although negative age stereotypes abound and employers continue to view age, not in terms of experience and stability, but as mental and physical deterioration as well as inflexibility and lack of enthusiasm, data supporting these stereotypes are nonexistent. The question remains: How can these stereotypes be excluded from the workplace? The ADEA has failed to resolve this issue; age-stereotypical thinking is as prevalent today as it was thirty-five years ago when the statute was enacted. The ADEA was intended to make people stop and think, Are these stereotypes rational, and do they have any basis in fact? But if the statute has failed, who or what can fill the void?

Older workers play a significant role here. Since better work performance is one of the most effective ways of dispelling these negative stereotypes, older workers must accept responsibility for keeping their knowledge and job skills current, for maintaining a high level of productivity, and for preserving a high degree of flexibility and adaptability. Through enhanced performance, the older worker will alert the employer to the positive attributes of age—experience, stability, maturity, and loyalty. Greater emphasis upon these qualities may lead to employer rejection of the negative qualities usually attributed to the older worker.

But the fact remains, employers continue to view age in terms not of experience and stability, but of deterioration and vapidity. Employment decisions based on stereotypes render it unnecessary for the employer to incur the cost of ascertaining the capabilities of each older employee. Stereotype-based decisions are thus more cost effective. It is incumbent upon older workers to undermine this rationale. Litigation is expensive. If age-based employment decisions are challenged in the courts, employers may find it more cost effective to repudiate reliance upon age stereotypes. Older workers, therefore, have the capacity to reduce, if not eliminate, age stereotypes from the workplace. It is incumbent upon older workers to assume a far more significant role in bringing to pass the elimination of age discrimination from the workplace.

3

Age Discrimination and Reductions in Force

Satchel Paige once observed that "age is mind over matter; if you don't mind, it doesn't matter." Unhappily, your age may matter to your boss.

Today, employers exhibit much less loyalty to their workers than they have in the past.[1] They appear far less concerned with their workers' general welfare than with the reduction of operating costs, short-term investment returns, and the survival of management. The continued presence in the workforce of older workers who have remained loyal to the company may result in higher salaries and increased pension and health plan costs. Frequently, the elimination of these workers is viewed as an appropriate means of reducing employee costs. The forced retirement of segments of a high-salaried older workforce constitutes a useful tool for achieving corporate financial goals.

Employers, of course, also are motivated to retain competent workers, regardless of their ages. Every worker represents an employer investment, and a productive worker continues to earn a return on that investment. Surveys of employers invariably show positive attitudes toward older workers, who are viewed as loyal, dependable, and conscientious. However, these same employers also express concerns about older workers' productivity.[2]

Workers nearing the end of their work careers may earn more than their current productivity warrants, and an opportunistic employer may take advantage of those circumstances to rid itself of older workers.[3] The older worker who tends to shirk his responsibilities and, consequently, is looked upon as less productive, surely marks himself for termination. A case in point involved Robert Goldman and his employer, First National Bank of Boston.[4]

Goldman had been employed by the bank for thirty-two years when he was terminated during the course of a reduction in force. The bank eliminated 119 of 252 positions in the department in which Goldman worked, and 3 of 15 positions in his unit. The three unit workers selected for dismissal were a twenty-four-year-old suspected of misusing a corporate credit card, and a thirty-seven-year-old and Goldman, then fifty-two, both of whom were considered to be the weakest performers in the unit. The bank claimed that Goldman was responsible for the fewest customer accounts with the lowest aggregate market value, and that his low volume resulted in large measure from the reassignment of some of his accounts because of client complaints.

During the trial of his age discrimination suit against the bank, Goldman presented substantial evidence that until his dismissal, the bank had considered his performance satisfactory. The bank, however, maintained that Goldman had been terminated only because he was the least productive worker in his unit. Because Goldman was unable to offer evidence refuting the bank's position, his case was dismissed. Goldman's failure to maintain a level of productivity commensurate with that of his co-workers proved to be his undoing.

We are not concerned here with the older worker who is largely to blame for the loss of his position. Regardless of a worker's age, discrimination is not a factor in his termination if the employer is motivated to end the employment relationship by reason of the worker's lack of productivity or because of some other failure to satisfy the employer's legitimate business expectations. Rather, we are concerned with the employer who treats his older workers adversely, solely as a means of re-solving other problems. Reductions in force and early retirement plans are two means of achieving employer financial goals that may also adversely affect the status of older workers. Either method may be undertaken as a legitimate business measure, and either may be used unlawfully to reduce or eliminate an older workforce.

Until the 1980s, the employer-employee relationship was analogous to a long-term contract, with the employee remain-ing with the employer for all or most of his or her working ca-reer. The worker's loyalty was rewarded with annual increases in compensation and generous health and pension plan ben-efits. Since the early 1980s, however, millions of workers have lost their jobs to downsizings or reductions in force (commonly referred to as RIFs), and a large proportion of these workers fall within the forty and over age group. Worker security vanished with these downsizings.

Employers now focus upon managerial flexibility in em-ployee relations, a flexibility that is characterized by dramatic increases in management's discretion over employment deci-sions. Rutgers University professor Alfred W. Blumrosen calls this "a cataclysmic change in the nature of labor relations—as significant as the recognition of collective bargaining in the 1930s."[5] Greater employer discretion over the fate of its work-ers makes enforcement of the discrimination laws far more dif-ficult, since a cost-cutting technique, such as a RIF, can readily be used by the employer to conceal discriminatory motives.

A RIF may provide for either voluntary or involuntary ter-minations. In a voluntary plan, workers are offered financial inducements to leave the company, and the employer achieves a payroll reduction without resorting to unpopular and pain-ful involuntary layoffs. Voluntary RIFs also reduce the incidence of lawsuits filed by departing workers, provided the employer conditions the receipt of financial incentives upon the worker's agreement to sign a waiver and release of all possible claims against the employer. From the employer's perspective, how-ever, the voluntary approach may not be the best choice, since it may fail to entice enough workers into retirement to satisfy the employer, and then again it may entice too many. It may also induce the resignation of the most valuable workers, and the employer ends up with an inferior workforce. By electing the voluntary approach, the employer loses control; the final outcome is far less certain than that of the involuntary plan.

In an involuntary plan, the pressure to fire older workers is enormous. Because older workers are more often higher salaried, greater savings may be achieved by selecting them for termination, thus reducing the need to dismiss younger, lower-paid workers. Because older workers are inviting targets, high-paid middle managers often suffer a large proportion of the terminations. From the employer's view, this may be eminently reasonable, but since most of these people fall within the protected age group of the Age Discrimination in Employment Act, the employer also opens the door to charges of age discrimination.

The employer who decides to resolve its financial problems by firing older workers because they have higher salaries is likely to be found guilty of age discrimination. But an employer who decides to resolve its financial problems by terminating higher-salaried workers, many of whom are older, may not be guilty of age discrimination. The difference is subtle indeed, for it is the employer's intent that makes the difference. The first employer selects older workers for termination. The second selects high-paid workers. If the older workers who lose their positions in a RIF are to succeed in proving their terminations were discriminatory, they must show that the employer *intended* to select older workers for termination. The employer thus charged undoubtedly will respond that it did not intend to select older workers for termination. Rather, it selected the higher-paid employees, whether old or young.

An employer planning a RIF will often have its lawyers develop detailed layoff and job elimination procedures. These procedures are designed not only to deter management personnel from making discriminatory selections for termination, but also to minimize the *appearance* of age discrimination in the implementation of the RIF. A major concern of the employer is the appearance of the RIF when it is analyzed from a statistical point of view. A statistical study that discloses a greater proportion of older workers marked for termination may present the appearance of an age discriminatory procedure, even if the employer had been bent on preventing age bias from corrupting the process. In many companywide RIFs, as just noted, high-paid middle managers in the age forty and above category suffer a disproportionate number of job eliminations. A statistical study may show that one of the consequences of the RIF was a dramatic lowering in the average age of the workforce, and this kind of showing usually spells trouble for the employer. Thus, even if the employer's intentions were beyond reproach, an unfavorable statistical showing may nevertheless spawn age discrimination lawsuits.

One of my clients charged her former employer with having implemented a discriminatory RIF. My sixty-four-year-old client, as well as several other workers in their sixties, lost their jobs as a result of the RIF, but several newly hired much younger employees also were terminated. The statistical evidence that the employer offered in defense of my client's age discrimination suit showed that prior to the RIF, the average age of the workforce was thirty-eight, and after nearly forty employees were terminated, the average age of the remaining workforce was still thirty-eight. If the employer had selected only the workers in their sixties for termination, the average age of the surviving workforce would have plunged, but by arranging for the firings of some younger workers as offsets to the firings of older workers, the workforce average age was maintained. However, it was fairly apparent that the employer had manipulated the RIF process to produce these favorable statistics. The manipulation was transparent even to those unsophisticated in these matters. One of the unfortunate younger workers terminated along with my client jokingly told her that in the future his resume would state that the reason for his termination was that he had been made an "offset for a nice old lady."

Statistical studies often tend to support a worker's claim that a RIF was unlawfully implemented. Andrew Quinn worked for twenty-four years as an account executive for Doremus & Company, a New York City advertising agency specializing in financial notice advertising, and was given successively more senior titles, culminating with senior vice president. Following a sharp contraction in its business due to a stock market decline, Doremus implemented a RIF that resulted in a 25 percent reduction in its workforce. Quinn, at first, held on to his position, but after one of his major accounts terminated its relationship with Doremus, he was offered a transfer to the post of night supervisor of the typesetting department. Quinn accepted the transfer on the promise that he would be permitted to return to his account executive position when business considerations warranted. Six months later, another RIF eliminated most of the typesetting department, and Quinn was terminated. Quinn, fifty-eight at the time, charged Doremus with age discrimination.

During the time between the two RIFs, Doremus hired or promoted five workers to the account executive position. Two of these workers were twenty-five years old, one was thirty-four, and two were thirty-nine. Thus, during the time Doremus claimed that its financial condition necessitated the removal of Quinn from the account executive position, it was engaged in hiring or promoting workers to that position, and, on average, they were twenty-six years younger than Quinn. Before the first RIF was initiated, the average age of the account executives was nearly fifty, but by the time Quinn was fired, the average age had been reduced to thirty-nine. When Doremus asked the court to dismiss Quinn's case, the court refused, pointing out that the comparison of Quinn's age with the average age of the workers hired and promoted to the account executive position, together with evidence of the sharp decline in the average age of the account executives as a result of the two RIFs, was a firm basis upon which to draw an inference that age discrimination played a major role in the implementation of the RIFs.[6]

Statistics also may be misused. In 1984, close to 150 of more than 3,000 Reader's Digest Association workers lost their jobs in a RIF. Twenty-three of those terminated, all of whom were over forty, contended that Reader's Digest had used the RIF as a pretext to eliminate older, better-paid workers, and therefore it was guilty of age discrimination. Reader's Digest, relying upon its statistical analysis of the RIF, argued that it had not discriminated against its older workers. Its study showed that prior to the RIF, 55 percent of Reader's Digest workers were age forty or over, and following the RIF, 54 percent of the remaining workers fell into that age category. The RIF, according to this study, had virtually no adverse impact upon the older employees. The twenty-three plaintiffs argued, however, that Reader's Digest's use of statistics was disingenuous. At the same time that Reader's Digest was terminating employees, it was hiring others. Hypothetically, Reader's Digest could have terminated a hundred workers, all over age fifty, while hiring a hundred new employees, all of whom were forty, and statistically, the number of workers in the forty and above group would not have changed. The RIF, the workers argued, should be analyzed, not by inquiring into the number of workers in age group forty and over who remained employed after the RIF, but by finding out whether a disproportionate number of older workers lost their jobs in the RIF. Examined in this light, the statistics showed that although 55 percent of Reader's Digest workers employed before the RIF were age forty and over, almost 70 percent of the workers terminated in the RIF were in that age group. Because Reader's Digest had selected a disproportionate number of older workers for dismissal, the court agreed with the workers that these statistics demonstrated a discriminatory impact on the older workers employed by the company.[7]

Even if the employer is well intentioned, a RIF may go awry, since a prejudiced manager may commit a discriminatory act even where a RIF is designed to exclude such acts. This is often the case where age-stereotypical perceptions abound in management, and in these circumstances it is not uncommon for older workers to be targeted for termination by management employees. Stereotypes may also play an unconscious role in formulating policy and in decision making. For example, where the selection of workers for termination is based on performance evaluations, unconscious stereotypes may lead a manager to apply discriminatory performance criteria favoring younger workers. All too often, the "less competent employees" selected for termination in a RIF turn out to be older workers.

Workers terminated in a RIF inevitably analyze it for evidence of age discrimination, because workers are well aware that RIFs, no matter how well intentioned, present the potential for age discrimination suits. Whether a RIF is actually discriminatory may depend on the perspective from which it is viewed. That was the case in a 1992 litigation involving Evans Chemetics, a division of W. R. Grace & Company.[8]

Evans hired Eugene Maresco in 1967 as a senior clerk. By 1986, he had advanced to the position of credit manager in Evans's office in Darien, Connecticut. In mid-1986, Evans, motivated by economic reasons, closed the Darien office and transferred its accounting functions to its offices in Lexington, Massachusetts, where most of the company's divisional operations were located. At the time it was closed, the Darien office had twelve workers, all but one of whom were over the age of forty. On the other hand, the opposite situation prevailed in the Lexington office, as only one of its twenty-person accounting department was over the age of forty. Four of the Darien workers were transferred to Lexington, and eight others, including Maresco, were terminated. No workers in the Lexington office were terminated in connection with the Darien closing.

Maresco charged Evans with age discrimination. Evans denied his charge, arguing that this was a simple case of closing the Darien office that resulted in a reduction in force of the Darien workforce. Since the age distribution of the four workers transferred to Lexington was approximately the same as that of the eight terminated workers, no age discrimination was involved. From this perspective, it appeared as if Evans's position was sound. But Evans had overlooked one fact. One of its officers had testified at his pretrial deposition that the transaction amounted to more than just closing the Darien office. Actually, a consolidation of the Darien and Lexington offices had occurred, with the accounting functions transferred from Darien to Lexington. From the point of view of a consolidation, there were more workers available in the two offices than there were jobs, and there was no reason to assume that all of the terminations should necessarily come from the Darien office. In these circumstances, the decision to terminate certain workers rather than others must be tested for discrimination by analyzing the ages of the workers in the combined work pool of the two offices. Viewed in this light, all nineteen of the under-forty group from the Lexington office were retained, whereas almost all of the over-forty group from Darien were terminated. These circumstances clearly supported an inference of age discrimination.

In other circumstances, the presence of age discrimination is more clearly apparent. Some employers invoke RIFs while recruiting new workers in other parts of the company. The newly hired younger workers are later transferred to the positions previously held by the older workers terminated in the RIF. It is not unknown for older workers to be transferred to a department that a short time later is eliminated in a RIF. Other employers more or less openly engage in discriminatory conduct, having made the decision to absorb the costs of an unlawful downsizing rather than to incur the greater costs of a lawful one. But the most insidious of the RIFs is one that on its face is lawful and is nearly impregnable to attack.

In this type of RIF, the employer selects those workers it wants to eliminate and then agrees to pay them a generous severance, provided, of course, the terminated workers agree to waive all rights against the employer. The selection process may be wholly biased, but the employer knows that the discrimination laws probably will not be enforced because the workers who are terminated will sign waivers and releases in order to receive the severance payments. In anticipation that this will occur, the employer may disregard the age discrimination laws and terminate its older workers with little fear of lawsuits. Even if an older worker later files suit for age discrimination, before he is allowed to proceed with the litigation the court will require proof that the waiver and release the worker signed was coerced or not signed voluntarily. This is a burden not easily sustained, and an early dismissal of the worker's case is likely.[9]

The employer is not required to prove that its RIF was free from discrimination. The burden of proof lies with the worker, and discrimination is difficult to prove. An employer may be awarded a favorable verdict merely because of the dismissed worker's failure to sustain the burden of proving the RIF was discriminatory. With the prospect that workers dismissed in a RIF will fail to sustain their burden of proof, an employer may be less concerned with the manner in which the RIF is implemented. In fact, an unlawful RIF may prove to be the most cost-effective way of reducing payroll. In these circumstances, our judicial system fails to redress acts of employment discrimination since it favors the position of the unscrupulous employer.

An employer may design a fair and age-neutral RIF, only later to discover that the management employees selected to implement the RIF have acted in a discriminatory manner. Elizabeth Brown (a pseudonym) graduated from high school when she was sixteen and spent the next thirty-nine years working for a large New York City bank. She started in an entry-level position and over the years worked her way upward through bookkeeper, loan clerk, credit clerk, and loan officer positions. She later was assigned to the bank's Real Estate and Mortgage Department as a credit officer, and she soon mastered the intricacies of mortgage financing. Brown was then selected by the bank to conduct real estate training seminars for her fellow workers, and she later assisted in restructuring the bank's Home Equity Department. Subsequently, she was appointed an underwriter in that department and made responsible for training its workers in home equity financing and the processing of mortgage applications.

One morning, after thirty-nine years with the bank, upon her arrival at her office, Brown was summoned to her department head's office. She was told that her job had been eliminated and that she was terminated. A few minutes later, she was ushered off the bank premises and found herself in the street, alone and in total shock. It had taken only a few minutes for the bank to destroy a relationship that had endured for thirty-nine years. Brown was fifty-five years old at the time. She sued for age discrimination.

The bank defended the suit by claiming that its financial problems had made it necessary to eliminate Brown's job, along with those of two thousand other workers, as part of a bankwide RIF. The RIF plan appeared to be age neutral, and no evidence was found that bank officers had deliberately targeted older workers for termination. How the RIF was handled in Brown's department, however, was another matter.

Prior to the RIF, the Home Equity Department had employed ten underwriters, including Brown. The bank officers assigned to implementing the RIF decided to eliminate seven of the underwriter positions, and the manager of the underwriters was charged with selecting the seven to be terminated and the three to be retained. Of the ten underwriters, four were over fifty years old, another four were in their forties, and two were in their thirties. The manager of the underwriters placed all four of the over-fifty-year-olds on the termination list, as well as two of the four in their forties and one of those in the thirties age group. Two of the retained underwriters were in their forties and one was in his thirties. From the point of view of the ages of the underwriters, this distribution was unremarkable except for the elimination of all those over fifty. This raised a few eyebrows, as did the fact that all three of the underwriters selected to keep their jobs had been trained by Brown, who had far more experience in mortgage financing than any of them.

The bank claimed that the selection process of the underwriters to be dismissed had been based upon the level of job performance of each underwriter as perceived by their manager, and that Brown's performance had been observed to have deteriorated in several respects. Brown's past annual performance evaluations, however, failed to substantiate that charge, so the bank offered another explanation. The manager, so it was said, reasoned that after the RIF, with only three underwriters processing mortgage applications rather than ten, the workload would increase significantly, and he would be well advised to select underwriters who worked well under conditions of high volume. According to the manager, Brown did not work well in high-volume situations. This spurious claim, as we shall see, proved to be the bank's undoing.

About one year prior to the RIF, Brown received warnings— at least she perceived them as warnings—that her job was in jeopardy. First, she was offered early retirement, an offer she declined. Next, her manager ceased inviting her and some of the other older underwriters to attend departmental staff meetings. Third, and most ominously, while she was on vacation, her desk was moved out of her office and placed on the main floor. Her office was then assigned to one of the younger underwriters who later was chosen to remain with the bank. In fear that she would be terminated on account of her age and that the bank was looking for ways to justify her dismissal or force her into retirement, Brown began to keep a daily handwritten log of her activities. This log, later presented to the court, showed that during a four-month high-volume period, Brown had processed as many mortgage applications as any of the other underwriters and in most instances had processed more. The log disproved the manager's explanation for selecting Brown for termination, and thus his credibility became a major issue in the case.

On the eve of trial, the bank agreed to settle the case and paid Brown a sum equal to approximately five years of her salary. Ultimately, the bank had to face up to the fact that the selection process used by the manager in dismissing seven of the underwriters had been contaminated with age bias and would not have withstood the scrutiny of the jury. If the bank had provided the manager with written criteria for evaluating the underwriters and had more closely supervised the selection process, perhaps it would have remained age neutral. The bank may have been well intentioned, but its manager of the underwriters was not.

Let us digress for a moment here. Why was Brown able to achieve such a good settlement? In developing an age discrimination case against an employer, whether it be a RIF case or otherwise, the worker's lawyer searches for direct and indirect evidence of discrimination. Direct evidence of discrimination, if it is available, ordinarily assures victory for the worker. Indirect evidence may or may not be decisive. A number of items of indirect evidence surfaced in Brown's case that made the attorneys for the bank uneasy. First, they were reluctant to present a case to a jury where the evidence showed that the manager's purported reasons for selecting Brown for termination in the RIF could not be substantiated. Second, they realized that after the jury heard of Brown's long and successful career with the bank, the jurors would be unlikely to accept the manager's characterization of her performance as less than adequate in any respect. The jury also would readily recognize Brown's exclusion from staff meetings and her office dispossession as transparent efforts to force her into retirement. But, in addition, the bank was confronted with direct evidence of age discrimination.

Brown lived some distance from her office and for several years had participated in a car pool with three or four fellow workers who lived nearby. One of the carpoolers worked in the bank's personnel department and had participated in implementing the RIF. About one week after Brown had been fired, her fellow carpooler in the personnel department stopped by her home to say hello and express his sorrow that she had lost her job. He did more than express his sorrow. He also told Brown and her husband, who was present, that Brown had been terminated because of her age

The bank's attorneys struggled unflaggingly to prevent this unambiguous statement of age discrimination from being heard by the jury once the trial started. They claimed the statement to be hearsay, and they argued that, even if it were not, it was not binding on the bank because the personnel officer had no authority to make such a statement about bank operations. These arguments were rejected by the court, and it supported Brown's position that the jury should hear this evidence. Thus, the bank was aware that the jury would hear Brown's and her husband's testimony that a responsible employee of the bank had told them, in clear and certain terms, that Brown had been fired because of her age. The impact of this testimony on the jury was foreseeable; the bank simply could not risk a jury determination. Minutes before the trial was to start, the bank agreed to a settlement.

A case in which an employer intentionally engaged in an age-biased RIF involved my client Virginia Green (another pseudonym), who created television commercials and magazine advertisements for a large advertising agency. Green was the oldest of twenty-three associate creative directors employed in the agency's Creative Department. When the agency experienced financial difficulties, it conducted a RIF, culminating in the termination of a number of workers, including Green, who was sixty-four at the time.

About one year prior to the RIF, while Green was making a presentation of a proposed television commercial to the staff, one of the agency's executive directors, on hand to view the presentation, began chanting, "We know how old you are, we know how old you are." Green, then sixty-three (with gray verging on near white hair), appeared in stark contrast to the surrounding younger work staff. Frightened and humiliated by the incident, from that point onward, Green feared for her job. Later, after the RIF had been announced, it was the chanting executive director who designated Green's position as one of those to be eliminated. Green sued for age discrimination.

The agency defended the suit on the ground that Green was terminated, not because of her age, and not because she was the oldest of the twenty-three associate creative directors, but on account of her rate of productivity, allegedly lower than that of the other associate creative directors. The agency purported to justify Green's dismissal on the ground that in the three years prior to her termination, Green had produced few television commercials and magazine advertisements that were ultimately sold to the agency's clients. The criterion for termination, according to the agency, was productivity, and those workers who were most productive and generated work acceptable to clients survived the RIF, while the less productive workers did not.

Both sides began to prepare for trial. In the litigation process, the time during which the parties prepare for trial is called the discovery period. Federal and state rules of court procedure provide each litigant the opportunity to "discover" the evidence of the opposing party. Typically, the depositions of opposing witnesses are taken, and each side provides the other with copies of relevant documents. It is during discovery that most discrimination cases are won or lost.

The right to examine the employer's files during discovery is a potent tool for ferreting out data in support of a charge of discrimination and in opposing a defense proffered by the employer. When the agency claimed that Green was less productive than her co-workers, it opened the door to an analysis of the agency's production records. These records disclosed that the agency had neglected to maintain an accurate count of magazine ads sold to clients, and thus worker productivity could not be measured by magazine ads but only by television commercials sold to clients. A wealth of information helpful to Green's case was discovered in these records. In the three years prior to Green's termination, eighteen of the twenty-three associate creative directors had produced fewer client-approved television commercials than Green. In fact, during the last two years of her employment, Green had produced and sold more television commercials than all but one of the associate creative directors, and in the last year she was employed, none of them produced and sold more television commercials than she did.

With this type of information in hand, we were able to argue forcefully that the agency had misrepresented Green's productivity in an attempt to justify her termination. When an employer misrepresents, exaggerates, understates, overstates, distorts, or tampers with the facts, it opens itself to claims of cover-up, a cover-up that age was the real reason for the termination of the older employee.

Even with all of this evidence at hand, the agency's lawyers informed the court that it planned to file a motion for summary judgment in an effort to have Green's case dismissed. A motion for summary judgment, undertaken in nearly every case by the employer's lawyers, is an attempt to have the case dismissed before trial on the ground that the worker, based upon the facts presented to the court, will be unable to establish a violation of the age discrimination statute. In this case, the court ruled that a motion for summary judgment was purely a waste of time and that the case should proceed directly to trial. At this point, the agency settled with Green.

Employers justify mass terminations of workers on economic grounds, such as trimming an inflated payroll. In these circumstances, one would not expect the employer to hire new workers during or soon after the RIF, but it happens. As we have seen, even employers as large and as sophisticated as the Reader's Digest Association fall into that trap. Counsel for employers find it necessary continuously to remind their clients who are engaged in RIFs to refrain from hiring new staff until some time has elapsed after the RIF has been concluded. To engage in hiring in the midst of mass firings invites speculation that the RIF is being conducted for a purpose other than that announced by the employer. A prominent employers' lawyer advises the corporate world, "Don't, Don't, Don't replace employees terminated in the course of a RIF within (at least) a year."[10] Carol Gallo's employer failed to heed that advice.

For several years, Gallo had been responsible for publishing employee newsletters for her employer, Prudential Residential Services. When Prudential experienced a downturn in its business, it conducted a RIF, eliminating Gallo's department, ending publication of four of the five newsletters for which Gallo had been responsible, and firing the fifty-year-old Gallo. Responsibility for publication of the surviving newsletter was assigned to the Marketing Department, but soon after, that department lost four of its employees. To fill these vacancies, Prudential ran a blind advertisement in a local newspaper asking for applicants for the position of communications editor in charge of internal publications. Unaware that Prudential had placed the advertisement, Gallo responded to the ad, but Prudential declined to interview her. Instead, it interviewed six other applicants, several of whom were in their twenties, and ultimately filled the position with one of the younger applicants. Later, Prudential hired another young applicant and reinstated the publication of the four newsletters. Thus, all five of the newsletters Gallo had been in charge of were again scheduled for publication and responsibility for their publication assigned to the two newly hired younger employees. Gallo cried foul and initiated a suit charging Prudential with age discrimination.

Prudential was successful in having the court grant it summary judgment dismissing Gallo's case, but an appellate court later reversed that decision, holding that Prudential's systematic resurrection of publications following Gallo's discharge and its hiring of younger workers to assume responsibilities formerly performed by Gallo strongly suggested that age was a factor in her termination. The appellate court went on to state that although it would not second-guess Prudential's business judgment in ordering a RIF, Gallo had the right to have a jury decide whether Prudential's reasons for firing her were pretexts and the real reason for her termination was her age. It was for the jury to search beneath the surface of the RIF to determine whether age bias underlay the employer's decision to terminate its workers.[11]

Very often, after a worker obtains a favorable ruling in a summary judgment proceeding, as in the Gallo case, the worker's attorneys are able to negotiate a favorable settlement with the employer (see chapter 10). Since the law reports are silent with regard to any further activities in the Gallo case, we may assume that her claims against Prudential were settled outside of court.

When issues of this sort are presented to jurors, they frequently determine that age played a significant role in the selection process of those who survive a RIF and those who do not. But, as Nelson Viola was to learn, every litigant does not succeed in having his case decided by a jury.

Viola was hired at the age of forty-six by Philips Medical Systems to work in the stockroom of its Spare Parts Department. Twelve years later, he was terminated in a RIF. Viola's performance ratings had been consistently satisfactory until three months prior to the RIF, when his supervisor rated his performance as "needs improvement," thus singling him out as one of the first workers to be dismissed in the RIF. Viola sued Philips for age discrimination, alleging that three RIF-related occurrences supported his claim:

1. His performance reviews had been satisfactory for the twelve years prior to the RIF, and it was only on the eve of the RIF that his performance was viewed as unsatisfactory.
2. While the RIF was in the planning stage, a much younger worker was transferred into the Spare Parts Department to fill a vacant position. If this transfer had not occurred, Viola could have filled the vacancy, thus rendering his dismissal unnecessary at the time of the RIF.
3. Eleven months after the RIF was concluded, Philips hired a new worker to perform the functions that Viola had performed prior to his termination, thus calling into question the economic reasons for his dismissal.

Despite this evidence, the court ruled that Viola had failed to adduce sufficient evidence to raise an inference of age discrimination, and upon Philips's application, the case was dismissed. Viola was thus denied the opportunity to present his case to a jury. If Viola's case had survived this stage of the proceedings, undoubtedly a jury would have given him a more favorable hearing.[12]

RIFs will remain a useful tool for employers. Those employers who design age-neutral RIFs, requiring procedures that minimize the possibility of the insertion of age bias into the selection process, will be subjected to fewer age discrimination suits. On the other hand, RIFs that are not designed to be age neutral or that are inadequately supervised are laden with problems for the employer and opportunities for the dismissed workers. With the aging of the workforce, employers may become even more inclined to use RIFs to eliminate high-salaried older workers. If, as has been predicted, the boomer generation is more likely to contest rather than accept age-motivated employment actions, then the battles over RIF dismissals have just begun.

4 | Age Discrimination and Early-Retirement Plans

Early-retirement plans have grown increasingly more popular with employers as useful means for reducing their personnel. Corporate downsizings that have continued in recent years—even during periods of near full employment and labor shortages—have prompted employers to use early-retirement plans as a relatively painless method of easing older workers out of the workforce.

Employers frequently offer generous benefits to induce retirement earlier than otherwise would occur under the provisions of their pension plans. Early retirement is most often offered to a limited group of workers, usually defined by age and service. Typically, early-retirement benefits are offered to workers over the age of fifty or fifty-five with ten or more years of service with the employer. The benefits offered may include severance, extended health and life insurance coverage, additional pension benefits, and bridge payments until the early retiree becomes eligible for Social Security. The severance payment alone may be equivalent to six months to a year or more of salary.

Although employer enthusiasm for these plans emerges from their use as a means of facilitating efforts to reduce payroll, all too frequently, these plans are also used to eliminate older, high-paid, long-term workers. Any employer that wants to set a limit on the number of its workers who exceed a certain age may achieve its goal by offering sufficiently attractive severance retirement benefits to induce employees to select early retirement.

Some employment law specialists would bar the use of these plans because, in their view, they are nothing more than thinly veiled attempts to eliminate older workers from the workplace.[1] Certainly, it is true that a plan that offers severance or other employee benefits as a means of inducing early retirement will create some degree of tension with the ADEA's goals of promoting the employment of older persons. Undeniably, these plans may be used by an employer to achieve precisely what the Age Discrimination in Employment Act seeks to eradicate: age-based elimination of older workers from the workplace. Not surprisingly, these employment law specialists contend that early-retirement plans, by their very nature, are antithetical to the ADEA, inasmuch as they foster acceptance of the ageist stereotype that older people are fit only for retirement. Early-retirement plans, they reason, reward only those workers who conform to that stereotype. They also argue that even if these plans on occasion benefit individual workers, they adversely affect the economy as a whole as well as older people as a group in that they deprive society of valuable work experience and negatively categorize older workers.

On the other side of the issue, other employment specialists, relying on the premise that the prohibition against age discrimination does not bar programs that benefit younger workers, argue that early-retirement plans ensure continuous opportunity for younger workers, for without such plans, the promotion of younger workers would be blocked by the continued presence of older workers in the workplace. With such plans in place, younger workers may advance more rapidly by filling the positions vacated by older workers who elect to accept early retirement.[2]

From the worker's perspective, the acceptance or rejection of an offer of early retirement constitutes a major career decision. Due to the importance of the decision, courts have emphasized time and again that the worker's acceptance of retirement must be wholly voluntary, and evidence of employer coercion will vitiate the worker's agreement to accept retirement. Whether participation in these plans is truly voluntary has become a major issue in the courts.[3]

Whether a plan is determined to be voluntary often depends on the point of view from which it is examined. Suppose a court is presented with this situation. An employer announces to its workers that due to financial pressures, it has decided to reduce its workforce by 25 percent over the ensuing six months. Simultaneously, the employer announces that in order to avoid as many involuntary layoffs as possible, it is offering generous early-retirement packages to all workers age fifty-five and over, provided they elect to retire during the next three months. It also announces that those workers who elect not to retire, but who are later selected for dismissal, will not receive the retirement package. The message conveyed to the workers is clear: they may well end up in a worse position if they reject the retirement option. Even though a worker may prefer to continue working, she will be hard-pressed not to accept this retirement offer. When she considers the possibility that she may be terminated even if she does not elect retirement—and in that event will depart the company empty-handed—there is little for her to decide.

Is the acceptance of early retirement in these circumstances voluntary? This presents a close legal question. Unless the court is provided with some additional evidence of an employer's coercive tactics, it may very well rule that a worker's acceptance of the offer is voluntary. But, from the worker's perspective, the offer of early retirement, coupled with the suggestion that the worker's position will be eliminated if the offer is not accepted, is not an option at all but a dismissal.

Let's change the facts a bit. A fifty-five-year-old worker is offered early retirement and is also advised that his position has been reclassified as "nonessential." The employer announces that following the period in which early retirement may be

elected, the company is planning a RIF. Is the worker's acceptance of early retirement voluntary? This is not a close question, since the worker has no real choice. Since the worker's
position has been reclassified as "nonessential," it surely will
be eliminated in the RIF. To elect to remain with the company
would be nothing short of suicidal.

How does this play out in the real world? Experiencing a
decline in advertising, the National Geographic Society decided
to reduce the number of its workers engaged in selling advertisements, and it offered every ad salesperson over the age of
fifty-five the option of early retirement. The offer included a
severance payment of one year's salary, retirement benefits calculated as if the retiree had remained employed until age sixty-
five, medical coverage for life, and supplemental life insurance
coverage. Twelve of the fifteen eligible workers accepted the offer and the three who declined remained employed with the
Society. Four of those who accepted the offer had second
thoughts and sued for age discrimination, arguing that because
they confronted the loss of their jobs if they had not accepted
early retirement, their acceptances were coerced rather than voluntarily selected.

In analyzing whether the offer of early retirement was voluntarily accepted, the court reviewed the circumstances from
a worker's perspective. If the worker was free to decline the offer and continue working, he was presented with a valuable
option. He could have retired, received the value of the retirement package, and either taken a new job or enjoyed the lei-
sure of retirement. Then again, he could have elected to continue
working and forfeit the package. "This may put him to a hard
choice; he may think the offer too good to refuse; but it is not
Don Corleone's 'Make him an offer he can't refuse.'" Unless the
employer "manipulated the option so that [a worker was] driven
to early retirement not by its attractions but by the terror of the
alternative," the acceptance of early retirement would be voluntary. Because these workers were not threatened with a job
loss or advised that their positions would be eliminated if they
failed to select early retirement, the court ruled they had vol-

untarily accepted retirement, and their case was dismissed.[4] But, in the cases that follow, evidence of employer manipulation of the process required different outcomes.

Thomas Dean Smith began working for World Insurance Company in 1950 as a stock clerk. For the next thirty-six years, he worked his way up through the company until World promoted him to assistant vice president for purchasing. In 1986, following changes in management, Smith was instructed to report to a newly hired vice president, Alan Jackson. One month later, Jackson told Smith he had the option of remaining with World and risk being dismissed or electing early retirement. Smith, age fifty-four at the time, chose retirement and then immediately filed suit, charging World with violation of the ADEA by forcing him into an early retirement.

At the trial, Smith testified that Jackson had told him that if he decided to stay on at World, Jackson "would start to turn the screws and build a file against him." Smith concluded that Jackson planned to make him look bad by assigning him projects he would be unable to handle adequately. A co-worker confirmed Smith's fears when she testified that Jackson had confided to her that he had been hired as an "axeman" to eliminate several of the older World employees, including Smith. The jury had little difficulty in finding in favor of Smith.[5]

The pressure upon Smith to accept early retirement was so great that his decision to retire could not have been freely made. Acceptance of an offer of retirement will be deemed to be voluntary only when the employee is free from coercion on the part of the employer, and here the coercion was flagrant.

As first viewed by the worker, an early-retirement package may appear quite generous. After all, how often is a worker offered a lump-sum payment equal to six months' or a year's salary without having to work for it? But the positive aspects of the offer must be measured against the negative—namely, the loss of a job. Thus, the worker's evaluation of the offer must factor in his prospects for future employment. The age of the worker obviously is crucial, for how likely is a sixty-year-old to obtain another position? Regardless of age, every worker must confront the likelihood that future employment will mean a smaller paycheck and, perhaps, less generous fringe benefits. Undoubtedly, the worker's pension benefits under her current employer's pension plan also will be adversely affected by the worker's acceptance of early retirement. Unless you have been confronted by similar circumstances, the enormity of the problem involved in arriving at a rational decision cannot be fully realized. Even if the worker is not subjected to any coercive measures to elect the retirement option, she normally will struggle over her decision. The struggle is only exacerbated if the offer must be evaluated in an atmosphere dominated by fear of what may happen to the worker if she elects to remain on the job. Tom Smith did not have that problem, since Jackson had made it clear that Smith had no choice. Smith did not voluntarily elect retirement; he was forced into retirement.

In 1969, Beebe Rubber Company, a subsidiary of the Mohawk Rubber Company, hired forty-three-year-old Andrew Hebert to serve as its controller. Thirteen years later, when its profits began to decline, Beebe was restructured, resulting in a material reduction in personnel. In October 1984, Hebert, then fifty-nine, was offered an early-retirement package. Although "extremely shocked" by Beebe's proposal that he retire, Hebert prepared a counterproposal, spelling out the terms of a retirement package acceptable to him. Beebe accepted the counterproposal, Hebert left the company, and he was replaced by a twenty-eight-year-old accountant. Hebert then sued, claiming that his "retirement" was, in fact, a discharge ordered by Beebe because of his age.

The offer of early retirement had been presented to Hebert by his manager. At his deposition, the manager admitted that when he approached Hebert with the offer, Hebert was, in fact, given no choice but to retire. Nevertheless, Beebe asked the court to dismiss Hebert's suit on the ground that Hebert, in formulating a counterproposal, had freely participated in designing a benefits package, and thus his acceptance of the early-retirement proposal was voluntary. The court ruled, however, that a worker's acceptance of an early-retirement package cannot be classified as "voluntary" when he is faced with a "choice between the Scylla of forced retirement or the Charybdis of discharge." An offer of early retirement is distinguished from a discharge by vesting in the worker the power to choose to continue working. Unless the worker is truly offered a choice, then acceptance of the offer of early retirement cannot be considered voluntary, even if the worker participated in the process in order to attain the best possible deal.[6]

Olga Cazzola also was given little choice about her future. After many years of contented and productive employment with Codman & Shurtleff, serving as its supervisor of office services, Cazzola was approaching her sixty-fifth birthday and a long-planned retirement. Then, she changed her mind and announced that she had decided not to retire. Two and one-half weeks after her sixty-fifth birthday, her job responsibilities were reduced, and she lost control of the word-processing department, a department she had set up and supervised from its inception. Although company officials claimed it was necessary to reduce her responsibilities because Cazzola was overworked, this issue had never been raised previously and had never been discussed with Cazzola.

Due to the change in her responsibilities, Cazzola was directed to report to a new supervisor. Try as she might, Cazzola could not please this supervisor in any respect; she could do nothing right. Despite many years of satisfactory performance evaluations, Cazzola was then given a poor evaluation, placed on probation, and told she would be fired if her performance did not improve immediately. A short time later, she was informed she had failed her probation, and she was given the choice of electing retirement or reassignment to a clerk's position in the word-processing department, the department she had previously created and later supervised.

Once Cazzola passed her sixty-fifth birthday and refused to retire, her world was turned upside down. Everything that she had done right before her sixty-fifth birthday was declared to be wrong after her birthday. When faced with the humiliation of assignment to the lowest position in a department she had created and supervised, she felt she had little choice but to elect retirement. She then sued her employer for age discrimination, and as you would expect, the jury found in her favor, ruling that she had been forced into electing retirement. It was simply inconceivable that her selection of the retirement option in those circumstances could be considered voluntary.[7]

Andrew Hebert's and Olga Cazzola's experiences with involuntary retirement are not uncommon. James Moylan's age discrimination lawsuit against National Westminster Bank is another case in point. In 1984, at age fifty-nine and after twenty-seven years of employment with the bank, Moylan held the position of assistant vice president and loan officer in the bank's commercial banking division. When Moylan's boss announced his forthcoming retirement, Moylan applied for his position. In January 1985, the bank promulgated the provisions of an early-retirement plan that included a package of enhanced benefits. Election of the plan was open to qualified employees from March through July of that year.

During his many years with the bank, Moylan had not received an unfavorable performance rating, but this enviable record came to an abrupt end in May 1985, when his performance was rated "less-than-favorable." Moylan was then advised that unless an immediate improvement was noted in his performance, he would be placed on probation. Shortly after, Moylan was contacted by a member of the bank's personnel department who, after speculating that termination would follow upon probation, suggested as an alternative that Moylan consider the possibility of early retirement. At about the same time, Moylan learned that his application for promotion to his former boss's position had been rejected, and, instead, the bank had assigned the position to an employee more than twenty years his junior. At this point, Moylan realized he had no future with the bank, and he decided to retire.

After six months in retirement, Moylan sued the bank for age discrimination. One of the issues in his case was the voluntariness of his election of retirement. The judge assigned

to the case described the circumstances—as he perceived them—
that confronted Moylan at the point that he decided to retire:

> After nearly thirty years of steady advancement, he is faced
> with a possible discharge—and its attendant income reduc-
> tion. . . . He realizes that if he is discharged, this fact, com-
> bined with his age, promises to make job hunting a dismal
> exercise. Management, however, quickly informs him that
> this scenario can be avoided if he retires within one month.
> Under these circumstances, I am unable to conclude . . . that
> a reasonable person would not have felt compelled to leave.

This is a polite, understated way of saying that Moylan was
booted out, that his election to retire was anything but
voluntary.[8]

Corporate restructurings and reorganizations nearly always
disproportionately affect aging workers. As we have seen, a company that cuts costs in a restructuring often thins out the ranks
of middle management, whose workers tend to be middle-aged
and older. Thus, reorganizations are looked upon as tools for
targeting the middle-aged and older workers, and frequently this
is the primary contention made in age discrimination cases
brought in their wake. Offers of early retirement, made in connection with a reorganization, may constitute the least expensive way for an employer to eliminate older workers from its
workforce. Less than generous benefits packages nevertheless
may engender a high employee acceptance rate, thus reducing
even further the cost to the employer of eliminating its older
workers. It has been suggested that it may actually pay an employer to engage in outright discrimination from time to time
in order to relieve its workforce of older, more highly paid workers.[9] Ample evidence exists to confirm that employers have acted
on suggestions of that type.

A few years ago, Sears, Roebuck decided on a reorganization to cut costs in its service centers. In Utah, Sears transferred
some of the clerical functions performed at its Ogden service

center to a larger service center in Salt Lake City, and simultaneously offered early-retirement packages to its Ogden workers who were age fifty and over. The older workers were then systematically pressured to accept retirement. As an example of the type of pressure that was exerted, two older salespersons were required to achieve sales quotas during the months preceding the offer that had never previously been met. When the quotas were not achieved, the salespersons were advised that if they refused to accept early retirement, they would be transferred to lower-paying positions. Three other salespersons were threatened with transfer from their current positions to high-pressure sales jobs with unattainable quotas.

After obtaining early-retirement acceptances from five of its older employees, Sears proceeded to hire predominantly younger, part-time employees to work in Ogden as well as in Salt Lake City. The court described this scene as "either an ill conceived and poorly executed efficiency move or a deliberate corporate attempt to reduce payroll costs by replacing experienced and well paid [older] workers with less experienced and lower paid younger workers." The jury decided it was the latter and awarded the Ogden workers substantial damages.[10]

Another attempt at eliminating older workers involved Montgomery Ward. In 1981, Ward was in serious financial trouble, and newly appointed executive officers tried to turn the company around by reorganizing it. The first priority of the reorganization was the age distribution of management personnel: Older unpromotable workers were said to be blocking the advancement of talented younger workers. As part of the reorganization, selected older workers were offered a newly initiated Voluntary Separation Plan. A worker accepting the plan received a separation payment if he agreed to sign a release waiving all claims against Ward and describing his departure as "voluntary." The departures, however, were far from voluntary.

Ward intended the separation plan to be a restaffing program, since those departing were to be replaced, in most part, by younger workers. Eighty percent of the management employees made eligible by the terms of the plan were over the age of forty. Ward did not simply submit the plan to eligible employees for them to consider acceptance or rejection. Rather, prior to presenting the plan to the workers, company officials reviewed the eligibility list and decided who they wanted to reject the plan and remain with the company and who they wanted to accept it and leave the company. Ward carefully scripted a procedure that, directly or indirectly, apprised each eligible employee whether to accept or reject. Ward coached supervisors on how they should go about advising a worker to say yes or no to the plan. Those who were on the retention list were advised that "they had a future with Ward" or that "your future is here," while those who were on the departure list were told the opposite. Numerous workers later testified that they had been given clear signals to accept or reject the plan and that it was common knowledge that company officials had informed those workers it wanted to keep and advised the others that they had no choice but to leave or face termination without separation benefits.

Some of the workers who accepted the plan and left the company later sued for age discrimination, claiming they had been forced into retirement. Ward argued that their cases should be dismissed, because they had left the company voluntarily and thus could not prove age had been a factor in their leaving. But the right to choose to remain or depart clearly was illusory. Ward's workers had no choice; the choice to remain or leave was made for them. Even though departing workers signed a document declaring that their departures were voluntary, in truth, they were coerced into leaving. The court permitted their age discrimination cases to proceed in the legal system.[11]

Was Ward guilty of poorly executing a plan to streamline its management, or did it deliberately force certain of its management personnel into retirement, thus allowing it to elevate younger employees to the positions vacated by the departing older employees? The reorganization targeted older workers, who were not permitted to choose freely between retirement and remaining with the company. They were forced to select retirement. A more direct violation of the age statute is difficult to imagine.

Robert Calhoun worked for Acme Cleveland Corporation for forty-two years, rising to the position of manager of the Product Design and Application Department located in Massachusetts. Every year, he received good performance reviews and annual pay increases. When the company began to experience operational and financial problems, it hired a new plant manager, who, as one of his first moves to reorganize the company, notified all workers eligible for early retirement that a forthcoming layoff of workers would be reduced to the extent that older workers accepted retirement. Calhoun, who was sixty-two, informed the new plant manager that he would not accept early retirement and that he intended to stay on with the company until he was sixty-five. A few weeks later, Calhoun was demoted, and a younger employee, who had been trained by Calhoun, was designated to replace him as department manager. Then the pressure was applied to Calhoun.

First, over a period of seven months, he was asked on three occasions whether he wanted to accept early retirement. Next, he was not invited to participate in a training seminar, although his department manager as well as workers holding positions junior to his were invited. Then he was soundly criticized and told it was grounds for dismissal for him to have brought a television to work on Patriot's Day (a holiday observed in Massachusetts and a day off for Acme's nonsupervisory employees) so he could watch the beginning and end of the Boston Marathon, as he had done for many years past without adverse comment from any of his superiors. At that point, the new plant manager told Calhoun the company was prepared to give him his severance and terminate his employment and that if he did not leave quietly, he would have to begin working twelve- to fourteen-hour days, six days per week. The following day, Calhoun retired. When Calhoun later sued Acme for age discrimination, his lawyers had little difficulty in persuading a jury to rule in Calhoun's favor.[12]

Pressures brought to bear upon older employees eligible

for early retirement are a common occurrence, as these cases demonstrate. Each employer has its own favorite instrument of persuasion. After years of good performance reviews, an older worker who has expressed a desire not to retire receives a poor review, totally out of character with all previous reviews. A reduction in responsibilities or compensation or both also are favorite employer tactics. Placing an employee on probation on account of purported job deficiencies is another strategy often found useful by employers. Eventually, these tactics make retirement look pretty good to the worker.

It took seven months for Acme Cleveland to get rid of Calhoun. Some employers take longer. Doris Stamey worked for Southern Bell Telephone and Telegraph Company for thirty-eight years. She was hired in 1943, when she was eighteen, as a long-distance operator. In 1955, Southern Bell assigned her to a position entailing visits to customers to instruct them on the use of the company's services. In 1973, Southern Bell restructured its Customer Service Division and established two new job titles: "service advisor," a nonmanagement position involving no direct customer contact, and "chief service advisor," a managerial position supervising the service advisors and exclusively in charge of direct customer contact. Stamey, then forty-eight, and almost all other Southern Bell employees in similar positions who were over the age of forty, were assigned to the nonmanagement service advisor positions. Southern Bell assigned the new chief service advisor positions principally to younger, newly hired employees.

For the next eight years, Stamey repeatedly applied for promotion to a chief service advisor position, but to no avail. In fact, during that period, no nonmanagement employee over the age of forty was promoted to a management position. Then, Southern Bell gradually phased out the service advisor position, and five workers holding that position were promoted to chief service advisor. However, all five were younger than forty.

When Stamey's position was phased out, she was fifty-six, and instead of promoting her to chief service advisor, Southern Bell offered her a transfer to an entry-level position with lower pay. Stamey declined the transfer, left Southern Bell, and filed a charge of age discrimination with the Equal Employment Opportunity Commission (EEOC). Several months later, Southern Bell announced that it had reassessed its needs and had decided it needed *one* service advisor, and Stamey was designated to fill the position. Stamey then withdrew her EEOC charge and accepted reassignment to her old position, but six months later, her position was again eliminated. By this time, Stamey must have wondered what Southern Bell could do next to make her life more miserable. She did not have long to wait. She was offered early retirement or transfer to another job, but she never learned the nature of the other job, for Southern Bell immediately presented her with retirement papers to sign. Stamey signed the papers, but then she filed a second age discrimination charge with the EEOC. Ultimately, the case was tried before a jury in federal court, and the jury decided in her favor.[13]

Offers of early retirement are not all bad. Obviously, the worker as well as the employer may benefit from the worker's acceptance of early retirement. As we have seen, however, the offer can easily be manipulated by an employer to coerce a worker or a group of workers to accept retirement rather than permit them freedom of choice. So long as the worker truly has freedom to accept or reject retirement, early retirement will remain a valuable option for the employer and the worker. However, the failure to provide freedom of choice can only result in a proliferation of age discrimination lawsuits.

5

Waivers of Claims and the Age Discrimination Law

Several years ago, one of my clients—we will call him John Black—upon being fired, was forced by his employer, a New York branch of a European bank, to sign a waiver of all claims he had against the bank.[1] Black was fifty-one at the time, had worked for the bank for about ten years, and held the title of vice president. Several months before Black's termination, his boss had been replaced by a much younger man. Subsequently, the bank relieved several other management employees and replaced them with newly hired younger workers. In light of the youth movement that appeared to be in process, Black was not overly surprised when he was confronted with the announcement that he was about to be terminated. The bank offered him one year's severance on the condition that he sign a release and waiver of any claims he had against the bank. The waiver form was given to him at about 9:00 A.M., and he was told he had until noon to make up his mind: "Either sign the waiver and receive one year's salary or don't sign the waiver and walk out of the bank with nothing."

During the three hours allowed him to decide what to do, Black accomplished little more than placing a call to his wife. He was unable to contact his attorney or arrange an immediate appointment with another attorney. Instead, he walked around downtown Manhattan, worrying about the state of his finances, and the more he worried, the more his problems seemed to mount. With one of his children in college and another about to enter, he had already arranged for a second mortgage on his home to help defray college costs, and his wife had recently accepted a part-time position. Still, his debts had mounted steadily. By the noon deadline, he had concluded that he had no choice. Even if he had a viable claim for age discrimination against the bank, he had to accept the severance. He had no other option. He walked back to the bank and signed the waiver.

If Black had been successful in reaching his lawyer that morning, his anxiety would have been relieved, at least to the extent of his concern about signing the waiver. Even though he had signed the waiver form presented to him by the bank, it was legally a worthless piece of paper. A worker's release and waiver of claims against his employer must be given voluntarily and knowingly; a waiver obtained through coercion is invalid. Although the bank acted within its legal rights in demanding a waiver of claims as a condition to its agreement to pay severance to Black, the waiver of claims obtained from Black would be legally enforceable only if the bank acquired it under circumstances that provided Black with a reasonable amount of time to consider whether to sign it or not. Obviously, three hours was not a reasonable amount of time. When Black later sued the bank for age discrimination, the bank's attorneys did not even argue that the waiver barred his claims. The waiver was not a factor in the litigation, and eventually Black settled his age discrimination claim and received payment of another two years' salary.

With the enactment of the ADEA and the concurrent growing tendency of terminated older workers to sue their former employers for age discrimination, employers have become increasingly more inclined to offer enhanced severance or retirement benefits to terminated older workers in exchange for releases and waivers of claims. These waivers generally are executed at the time of the worker's termination, and in addition to providing for waivers of all claims against the employer, they also typically specify that the worker will not sue the employer for age discrimination.

Sometimes, however, an employer's request for a waiver proves counterproductive. The mere act of asking for a waiver of claims may arouse a worker's concerns and suspicions where previously none had existed, and a worker thus alerted may conceive of a claim that had not previously occurred to him. A request for a waiver also may create an environment in which the employer feels required to enter into negotiations with the worker, negotiations that may conclude with the payment of more severance than the employer initially contemplated. Most employers, nonetheless, are firmly in favor of obtaining waivers from all dismissed older workers.

Waivers have grown even more common with the wave of RIFs and downsizings begun in the early 1980s. Periodic downsizings have become modus operandi with some companies, and affected workers, especially workers in their fifties who face long periods of, if not permanent, unemployment, have reacted negatively to losing their jobs in a restructuring designed not to ward off impending financial disaster, but to increase company profits. These older workers have become less and less hesitant to allege age discrimination against the downsizers. To discourage these age discrimination suits, employers have resorted to requiring the workers dismissed in the downsizings to sign waivers of age discrimination claims as a condition of the employer's commitment to pay them severance benefits. Because a worker may freely choose to retain his right to sue the employer for age discrimination or, on the other hand, give up the right in exchange for a package of severance benefits, the courts consider a waiver given under these circumstances to be voluntary and thus enforceable.

The use of waivers in downsizings has come under the critical view of such writers as Rutgers University professor Alfred W. Blumrosen. He points out that an employer may select workers for termination knowing that the discrimination laws will not be enforced because those terminated will sign waivers of claims in order to receive severance benefits. The employer may thus disregard these laws and freely discriminate against older workers in deciding who will fall victim to the downsizing.

> These employer decisions are made on the basis of judgments as to who will best fit in the reduced structure— judgments that have a major element of subjectivity and may be influenced by conscious or unconscious bias against . . . long-time workers who are too old to hunt. Because of the waiver, the employer need not fear the enforcement of . . . equal opportunity laws. The laws have little *in terrorem* effect because management knows that their decisions as to whom to discharge will not be litigated.[2]

From a business perspective, however, the employer should be free to terminate the employment relationship and obtain a waiver, provided the waiver is voluntarily given by the worker. In any event, an employer almost always holds the dominant position in establishing the terms of parting, and this, in some instances, has led to abusive tactics, such as those used to obtain a waiver from Black. With the growth of downsizings and the ever increasing role of workers' waivers of claims, Congress intervened in 1990 with the adoption of the Older Workers Benefit Protection Act (the Older Workers Act).[3]

Prior to 1990, the courts had upheld workers' waivers of age claims provided they were given knowingly and voluntarily by the workers. The standard most frequently applied by the courts to determine whether a waiver had been given knowingly and voluntarily was one that considered the "totality of the circumstances" under which the waiver was given. In applying this standard, the court reviewed the worker's education and experience, the amount of time given to the worker to make a decision, the clarity of the waiver agreement, and the benefit the worker received in exchange for the waiver, as well as whether the worker was represented by counsel and whether the employer allowed any negotiation of the terms of the waiver. The Older Workers Act adopted the "knowingly and voluntarily" criterion and specified eight separate conditions a waiver must include to be considered to have met that criterion.

1. The waiver must be written so as to be understood by the worker. Clarity is of the utmost importance.
2. The waiver must specifically refer to rights and claims arising under the ADEA. The employer must advise the worker that by signing the waiver the worker is relinquishing rights provided by the law.
3. The waiver must relate only to those claims that arose before it was signed. An employer is barred from obtaining waivers of future claims. Otherwise, as one court expressed it, an employer could purchase a license to discriminate in the future.
4. In exchange for the waiver, the worker must be furnished with a payment or benefit to which she would not otherwise be entitled. If the employer has an established severance policy, the worker must receive something in addition to the normal severance benefits.
5. The employer must warn the worker that the signing of the document has legal consequences, and that the advice of counsel may be required.
6. The worker may not be rushed into signing the waiver but must be given at least twenty-one days to think about it.
7. After signing the waiver, the worker must be given another seven days in which to change her mind, and should she wish to, she may then revoke the waiver.
8. Where a group of workers is dismissed, as in a RIF, the employer must provide the dismissed workers with additional information, including the job titles and ages of all persons included in the group of dismissed workers.

When an employer offers a group of workers retirement or dismisses them in a RIF, members of the group may be even more concerned about the circumstances of their terminations. The information prescribed by item 8 is designed to give those older workers a clearer picture of what the employer is up to and the circumstances under which the workers are being asked to sign a waiver. Prior to the Older Workers Act, the workers did not have available to them information pertaining to the scope of an early-retirement plan or a RIF, nor did they have information regarding the number or the identity of the workers affected. If a RIF targeted only older workers, a worker could sign away his rights without being aware that the employer was guilty of age discrimination on a massive scale. Similarly, if an employer used an early-retirement plan to eliminate older workers in a particular department, those workers might learn of the employer's designs only after waivers had been signed.

If a worker signs a waiver and later challenges its validity, the employer has the burden of proving the waiver was made knowingly and voluntarily by demonstrating that the conditions of the Older Workers Act have been fully satisfied. Even then, a worker may challenge the waiver if other circumstances suggest that its signing was in some respect coerced or obtained by misrepresentation or fraud.

One aspect of the Older Workers Act has been hotly disputed in the courts: Is a worker who signs a waiver of claims in exchange for a monetary payment and who later challenges the waiver's validity and sues the employer for age discrimination obliged, as a condition of continuing his age discrimination suit, to return the money to the employer? This is not an uncommon occurrence. For example, subsequent to the dismissal of an older worker in a RIF, the dismissed worker learns that the employer has hired a younger worker to fill his former position, a position supposedly eliminated in the RIF. The older worker contends that the employer has lied to him and has fraudulently induced him to sign a waiver of Age Discrimination in Employment Act (ADEA) claims. He then sues the employer for age discrimination, but the employer demands that the court dismiss the suit on the ground that the worker signed a waiver of all claims, including age discrimination claims, in exchange for an additional severance payment, and the worker has not repaid the severance payment to the employer. The employer argues that if the older worker is allowed to proceed with the suit without returning the additional severance payment, the employer will have lost the benefit for which it paid. But the older worker, having been dismissed in the RIF, has already used up his severance in payment of living expenses. If the court orders the older worker to tender back or return the severance as a condition of continuing the suit, the older worker will be unable to comply. Although having apparently committed a flagrant act of age discrimination, the employer obtains a dismissal of the worker's suit.

A closely related issue, also ardently contested in the courts, focuses on an older worker's ratification of a waiver that may be invalid. Can an invalid waiver be ratified by the actions of the worker who signed it? Laura Grillet had been employed as a personnel officer by Sears, Roebuck for twenty-six years when Sears informed her that her position and all positions comparable to hers were to be eliminated. Sears offered her an additional forty weeks of severance if she agreed to sign a release and waiver of all claims against Sears. Within a week of signing the waiver and of electing to take the enhanced severance package, Grillet learned that Sears had offered positions in the personnel department in which she had worked to three younger workers. Concluding that Sears had been dishonest in its dealings with her, Grillet decided to sue for age discrimination. Grillet, however, delayed starting her suit until after she had received the last of her forty weekly severance payments. She then filed suit, but Sears, relying upon the waiver, asked the court to dismiss her case. Grillet argued that the waiver was invalid because Sears had falsely represented to her that all positions comparable to hers would be eliminated. The court, however, rejected her suit, stating that even if the waiver was invalid, by waiting to receive all her severance payments before contesting the waiver's validity, she, in fact, had ratified it.[4]

The courts have come down on both sides of the tender-back and ratification issues. Both issues were presented to the court in a lawsuit filed by Gerald Oberg and two other former workers of Allied Van Lines. They had signed waivers of all claims arising during their employment with Allied and had also promised not to file suit against the company. In exchange for the waivers and the promises not to sue, they were each granted severance and, like Grillet, waited until after receipt of the last severance payment before filing suit. Moreover, they did not return the severance payments to Allied prior to filing suit. Allied admitted that the waivers did not fully comply with the eight conditions of the Older Workers Act but argued that the waivers had been ratified by Oberg and the other former workers as a consequence of their retention of the severance payments. The court would have none of this, ruling that a defective waiver cannot be ratified; it is void and without legal effect. The court also refused to order Oberg to tender back his severance as a condition to proceeding with the litigation.[5]

These issues arose again in another case involving Sears. Vernal Forbus and other Sears workers accepted offers of early retirement and signed waivers after they had been told that the site at which they were employed was to be converted to another line of work and that many of their jobs were to be eliminated. After the workers retired, Sears modified the plans for the site and eliminated fewer jobs than it originally contemplated. Upon learning of this, Forbus and the others asked for their jobs back, but Sears told them that none was available. They then started litigation, claiming that their decisions to retire and sign waivers were based on misrepresentations made by Sears. Sears countered with the argument that even if the waivers were invalid, Forbus and the others had ratified them by retaining the early-retirement benefits.

The court rejected Sears's argument. It first stated that forcing older workers to pay back their early-retirement benefits as a condition to pursuing their ADEA rights is inconsistent with the purposes of the statute. Such a rule would have a "crippling effect" on the workers' ability to challenge waivers obtained by misrepresentation. "Such a rule," the court continued, "would, in our opinion, encourage egregious behavior on the part of employers in forcing certain workers into early retirement for the economic benefit of the company." The court thus rejected the concept that a tender-back requirement is a prerequisite to challenging a waiver of ADEA claims.[6]

Other courts have concluded to the contrary. Arthur Reid agreed to accept an early-retirement package offered by IBM and signed a waiver that included a provision that he would "never institute a claim of any kind against IBM," and if he did sue IBM, he would be required to "pay all costs and expenses of defending against the suit incurred by IBM . . . including reasonable attorneys' fees." Several months after signing the waiver, Reid changed his mind about retirement and applied for a position at IBM. When his application was rejected, he sued IBM, alleging that acts of age bias had occurred at the time he had been offered early retirement. He also claimed that the waiver he signed was invalid. The court rejected the latter claim, stating that even if the waiver was invalid, Reid's failure to tender back to IBM the early-retirement benefits he had received in the interim acted as a ratification of the waiver.

Here, the court gave precedence to the rights gained by IBM in contracting with Reid to provide him with an early-retirement package in exchange for a release and waiver of all claims. The court dismissed the argument that had proved successful in the Forbus case, namely that a tender-back requirement is inconsistent with the purposes of the ADEA. In addition to dismissing his suit, the court ordered Reid to pay IBM's costs in defending the suit.[7]

Here we have two courts examining basically the same issue from opposite perspectives. The Forbus court was concerned primarily with the broader aspects of the ADEA. It gave precedence to the general purpose of the act in barring discrimination in the workplace against the older worker, and it refused to permit the employer's contractual rights to interfere with that purpose. To rule otherwise, the court reasoned, would undermine the national policy against discrimination in the workplace, since the older worker would be required to tender back that which he most likely has already spent. The Reid court, on the other hand, refused to interfere with the contractual rights of the employer. It reasoned that it would be unfair to permit a worker who had received a payment for the waiver to keep that payment while at the same time to pursue a lawsuit the waiver was intended to obviate.

Courts have continued to wrestle with the issues of tender back and ratification, and in the interest of balancing the rights of the parties, some courts have fashioned innovative procedures. Patricia Kristoferson and Terry Lewis sued their former employer, Otis Spunkmeyer, Inc., for sex discrimination. Although this was a Title VII and not an ADEA case, the issues of tender back and ratification are not dissimilar. To be valid under Title VII, a waiver must be given knowingly and voluntarily, as under the Older Workers Act, and whether Kristoferson and Lewis had acted knowingly and voluntarily when they signed waivers was very much in doubt. Without advance notice, both were told that they were to be immediately terminated and that if they wanted to receive any severance, they would be required to sign an agreement releasing Spunkmeyer of all claims. Given little time to consider their options, both signed without really knowing what they were signing.

Spunkmeyer asked the court to dismiss their suit on the ground that even if the waivers were not given knowingly and voluntarily, both Kristoferson and Lewis later had knowingly and voluntarily ratified the waivers by choosing not to pay back the severance before filing suit. While recognizing the conflict between the discrimination statutes and traditional principles of contract law, the court appeared to be more concerned with the ability of Kristoferson and Lewis, as with that of other dismissed workers, to repay the severance as a condition for proceeding with their case. As noted earlier, dismissed workers are likely to have used their severance just to survive and are not likely to have it on hand when they later decide to sue. Rather than foreclose Kristoferson and Lewis from proceeding with their case, the court required each to sign an agreement promising to repay the severance if the court later ruled that the waivers were, indeed, invalid. If Spunkmeyer proves the waivers to be valid, the suit ends there, and Kristoferson and Lewis will not have to repay the severance. On the other hand, if the court ultimately rules that the waivers are invalid, as a condition for continuing with their suit, Kristoferson and Lewis will be required to pay back the severance each had received.[8]

The court's rationale is consistent with the Older Workers Act. The act provides that the burden of proving the validity of a waiver falls on the party that asserts its validity. In most cases, this means that the employer has the burden of proving that a waiver meets the requirements of the Older Workers Act and that it was given knowingly and voluntarily. Requiring an older worker to tender back the benefits before the validity of the waiver is litigated in effect relieves the employer of that burden. By delaying the repayment, the court reestablished the burden of proof demanded by the statute. But at best, the court found only a partial solution to the problem.

With a clear split among the courts, ultimately only the Supreme Court could resolve the tender-back and ratification issues, and these issues reached that court in Dolores Oubre's age discrimination suit against Entergy Operations, Inc. Oubre had worked as a scheduler in Entergy's power plant in Killona, Louisiana. In 1994, she received a poor performance evaluation, and early the following year, her supervisor gave her the option of either improving her performance or accepting a severance arrangement. After consulting with her attorney, Oubre decided to accept the severance arrangement. As part of the severance package, Oubre signed a release and waiver in which she agreed "to waive, settle, release and discharge any and all claims, demands, damages, actions, or causes of action" she had against Entergy.

In procuring this waiver and release from Oubre, Entergy failed to comply with three of the eight conditions required by the Older Workers Act: She was given fewer than twenty-one days to consider whether to sign the release (item 6); she was not given an additional seven days to revoke the release (item 7); and the release did not specifically refer to ADEA claims (item 2).

Oubre later filed suit against Entergy, alleging she had been forced to resign in violation of the ADEA. When Oubre failed to return the severance payments, Entergy moved to dismiss her case on the ground that her failure to return the severance constituted a ratification of the defective waiver. The lower courts dismissed Oubre's case, and she appealed to the Supreme Court.

In reinstating Oubre's claim, the Supreme Court relied upon the precise wording of the Older Workers Act: A worker "may not waive" an ADEA claim unless the waiver or release signed by the worker satisfies the conditions of the act. The court ruled:

> The [Older Workers Act] implements Congress' policy via a strict, unqualified statutory stricture on waivers, and we are bound to take Congress at its word. Congress imposed specific duties on employers who seek releases of certain claims created by statute. Congress delineated these duties with precision and without qualification: An employee "may not waive" an ADEA claim unless the employer complies with the statute. Courts cannot with ease presume ratification of that which Congress forbids.

Since the waiver Oubre signed failed to comply with the act, it was unenforceable against her, and it could not stand as a bar to her suit against Entergy, whether she returned the severance payments or not.[9]

The use of the release and waiver of claims will continue to be a powerful weapon in the hands of the employer. As observed by Professor Blumrosen, a release and waiver may be used by an employer intent on eliminating an older workforce to insulate itself from valid age discrimination claims. Although the Older Workers Act affords the older worker relief against a defectively executed waiver, an employer who successfully conceals its discriminatory conduct from the worker prior to her signing of the waiver may later rely upon the act to prevent the worker's age discrimination suit from proceeding.[10] If the waiver is valid under the provisions of the Older Workers Act, before the worker will be allowed to proceed with a case against her employer, she would have to prove that the waiver was obtained from her by fraud, misrepresentation, or duress, each of which is very difficult to establish. In these circumstances, an employer may actually use the act to further its discriminatory conduct. Certainly, Congress never intended this result, and thus further legislative action may be necessary.

6 Age Discrimination and the Hiring of Older Workers

Viewed from a broad perspective, the Age Discrimination in Employment Act has achieved some success in combating age discrimination in the workplace. After its enactment in 1967, the ADEA at first remained an obscure, little-used piece of legislation.[1] Beginning in the late 1970s, however, ten years after its enactment, workers began to file age discrimination claims with increasing frequency. By the mid-1980s, workers were filing age claims with the Equal Employment Opportunity Commission at the rate of more than 20,000 per year, nearly equaling the number of race and sex discrimination claims filed annually. But, despite the fact that many thousands of these victims of age discrimination have obtained some measure of relief under the provisions of the ADEA, the law's primary goal, namely, the elimination of commonly held attitudes that falsely depict the capabilities of older workers, has not been realized. Widely held false assumptions pertaining to older worker capability supposedly were to disappear from the work site once the U.S. populace was made aware that these assumptions were, indeed, false. In this respect, the ADEA has failed dismally.

It is doubtful that a study conducted by the current secretary of labor would find age stereotyping today any less prevalent than that prevailing thirty years ago when Secretary of Labor Wirtz reported his findings to Congress. Walter K. Olson—widely published, but not known as a friend of those advocating the elimination of workplace discrimination—accurately reflects the view of the business world when he writes:

> Reformers ask much of human nature when they demand that preconceptions based on age be done away with. Indeed, the impulse to generalize about people based on age is so strong that even ageism buffs probably never manage to resist it for long. . . . All of us rely constantly on age to "place" someone's likely attitudes, interests, and behavior; this is one reason we have grown to expect unfamiliar personages to be introduced in casual conversations and news stories with some signal as to whether they're nineteen or seventy-four years old.[2]

Olson's "impulse to generalize" reflects the business world's general attitude toward older workers. It requires much less effort for an employer to rely upon the assumption that all older workers possess identical attitudes and capabilities than it is to specifically identify each individual older worker's *particular* attitudes and capabilities. It also is more cost effective. The employer's cost of evaluating the capabilities of each of its sixty-year-old workers will, in most instances, far exceed the cost of eliminating the age sixty and older crowd from the work site by simply offering them the choice between early-retirement benefits or outright dismissal.

Secretary Wirtz attributed the prevalence of age stereotypes in the workplace to ignorance. Today, we might more accurately ascribe the continued use of age stereotypes to employer desire for lower costs. Thus, in the nearly thirty-five-year existence of the ADEA, we have moved from age discrimination as a product of ignorance to age discrimination as a product of corporate economy. Discrimination emanating from ignorance may in some instances be excusable, but discrimination motivated by employer cost savings is always pernicious.

Some economists argue that age discrimination has always been more a product of economics than of ignorance. They rely upon the life-cycle model of career development that holds that worker salaries generally exceed worker productivity at the beginning and at the end of the work life of an employee, but that salaries are generally lower and productivity higher during the middle years of the work cycle. Thus, they argue, since the productivity of the worker decreases with age, an opportunistic employer is strongly motivated by cost savings to terminate the relationship at that point of the work cycle. Their position, of course, is grounded on the assumption that worker productivity necessarily decreases with age. Since this is a false assumption, their theories can be said to be based as much on ignorance as on economics. On the other hand, employer acceptance of these theories explains why they tend to eliminate their older workers from the workplace.

In addition to failing to eradicate age stereotyping from the workplace, the ADEA has failed in another significant respect. Following the submission to Congress of the report prepared by Secretary of Labor Wirtz, President Johnson transmitted to Congress proposed legislation that ultimately was adopted as the ADEA. In his accompanying message to Congress, the president expressed concern with the secretary's findings that workers over fifty-five were barred from a vast number of jobs in the private sector:

> Hundreds of thousands not yet old, not yet voluntarily retired, find themselves jobless because of arbitrary age discrimination. . . . In 1965, the Secretary of Labor reported to the Congress and the President that approximately half of all private job openings were barred to applicants over fifty-five; a quarter were closed to applicants over forty-five. In economic terms, this is a serious—and senseless— loss to a nation on the move. But the greater loss is the cruel sacrifice in happiness and well-being which joblessness imposes on these citizens and their families.[3]

Because employers tended to exclude job applicants over

a certain age, usually forty-five, even from nonstrenuous positions, older workers found themselves severely disadvantaged
in regaining employment once they were displaced from their
positions. In recognition of this widespread practice, congressional committee reports emphasized the principal purpose of
the ADEA as the exclusion of age discrimination from the *hiring* process.[4]

Although the ADEA has successfully eradicated age-biased
employment advertising—such as job openings for "workers
between ages twenty and forty"—the refusal to hire older workers remains as serious a concern today as in 1967. The ADEA
has accomplished nothing of consequence in resolving this concern, since more than 75 percent of all ADEA claims filed with
the EEOC involve the termination of employment and a mere
9 percent deal with refusals to hire.[5] Even fewer refusal-to-hire
claims ever get to the courts.

Various reasons have been offered to explain the dearth
of failure-to-hire lawsuits. One is based on the lack of relevant
information available to the job applicant. Terminated workers
generally have a fair amount of information available to them
concerning the circumstances existing at the time of their terminations. Even after being discharged, a worker may have a
source of information in the friends left behind at the workplace.
If a newly hired younger employee appears on the scene to perform the responsibilities of an older worker terminated a few
weeks earlier, purportedly because his job was eliminated in a
RIF, the older worker will soon learn of it. A job applicant, on
the other hand, has none of these advantages. Thus, an
employer's discriminatory conduct may be more readily concealed from the job applicant than from one of its terminated
workers.

Proving that age discrimination has infected the hiring process is especially difficult. Little evidence of discrimination is
usually available in the first instance, and, unfortunately, little
evidence later becomes available during the discovery phase of
the litigation process. Consequently, lawyers are reluctant to take
on these cases.

The employer's defense, invariably offered in response to a failure-to-hire claim, is based upon its contention that "the person hired was better qualified, and the older job applicant less qualified, for the vacant position." A myriad of factors may be included in the decision to hire Ms. X rather than Mr. Y, many of which are wholly subjective. Indeed, the hiring decision is generally a product of a highly subjective process. Subjective employer decisions are rarely upset by the courts because, historically, judges have been extremely reluctant to substitute their judgment for that of the businessperson. In these circumstances, it is readily apparent that an employer bent on discriminating against an older worker job applicant may easily conceal its illegal intentions.

Even when a rejected applicant suspects age bias may have played a role in her rejection, she may be reluctant to file a discrimination claim with the EEOC and even more hesitant to become involved in litigation later. Obtaining a job is the primary interest of the unemployed worker, and in most instances, the older worker will not allow the mere suspicion of unlawful employer behavior to deflect her from the job search. Also, the bitterness suffered by the wrongfully discharged long-term worker is less often experienced by the unsuccessful job applicant, and thus the latter's motivation to become involved in allegations of age discrimination is less compelling. And, as many of us have experienced, the employer's rejection is invariably accompanied by the promise that the applicant's resume will remain on file in the event another position opens up. It almost never does, but hope springs eternal. Why charge an employer with discrimination when, if you don't, it may offer you another position next week?

The reluctance of the older worker to file a failure-to-hire suit combined with the difficulties ordinarily endured in prosecuting such a suit serve to insulate the employer from liability for failing to hire an older worker. Since employers are clearly aware that the prospect of a failure-to-hire discrimination charge is remote, they are less inclined to concern themselves with compliance with the ADEA in making hiring decisions. The employer also is aware that a worker not hired cannot later sue for being fired. Therefore, in deciding whether to hire an older worker, the employer may take into account its anticipated cost of defending against a future termination suit, and then the odds against the hiring of an older worker increase dramatically. By some estimates, the probability that an employer will have to defend itself against an age discrimination suit arising from a termination of employment is thirty times greater than the likelihood that it will have to defend itself against a suit arising from a failure-to-hire.[6] Thus, the employer is strongly motivated *not* to hire an older employee. Not only has the ADEA failed to afford the older worker protection from an employer bent upon denying him employment because of his age, it actually may motivate employers to engage in such unlawful conduct.

From the employer's perspective, the rejection of the older worker applicant may be justifiable, even if the applicant appears eminently qualified for the open position. The older worker's work experience may be too closely allied with that of her former employer, and some employee skills simply are not readily transferable from one position to another, while still other skills may prove to be obsolete. Some employers may experience difficulty in placing an older worker in a position subordinate to a younger supervisor. And then there is the question of the proximity of retirement. Is the older worker likely to remain on the job long enough to justify the cost of any retraining that may be required?

In most instances, a failure-to-hire age discrimination case is destined for failure unless the rejected applicant is able to provide the court with direct evidence of age discrimination. This occurs rather infrequently, but some employers don't even bother to cover up their illicit intentions. A fifty-five-year-old licensed engineer applied for a mechanical engineering position with a U.S. Navy shipbuilding facility in Bath, Maine. During his interview, he was advised by the chief engineer that he was looking for a "younger engineer." When pressed as to whether age really made a difference, the interviewer responded, "I think so. We have a couple of older engineers that will be

retiring in a couple of years, and we want to hire a younger engineer and train him to take their places."[7] Most employers are
far more discreet and less likely to express their age bias in such
explicit terms. But this is the type of evidence a rejected applicant needs in order to prosecute a hiring discrimination claim
successfully.

If direct evidence of age discrimination is unavailable to
the worker, then he had better have some very strong circumstantial evidence pointing to the presence of age bias. Isaac
Punahele was fortunate in that regard. After Punahele submitted an application to United Airlines for a ramp service position, United hired thirty-eight persons who had less experience
than Punahele in this type of position, and each of the thirty-
eight was younger than he. In these circumstances, an employer,
even with the advantages it has in a hiring case, will be hard-
pressed to persuade a jury that age discrimination did not play
a prominent role in the worker's rejection.[8]

With the proliferation of corporate downsizings, rehiring
cases have appeared on court calendars with increasing frequency. An employer who terminates a worker in a RIF sometimes assures the worker that in the event a suitable position
opens up in the future, the worker will be considered for that
position. Disputes over rehiring following a RIF may also occur under other circumstances, as when Carol Gallo tried to re-
claim her position from Prudential Residential Services (chapter
3). In another case, George Reed worked for Signode Corporation as general manager and vice president of its electrical division. When he was fifty-eight, Reed experienced serious health
problems and requested a one-year leave of absence. Signode
advised him that company policy precluded such leave, and
Reed was left with the choice of continuing to work with his
illness or resigning. He chose to resign, and Signode replaced
him with a newly hired Canadian citizen.

Six months later, Reed's health improved, and he wrote
to Signode expressing his desire to return to work in a suitable
position. A short time later, he responded to a blind employment advertisement appearing in the *Wall Street Journal*. He

subsequently learned that Signode had arranged for the advertisement to find applicants to fill his former position in Signode's electrical division. When Reed asked to be considered for the position, Signode informed him that the *Wall Street Journal* advertisement was merely a "dummy" advertisement, placed by Signode to satisfy immigration requirements so as to permit Reed's Canadian replacement to obtain a permanent visa. Soon after, Signode transferred the Canadian replacement to another position, leaving Reed's former position again vacant. Despite Reed's availability, Signode actively sought another general manager.

Reed persisted. Letters to Signode requesting a managerial position were met with the response that no positions were available, even though Reed's former position was yet to be filled. Signode again advertised in the *Wall Street Journal*. Reed again applied for the position, and again he was rejected. Ultimately, Signode considered three candidates for the position, each much younger than Reed, and one of these, thirteen years younger than Reed, was hired. Signode never offered to rehire Reed for any position.

In Reed's subsequent suit for age discrimination, Signode argued that Reed was not rehired because of his weak sales and marketing orientation. This was a strange position to assert since Reed had extensive sales and marketing experience, both before being hired and while working for Signode, and the person Signode hired for Reed's former position had limited sales experience.

Given the difficulties confronting the older worker in hiring and rehiring cases, it is remarkable that Reed was able to assemble such an array of evidence tending to show that he had, in fact, been a victim of age discrimination.[9] As we shall see later (chapter 11), indirect evidence of discrimination, properly presented, may be nearly as persuasive as direct evidence of discriminatory conduct. Whether it be direct or indirect, evidence of age discrimination in the hiring process must be nearly overwhelming to achieve a successful outcome. Without such evidence, the older worker and his attorney are well advised to consider seriously whether or not litigation should be pursued. Gary Senner and his attorney would undoubtedly agree.

Senner was fifty-four when he applied for a psychology instructor position at Northcentral Technical College in Wausau, Wisconsin. There were forty-eight applicants for the position, but after the college eliminated those not qualified and those who had submitted incomplete or defective applications, nine applicants remained for consideration for the position. Two males, one over forty (Senner), and seven females, one over forty, were given numerical ratings based on academic credentials and experience, and of these nine, the three with the highest numerical ratings were granted interviews. Even though Senner was the only one of the nine who had a doctorate, the college did not select him for an interview. All three to whom the college had granted interviews were women under forty, and one of them was eventually hired.

The successful candidate previously had not taught full-time but had taught psychology courses part-time on the college level. Senner's doctorate was in education, but he had taken courses in psychology. Although Senner had never previously held a full-time teaching position, he had taught as an adjunct professor in nearby universities in Wisconsin. Believing that he was the better qualified candidate, Senner filed suit, charging age and sex discrimination. He did not prevail on either count.[10]

In his suit, Senner argued that the college's numerical rating system was overly subjective and that many of his attributes could have been better assessed in an interview, which he had been denied. But he could offer no evidence that the college's denial of an interview was discriminatory. Even if the college had unfairly evaluated or underevaluated his credentials, Senner could establish only that the college's criteria were subjective, but not that they were discriminatory. Even though the evidence suggested that Senner may have been treated unfairly, it was insufficient to persuade the court that he was a victim of discrimination. As Senner discovered, absent direct or highly persuasive circumstantial evidence of age bias, a failure-to-hire suit will not succeed.

Ann Hertz had very persuasive evidence of age bias to offer the court in her age discrimination case against The Gap. At the age of sixty-one, Hertz submitted a written application for a sales or office position with the Gap store located in Bayside, New York. In the application, Hertz indicated that she was available to work between the hours of 9:00 A.M. and 5:00 P.M. on Mondays, Tuesdays, and Fridays. Hertz later testified that she listed these hours on the application because she felt it was more likely that she would be selected for a part-time position, and perhaps this would later develop into a full-time position. After Hertz submitted her application, the Gap's store manager contacted her and they agreed to a date and time for an interview. The following account of the interview was reported by Hertz at her deposition taken some time later.

On the day of the interview, Hertz arrived at the store and was asked by the associate manager, "May I help you?" Hertz responded that she was to be interviewed by the store manager. The store manager, who at the time was standing on a ladder shelving merchandise, was informed by the associate manager that Hertz had arrived for the interview. As you visualize this scene, you should be aware that Hertz had not listed her age on her application, and thus the first knowledge the store manager had that Hertz was a woman in her sixties was when she looked down from the ladder and saw Hertz for the first time. The store manager immediately said to the associate manager, "I'm busy now. You handle it."

The associate manager then beckoned Hertz to follow her, and she preceded Hertz out of the store, where they sat down on a park bench. "Why do you want to work for the Gap?" Hertz was asked. This was followed by a question about her experience. At that point, after asking Hertz two questions, the associate manager looked at Hertz's application and said, "Well, we really want someone to work nights and weekends." Hertz then asked, "Why did you call me then?" The associate manager then stood up and said, "That's the way it is. If we need someone around holiday time . . . we'll get in touch." The associate manager then walked back into the store, leaving Hertz on the park bench. End of interview.

Hertz filed a suit for age discrimination, alleging that when the store manager discovered she was an older woman, she was given only a perfunctory interview and then falsely informed that the open position required work hours different from those indicated in her application. The Gap asked the court to dismiss Hertz's case on the ground that insufficient evidence existed showing that the decision not to hire Hertz was based upon her age. The court disagreed.

The court first observed that the Gap store manager had screened Hertz's application before scheduling an interview, and thus the manager was aware of Hertz's listed hours of availability. In addition, the associate manager refrained from asking Hertz at the interview whether she was available to work at times other than those listed in her application, nor did she ask Hertz whether she was willing to work nights and weekends. The associate manager abruptly ended the interview after just two questions and then left Hertz sitting on the bench outside the store. At the very least, this occurrence raised an inference of discrimination, thus permitting Hertz to continue with the case. Her case was later settled.[11]

When the store manager looked down from her ladder and saw below an elderly lady seeking a job, her first thoughts were probably negative—I don't want an old woman like that working in my store. She reacted without thinking and may not have been fully aware that what followed was in violation of the law. A store manager more attuned to the discrimination laws would have carried out the interview in an ordinary fashion and then found some excuse, such as lack of relevant experience, to reject Hertz's application. If the manager had proceeded in this manner, it is likely that Hertz never would have been able to show even a trace of discriminatory conduct. Only because Hertz was humiliated by the conduct of the manager and associate manager was she able to establish a case of age discrimination. Less egregious conduct undoubtedly would have produced a different result. The lesson to be learned from this case is that if you have any thoughts about filing a failure-to-hire age discrimination lawsuit, it would be very advantageous if you were able to show that you were grossly mistreated or humiliated by the employer.

The ADEA has not worked well in failure-to-hire cases. The litigation process developed over the past thirty-five years simply does not lend itself to hiring cases. Except in unusual circumstances, such as those confronting George Reed and Ann Hertz, the unemployed older worker will receive little help from the ADEA.

7 | Promotions, Demotions, Transfers, and Age Discrimination

An employer may subject an older worker to acts of age discrimination in connection with any aspect of the employment relationship at any time between hiring and firing. Older workers have charged their employers with age discrimination in connection with failures to promote, demotions, failures to transfer, assignments of undesirable transfers, on-the-job harassment, reductions in compensation, and other matters relating to the worker's terms and conditions of employment. As in hiring cases, older workers have had far less success in proving violations of the Age Discrimination in Employment Act (ADEA) in these areas of the employment relationship than in cases involving terminations of employment. Decisions to promote or not to promote, to demote, and to transfer or not to transfer usually entail highly subjective decision-making factors, thus affording employers a ready means of concealment of their discriminatory motives. As in failure-to-hire cases, the court's traditional reluctance to interfere with an employer's business decisions made upon subjective factors, and its disinclination to substitute its judgment for that of the businessperson, may actually assist the employer in perpetuating its concealment of age bias.

Unlike the case of a worker not hired or one recently fired, an older worker charging his employer with acts of discrimination attendant to a promotion, demotion, or transfer remains anchored in the employment relationship. The worker must continue his daily life as an employee, regularly encountering those he has charged with discriminatory acts. Although (as we shall see in chapter 8) the law bars an employer from retaliating against a worker who has charged it with discrimination, the employer-employee relationship is irreversibly altered once the worker has asserted a claim of discrimination. Workers are generally reluctant to confront this situation. Having been denied a promotion, a worker is much more likely to suffer the pain of rejection in silence than to open the door to an even more contentious relationship with his or her employer. On the other hand, some workers who have been denied a promotion or transfer conclude that a viable employment relationship is no longer possible, and it is these workers who are less likely to be deterred from asserting an age discrimination claim.

A promotion case, similar to a failure-to-hire case, is rarely successful unless the worker is able to furnish the court with compelling evidence of age discriminatory conduct. Almost always, the only available evidence of discrimination of this type is indirect or circumstantial in nature.

Joseph Bartek began his employment with the Urban Redevelopment Authority of Pittsburgh (URA) as a cost estimator and later was promoted to deputy director of the Housing Rehabilitation Department. After thirteen years in that position, URA personnel informed him that his position was being eliminated for budgetary reasons and that he had the choice of resigning or accepting a subordinate position. He decided on the latter, but only on the condition that he would be fairly considered for promotion in the future. Five years later, the URA selected a twenty-eight-year-old worker over Bartek for the position of the administrator of the Mortgage/Home Improvement Loan Program. At the time, Bartek was sixty-two. Although Bartek had superior qualifications for the position, the URA alleged that the younger employee had been chosen because she had experience in finance, but it later admitted the position did not require an extensive financial background. Subsequently, the URA again chose this same twenty-eight-year-old employee instead of Bartek for the position of residential finance section manager. Not long after, two other younger employees, both in their thirties, were promoted to positions for which Bartek was qualified. Finally, the URA designated a twenty-seven-year-old totally unqualified, newly hired employee to fill the position of the administrator of the Agency/Emergency Loan Program, a position for which Bartek was eminently qualified. Following this series of rejections for promotion, Bartek filed an age discrimination suit against the URA, and a jury ultimately ruled that the URA had intentionally discriminated against him in denying him promotions to these positions.[1]

Although Bartek was unable to offer any direct proof of age discrimination, the evidence he offered, showing repeated denials of promotions in favor of much younger employees, persuaded the jury that the URA's explanations for not promoting him simply were not believable. A pattern of employer behavior that implies unlawful conduct is often sufficient to establish a discriminatory motive. This is particularly so, as in Bartek's case, when an older worker is denied several promotion opportunities over a relatively short period of time. However, in those instances where the promotion denials occur over an extended period of time, the employer may be able to establish that different supervisory personnel were involved with each promotion denial and that each decision maker acted independently of every other decision maker. The employer then argues that a general discriminatory motive cannot be attributed to all the decision makers, because their independent actions were not part of any pattern of discrimination. Failing to establish a pattern of common behavior, the worker is reduced to trying to establish that each decision maker was individually motivated by age bias. This is a burden difficult to sustain.

In response to a worker's allegations that repeated denials of promotion were discriminatory, an employer will often argue that the worker was not selected for promotion because she was unqualified or was not the best qualified for the positions at issue. The worker argues in return that if she, in fact, is unqualified or less qualified than others, it is because the employer refused in the past to promote her to positions where she would have gained the experience that would have qualified her for the higher positions. Workers argue this point especially with regard to the denial of a promotion to a supervisory position, the worker contending that she was denied the opportunity to gain the experience in lesser supervisory positions that would have qualified her for the higher supervisory position. If the worker is able to offer evidence of age bias in the employer's past conduct in denying her this experience, then she may very well succeed in showing that the later denial of promotion also was discriminatory.

Absent a pattern of repeated rejections for promotion, the older worker, on occasion, may be able to rely upon direct evidence of age bias to prove discriminatory intent. Dolen Lindsey's suit against his employer is a case in point. Lindsey filed suit against American Cast Iron Pipe Company for failing to promote him to assistant manager in its data processing department, allegedly because of his age. Lindsey had been a member of the data processing department for twenty-five years, working his way up from clerk to a level four programmer, the highest programming classification attainable in the department. When he heard that an assistant manager position was about to become available, he asked to be considered for promotion to that position. He was fifty-one at the time. Although his supervisors affirmed that they held him in high regard, they also told him that they were looking for a younger person to serve as the assistant manager, and not long thereafter, a thirty-four-year-old level three programmer was promoted to the position.[2]

For the most part, employers and their supervisory personnel avoid statements evidencing unlawful motives, and when they wish to conceal the basis for an employment decision, they will carefully document what appears to be an age-neutral decision-making process. Statements like that relied upon by Lindsey are rare, but when they surface, they usually spell success for the older worker's age discrimination suit. Indeed, the jury in the Lindsey case was persuaded that he had been a victim of age discrimination and its verdict was in his favor.

Cases involving demotions are very much like discharge cases. Age discrimination allegations relating to a demotion generally occur in one of three situations: a demotion arising out of alleged deteriorating job performance; a demotion occurring as a consequence of a company reorganization; or a demotion resulting from a downgrading or the elimination of the worker's position. David Weihaupt's demotion occurred after his employer reorganized his department.

Weihaupt began working for the American Medical Association in Chicago as a field representative when he was thirty-three, and twelve years later the AMA promoted him to special assistant to the director of the Public Affairs Division. His success in that position led to a further promotion, this time to director of the Office of Corporate Liaison, and his performance continued to be rated high. At that point, the section of the AMA in which Weihaupt worked was reorganized, his position was restructured, and he found himself reporting to a new supervisor. He did not know it then, but rocky times lay ahead. Weihaupt was fifty-one at the time.

After evaluating Weihaupt's job performance, the new supervisor decided that Weihaupt was not qualified for the restructured position. Specifically, the new supervisor expressed lack of confidence in Weihaupt's ability to develop and implement AMA goals. Weihaupt was then demoted and replaced by a newly hired employee, age thirty-six. Thereupon, Weihaupt resigned and sued the AMA for age discrimination.

The AMA readily admitted that, prior to the reorganization, Weihaupt was well qualified for his position, but it argued that this was irrelevant in determining whether Weihaupt was qualified to remain in that position after it was restructured. As the court observed: "Whether one is qualified may change from time to time. The fact that an individual may have been qualified in the past does not mean that he is qualified at a later time."

The AMA contended that Weihaupt was no longer qualified for the position because he lacked substantive knowledge of health care policies and was deficient in the organizational abilities required of the new position. In response, Weihaupt could do no more than challenge the judgment of his superiors by asserting his qualifications for the position, as he perceived them. This was not enough. Weihaupt could not show that his employer's judgments were age biased. His case was dismissed.[3]

For Weihaupt to have succeeded, he would have had to prove that the restructuring of his position was part of an AMA plan to remove him because it was felt he was too old for the position, or because the AMA wanted to place a younger worker in his position. If either had been the object of an AMA plan to eliminate Weihaupt, then clearly the plan would have been motivated by age bias. But Weihaupt offered no evidence, direct or indirect, showing an unlawful motive on the part of the AMA.

Demotion cases are rather rare, representing a small fraction of the age discrimination suits filed in the courts. Unlike discharge cases, in a demotion case the complaining employee usually remains employed after the alleged discriminatory action (Weihaupt represents the exception). The prospect of suing one's current employer ordinarily constitutes enough of a deterrent for the worker to live with the demotion. Even if the worker sues and wins, the relief normally granted to the worker does not justify the effort involved to obtain it. The courts are unlikely to require the employer to restore the worker to his or her old position, since judges generally look upon such action as an ill-advised intervention in the business affairs of an employer. It is more likely that the court will assess damages against the employer, but these damages will be computed as the difference in salary and benefits paid to the worker before the demotion and those paid after—in most cases, a rather small sum, or at least generally not large enough to warrant litigation. The rewards being small, little inducement exists to proceed to litigation in matters of this type. Demotion cases probably will continue to be a rarity on court dockets.

Intracompany transfers have been the subject of age discrimination litigation in two areas. The first is an employer's decision to deny a desirable transfer to an older worker, a decision made on the basis of the worker's age. Frequently, an age claim will arise in which an older worker requests a transfer to a more desirable position but then discovers that a much younger and less qualified employee has been given the position. The second is the imposition of an undesirable transfer upon an older worker. Transfers that result in loss of promotional opportunities and transfers to distant localities are usually denominated as "undesirable," and if age is a material factor in an employer's decision in ordering such a transfer, it is guilty of age discrimination. But as in the case of demotions, the worker complaining of a transfer or its denial is well advised to analyze the circumstances carefully before committing to litigating against his or her own employer.

Lawrence Jackson was denied a transfer in circumstances that made it easy for him to decide to file an age claim against his employer. Jackson worked for twelve years as a sales representative for an animal health business operated by Shell Oil Company in St. Louis. Shell later sold this portion of its business to Diamond Shamrock Corporation, which agreed to hire most of Shell's workers employed by the animal health business. Some of Shell's workers, including Jackson, expressed a desire to stay with Shell and inquired about the possibility of transferring to other positions within the company. Jackson refused to apply for employment with Diamond Shamrock, and Shell denied his request for transfer to another position. When the sale with Diamond Shamrock was completed, Shell dismissed Jackson.

Shell granted only one of the animal health sales representative's requests for transfer. This worker was thirty years old, had been with the company for two and a half years, and had an indifferent sales performance record. Jackson, on the other hand, was forty-three, had twelve years' experience with Shell as a sales representative, had been the senior sales representative for the preceding two years, and had been highly regarded for his work. Of the two, the less qualified, less experienced, and substantially younger employee was granted a transfer, while the other, who was more highly qualified with far more experience but also significantly older, was not. The jury's decision to award damages to Jackson in his age discrimination suit was affirmed by an appellate court that noted that substantial evidence supported the jury's conclusion that, but for Jackson's age, his request for transfer would have been granted.[4]

Generally, an employer is not obligated to create or locate another position for a worker displaced in a RIF or in connection with some other company reorganization. However, if the employer has maintained a policy of transferring workers to other positions whenever possible so as to minimize terminations following a RIF or a reorganization, then that employer is obligated to administer that policy without regard to age, as transfers favoring the younger at the expense of older workers are obviously not acceptable.

Frank Curto began working for Sears in 1970 as the administrative assistant to the vice president of the Sears department overseeing its leases. Curto's responsibilities included leases for Sears Tower in Chicago as well as other leases in Chicago and New York City. In the late 1970s, the need for Curto's services began to diminish, as rental properties were close to fully occupied and Sears had engaged an independent leasing agent for the Sears Tower. Eventually, Curto's position was eliminated, he was not offered another position, and he was terminated. Curto was fifty-nine at the time.

Curto claimed that Sears had previously maintained a policy of transferring workers whose positions had been eliminated to other jobs, and Sears had declined to transfer him to another position on account of his age. Moreover, Curto claimed, other jobs were available at the time his position was eliminated, but they were offered to younger workers. Sears argued that it had no duty to find Curto an alternative position, and that even if it had such a duty, no positions were then available for which Curto was qualified. Ultimately, Curto's case was dismissed on the ground that he was unable to identify specific job openings he was qualified to fill. Curto failed to establish one of the fundamental elements of his claim, and thus his charge that Sears favored younger workers by transferring them rather than him never reached the trial stage.[5]

Age discrimination claims arising out of an undesirable transfer have not met with much success. As a result of a reorganization and the subsequent elimination of his position, an older worker was ordered transferred from Pittsburgh to Harlingen, Texas. Although his pay and benefits remained unchanged, the worker resisted the transfer since he had no desire to move to Texas, far from his family and friends. He contended the transfer was motivated by his age, but the court was wholly unsympathetic to his position. Despite the worker's protestations, the court dismissed his claim, primarily because he had failed to prove that he had been subjected to any "adverse" employment decision: "Although [the worker] may have concluded that such a relocation would adversely affect his personal life, the ADEA *only addresses those business decisions which adversely affect one's business opportunities.* Furthermore, while it may be that Harlingen is not the Garden of Eden, no objective evidence of its undesirability was presented . . . except for . . . [the worker's] subjective and conclusory antipathy toward a reassignment there."[6]

Denials of promotions, demotions, unwillingness to grant transfers, and assignments of undesirable transfers do not exhaust the areas of the employment relationship in which workers have charged their employers with age discrimination since any other of the general terms and conditions of a worker's relationship with his employer also may give rise to an age claim. Eneas D'Aquino's nineteen years of employment with Citicorp/Diner's Club were relatively uneventful until he turned sixty. Thereafter, D'Aquino's performance was rated average or marginal, his annual salary increases were only minimal, and his applications for advancement were rejected. Ultimately, he filed an age discrimination suit, alleging that once he turned sixty, Citicorp/Diner's Club had given him unfavorable performance evaluations and minimal salary increases, had assigned him difficult work projects, and had denied him all opportunities for advancement. D'Aquino lost on all counts.

The court spelled out D'Aquino's burden of proof as one requiring him to establish that he had suffered "a materially adverse change in the terms or conditions of his employment" and that he would not have been subjected to such adverse treatment except for his age. The problem with D'Aquino's case, according to the court, was that he could not prove that any of the changes in the terms and conditions of his employment that occurred after he turned sixty actually were adverse. For example, the average and marginal performance evaluations were not much different from the evaluations given him before he turned sixty, and to the extent that they were different, the court accepted the explanations given by those evaluating his performance. Although D'Aquino presented evidence that younger workers were given salary increases exceeding his, the court stated in its ruling that this was not conclusive: "The law forbids employment discrimination on the basis of age; it does not require that the old be paid higher salaries than the young." D'Aquino's other claims met a similar fate because he failed to produce persuasive evidence of any age-motivated actions.[7]

Workers claiming discriminatory treatment with regard to other terms and conditions of employment, such as a failure to retrain or the imposition of inappropriate discipline, often do not succeed for the same reason that D'Aquino failed. For example, a part-time commission shoe salesman, charging that his work hours should not have been reduced, was unsuccessful in proving his employer had acted out of age bias, inasmuch as he was unable to offer convincing evidence that the reduction in hours occurred because the store's management considered him too old for the job.

In contrast to the cases we have been reviewing, courts have strongly reacted to an employer's harassment or base mistreatment of an aging worker. Monarch Paper Company hired Richard Wilson when he was forty-eight. After eleven years with the company, Wilson had advanced to the position of vice president and assistant to the president. At that time, Monarch placed

Wilson in charge of the completion of an office warehouse building in Dallas, the largest construction project ever undertaken
by Monarch. Wilson successfully completed the project within
budget.

Wilson later became aware that Monarch's long-range planning favored the advancement of younger workers at all levels
of management. When the president of the company fell ill, he
was replaced with a forty-two-year-old, who later refused to
speak to Wilson, now fifty-nine. This silent treatment was apparently tactical and part of a plan to get rid of Wilson. The
new president's planning proposals emphasized youth. In ordinary conversation, he frequently referred to the ages of company workers and expressed a desire to hire "new blood" and
develop a "young team." In the meantime, Monarch was dis-
mantling Wilson's position by transferring many of his responsibilities to others. Wilson was then presented with three
options: (1) accept a sales position at one-half his current compensation; (2) agree to termination, with the payment of three
months' severance; or (3) accept a position in the company's
warehouse in Houston at the same salary, but with a reduction
in benefits. In the belief that he was being offered the position
of warehouse manager, the only vacant position in Houston at
the time, Wilson elected the last option.

When Wilson reported for duty in Houston, he found, to
his dismay, that he had not been assigned to the position of
manager as he had been led to believe, but rather he had been
relegated to an entry-level supervisory position that required
no more than one year's experience in the paper business. Wilson had thirty years' experience in the paper business, had a
college degree, and was vastly overqualified for his new position. Immediately upon assuming this position, Wilson was subjected to continuous verbal abuse by the newly named Houston
warehouse manager, who routinely referred to him as the "old
man." Wilson was further demeaned when he was placed in
charge of housekeeping at the warehouse but was not provided
with any employees to perform housekeeping duties. Thus we
are presented with the picture of Wilson, formerly a vice

president and assistant to the president, reduced to sweeping floors and cleaning the employees' cafeteria.

A few months later, Wilson fell ill and was diagnosed as suffering from reactive depression resulting from on-the-job stress. As his condition continued to deteriorate, he was involuntarily hospitalized. Wilson's emotional illness was severe and long lasting. After his first hospitalization, he fell into a deep depression and again was hospitalized, and another five years elapsed before he was able to return to a normal life. Wilson had no history of emotional illness prior to his assignment to the Houston warehouse.

Wilson filed suit for age discrimination, alleging that Monarch had eliminated his former position, had reassigned him to an entry-level position, had intentionally inflicted emotional distress upon him, and had later terminated his long-term disability benefits in retaliation for his filing an age discrimination claim against the company. The jury awarded him damages in excess of $3,400,000.

It is difficult to imagine a more outrageous case than Wilson's. When Monarch appealed the jury's determination, the appellate court readily affirmed the decision in Wilson's favor:

> What takes this case out of the realm of an ordinary employment dispute is the degrading and humiliating way that [Wilson] was stripped of his duties and demoted from an executive manager to an entry-level warehouse supervisor with menial and demeaning duties. . . . We find it difficult to conceive a workplace scenario more painful and embarrassing than an executive, indeed a vice president and the assistant to the president, being subjected before his fellow employees to the most menial janitorial services and duties of cleaning up after entry-level employees: the steep downhill push to total humiliation was complete.[8]

Wilson won his case, but at what a personal cost! This is surely a unique case, but how often do management personnel consider the possible, or even probable, consequences following on their decisions that affect older workers? As we have seen repeatedly, far too often employment decisions are made with little regard for their effect upon the older worker and the resultant personal suffering endured by the worker and his or her family.

The harassment of a worker, such as that experienced by Wilson, is a tool used by employers bent on pressuring an older worker to resign or accept an earlier than planned retirement. An employer also may use the denial of a promotion or a demotion as a means of persuading, if not compelling, an older worker to resign. If the employer successfully induces a worker's resignation, the worker, later charging the employer with age discrimination, may be materially limited in the damages and other relief he may obtain under the law. This limitation, however, will not apply if the worker is able to show the court that his resignation was in effect an involuntary resignation, commonly referred to as a "constructive discharge."

A worker's resignation will be considered a constructive discharge if the employer required the worker to perform job functions under conditions so difficult that any reasonable person, working under those conditions, would feel compelled to resign. In other words, a worker is constructively discharged if she is forced to quit because of the intolerable working conditions she is compelled to endure.

What a reasonable person considers to be tolerable or intolerable is an issue often litigated in the courts. This issue frequently becomes a significant factor in an age discrimination case, for if the court determines that a worker's resignation occurred under circumstances considered by the court to be less than intolerable, back pay and other damages may be denied the worker, even if the employer is found guilty of age discrimination. Conversely, if constructively discharged, the worker may be eligible for the entire panoply of damages and other relief available to any worker unlawfully discharged because of his or her age.[9]

As related in chapter 4, shortly after Olga Cazzola's sixty-fifth birthday, her company was reorganized, her responsibilities were reduced, and she was ordered to report to a person she genuinely disliked. She immediately asked for a transfer, but her request was denied. Although she tried to please her new supervisor, she could do nothing right, and later was given a negative performance evaluation. Cazzola was then advised that if she failed to elect retirement, she would be further demoted. She decided to retire, but when later she sued for age discrimination, the court held that she had been constructively discharged for the reason that it could not be said that she had freely accepted retirement when her only other alternative was another demotion. Her situation had become intolerable.[10]

Harold Jacobson was the manager of International Sales of Ecko Housewares Company, a subsidiary of American Home Products. When Jacobson was fifty-seven, Ecko's president began to bypass him in favor of four younger sales managers under Jacobson's supervision. Then Jacobson was transferred to another subsidiary of American Home Products and was relegated to performing meaningless work, while his former responsibilities were divided among the four younger sales managers. Jacobson eventually resigned and sued for age discrimination. American Home Products asked the court to dismiss his case, asserting that Jacobson had voluntarily resigned and thus he had not been constructively discharged. If that argument had been successful, Jacobson would have been barred from the recovery of any damages that accrued after the date he left the company. The company contended that Jacobson could not have been constructively discharged because his working conditions were far from intolerable. He merely was unhappy with his new assignment, the company argued, and besides, his pay and benefits had not been diminished in the transfer.

The court viewed the matter differently. It ordered the case to proceed to trial to determine whether the company had tried to force Jacobson to resign because he was considered too old, and whether it constructively discharged him by transferring him from a powerful, influential position in one subsidiary to a sham position in another. The court also placed the pay and benefits issue in proper perspective: "It would be inconsistent with . . . the ADEA . . . to allow discriminating corporations to immunize themselves from the strictures of this . . . statute simply by maintaining . . . compensation at a comparable level when putting older employees out to pasture with little to do."[11]

You will recall that Wilson also continued to receive his vice president's salary after he had been assigned janitorial duties, but this did not render his working conditions any less intolerable. However, courts have differed on this issue. Contrary to the decisions in the Wilson and Jacobson cases, other courts have questioned whether a demotion with no change in pay can amount to a constructive discharge.[12]

Even when an employer resorts to the use of offensive working conditions as a means of forcing a worker's resignation, the worker must endure such conditions for some period of time before deciding that resignation is the only practicable alternative. The worker cannot act too quickly, lest the court rule that the worker did not endure these working conditions for a sufficient duration to render them intolerable.[13] When working conditions truly become intolerable, the worker will successfully establish his age discrimination case, provided he is able also to prove that the intolerable conditions derive from age bias.

When denied a promotion or transfer, forced to accept an undesirable transfer, or subjected to a demotion, disappointed older workers undoubtedly will continue to charge their employers with age discrimination, but the probability of success will continue to remain low. Here again, the ADEA as it has been interpreted by the courts has failed the older worker. These types of employment decisions evade the proscriptions of the ADEA since the underlying discriminatory motives are too easily concealed from view. Except in the most outrageous cases, the courts have done little to assist workers in their attempts to uncover employer discriminatory motives in these areas of the employment relationship.

8 Employer Retaliation against Age Discrimination Claimants

In more than forty years of practice as a lawyer, I never have had a more difficult client than Barbara Jones.[1] She was overly critical, obstinate, intransigent, and uncompromising. Nearly all of our meetings ended in anger and frustration. On at least four occasions, I pleaded with her to find another lawyer. At first, she tried, but she was unsuccessful in persuading any other lawyer to take her case. Subsequently, she refused even to consider the possibility of changing lawyers. She stated her position very clearly: "You are stuck with me; better make the best of it."

Jones had recently been fired and had sued her former employer for age and sex discrimination. She had been unable to find other employment and had far too much free time on her hands. Her job loss occurred just as the O. J. Simpson trial was beginning, and she spent a good portion of her day following the trial on television. At our meetings to discuss her case, my plans for conducting discovery and other aspects of the litigation were invariably met with "that's not the way the lawyers in the O. J. Simpson case do it." With consummate patience, I would explain to her that the Simpson case was a criminal matter and hers was not, that the statutes governing the respective cases were dissimilar in all respects, and that the rules of the California court where the Simpson case was being tried had no relevance to a proceeding in a federal court in New York City, where her case was pending. She would leave my office declaring she now understood the difference between the two cases, but at our next meeting, I would be informed "that is not the way the lawyers in the O. J. Simpson case do it."

Jones first came to my office convinced she was about to be fired, and not long after, she indeed was terminated. During her last few months on the job, she felt that both age and sex bias had undermined her employer's decisions affecting her status as an employee. Initially, I evaluated her case as rather weak, but sufficient evidence was on hand to justify proceeding with the case, at least through the discovery stage. If we were unable to develop more compelling evidence of discrimination, we would be confronted with the prospect of withdrawing the case or suffering a court-ordered dismissal. As we proceeded with discovery, the likelihood of proving age or sex discrimination grew less and less certain. But in addition to age and sex discrimination, Jones also had charged her employer with retaliation, claiming that her supervisor had undermined her status with the company because she had filed discrimination charges with the Equal Employment Opportunity Commission (EEOC). As the case proceeded, the evidence supporting the retaliation charge began to mount.

Workers who exercise the rights granted them by the Age Discrimination in Employment Act (ADEA) are protected from retaliatory actions by their employers.[2] It is unlawful for an employer to retaliate against a worker who has opposed an act of age discrimination, or who has filed a charge of age discrimination, or who has testified or participated in any proceeding or litigation relating to a charge of age discrimination. These actions are defined as "protected activities," and the statute has been broadly interpreted by the courts to maximize the protection of workers engaged in such activities. These protections fall into place with the first hint of an age claim. Even an informal, crudely drafted letter claiming discrimination and addressed to the company's human resources department is sufficient to trigger the statute's protections.

The Supreme Court has extended these protections to an employer's former workers.[3] If a discharged worker files a discrimination charge with the EEOC and the ex-employer later interferes with the worker's search for new employment, such as by withholding a letter of recommendation or by providing false and negative information to a prospective employer, the employer may be guilty of unlawful retaliation. The employer will find itself in even more difficulty if the worker then formally charges it with retaliation. Even if the employer prevails on the discrimination claim, it still may be held liable for retaliation.

Charging an employer with retaliation is one thing; proving it is another. The worker is required to prove a causal connection between her participation in a protected activity and the adverse or allegedly retaliatory action affecting her employment. A causal connection may be demonstrated through indirect evidence, such as the close proximity in time between the worker's participation in the protected activity and the employer's adverse employment action affecting that worker. The closer the proximity in time, the greater the likelihood the worker will successfully establish a retaliation charge.

A sudden change in the employer's attitude toward the worker following her participation in a protected activity also may constitute evidence of a retaliatory motive. Proximity in time and change in attitude are the basic elements of proof of causation, necessary to establish a retaliation charge.

Jones's employer argued that her termination occurred, not as a result of any discriminatory conduct on its part, but rather because of interpersonal problems she had with her co-workers and supervisors. She was described as generally uncooperative, insubordinate, overly opinionated, and argumentative and was portrayed as creating such a disruptive force in the office as to require her termination. My own experience with Jones led me to conclude that this description was not wholly unjustified, and that many of her problems were of her own making and not the result of discriminatory acts committed by her employer. Apparently, a host of Jones's former co-workers were prepared to testify on the employer's behalf and against her at the forthcoming trial. Since our case for age and sex discrimination was not developing as we had hoped, we decided to shift gears and focus our efforts on proving Jones's retaliation charge.

Unlike most workers who have been subjected to discriminatory conduct, Jones had filed a discrimination charge with the EEOC *before, not after*, her employment was terminated. Many workers delay the filing of a charge until after they have been fired, but in almost all cases, that is a mistake. Understandably, an older worker has no desire to alienate an employer by filing a discrimination charge, for an employer—guilty or not—will almost always react negatively in these circumstances. Thus, the charge itself may precipitate additional adverse actions against the worker. But on occasion, the filing of a charge may generate positive results for the worker. In a large company, the filing of a discrimination charge may alert upper management to the existence of discriminatory conduct among lower- and middle-management employees, conduct upper management was unaware of and which it finds reprehensible. Even an employer bent on discriminating against an older worker may suddenly desist from such conduct upon realizing that continued adverse treatment of the worker may result in a further charge of retaliation. Although Jones realized none of these benefits, the filing of a charge before being terminated had been an astute move, and she was about to reap other benefits.

Jones filed her charge with the EEOC in December 1993, and in early January 1994, the EEOC advised her employer of the contents of the charge. Two weeks later, Jones suffered the first in a series of adverse actions by her employer. The layout of the office in which she and the other employees worked consisted of two parallel rows of four cubicles. Each cubicle was just large enough for a desk and chair, and the cubicle walls were little more than waist high, thus affording little privacy. Until that time, the assignment of cubicles was done randomly, not on the basis of any preconceived plan. Jones's supervisor occupied one of the front cubicles, and Jones sat in one in the rear. Now, the seating arrangement was changed. Her supervisor moved to a rear cubicle, and Jones was assigned to a cubicle located immediately in front of his. The change enabled the supervisor to monitor Jones's daily activities, and thereafter she was compelled to endure the humiliating experience, as the company's most senior worker, of having her supervisor peer over her shoulder and record her every move. It was apparent that after Jones filed the EEOC charge, her employer had decided to fire her, and the change in seating arrangements was undertaken to facilitate the gathering of evidence in support of her forthcoming discharge.

After scrutinizing her work for nearly two months, Jones's supervisor issued her a warning notice, citing three incidents of "improper conduct demonstrating a lack of responsibility." All three incidents were based on false premises, as Jones was able to demonstrate. In fact, while preparing a response to the warning notice, Jones learned that a fellow worker had witnessed one of the cited incidents and had confirmed the falsity of the supervisor's account.

Not long after, Jones received her annual performance evaluation and was given a rating designated as "marginal." Her supervisor had manipulated the evaluation to support the allegations asserted in the warning notice, and he had given no recognition to any of Jones's achievements during the previous year. A few weeks later, as Jones was entering her cubicle, she accidentally brushed against her supervisor. She was then accused of assaulting him. Jones, at least a foot shorter and 150 pounds lighter than her male supervisor, certainly was no match for him, and although the accusation obviously was spurious, Jones was fired the following day.

Once these facts were assembled, a clear picture of retaliation emerged, as the two basic elements of a retaliation claim were present. First, after Jones had engaged in a protected activity, the filing of a discrimination charge with the EEOC, her employer had taken adverse employment actions against her. The causal connection was apparent in the close proximity in time between her filing of the EEOC charge and the first adverse action taken against her, as well as in the sudden change in her employer's attitude toward her.

Ultimately, Jones's case was settled for nearly $400,000—equal to more than seven years' salary—a sum far in excess of my original evaluation.[4] We probably never will learn from the employer or its counsel the reason the employer agreed to settle for such a large figure, but I believe the strength of our retaliation case had to have been a significant factor in their calculations. If the case had proceeded to trial, we may very well have been defeated on the age and sex discrimination charges, but the retaliation charge appeared to be solid. The employer was unwilling to let a jury decide that issue.

On occasion, juries have rejected a worker's claim of age discrimination while ruling in favor of his retaliation charge. This occurred in Joseph Dominic's case. After he was terminated, Dominic sued his employer, the Consolidated Edison Company of New York, for age discrimination and retaliation. Dominic had joined Con Ed in 1971, and by 1976 he had risen to the position of training director. In that position, he had been placed in charge of Con Ed's Training Center, where he oversaw seventy course offerings, developed new courses, and supervised between twenty and thirty workers. Each year, he received excellent performance ratings and substantial merit increases.

As part of a reorganization conducted in 1981, Con Ed merged Dominic's position with a newly created position designated "manager of training and safety." Although Dominic had been promised assignment to the new position, Con Ed gave it to Dominic's fellow worker Henry Howe, and shortly thereafter, Dominic was demoted. At the time, Dominic was forty-eight and Howe thirteen years younger. Dominic complained to his manager that age bias had infected the decision assigning Howe to the new position as well as the decision demoting Dominic.

As Dominic later learned, just prior to Howe's appointment to the new position, Con Ed had retroactively lowered Dominic's performance evaluation rating and had raised Howe's rating. Upon learning that the performance evaluations had been manipulated, Dominic again accused Con Ed of allowing age discrimination to contaminate decisions made in connection with his employment.

Some time later, Dominic noticed that his supervisors were assigning him minor tasks normally performed by clerical staff. Then, in his next performance review, his supervisor cited him for nine specified deficiencies and placed him on a short-term review schedule. At this point, Dominic decided to file an age discrimination charge with the New York State Division of Human Rights.[5] The day after he filed the charge, Dominic's supervisor again evaluated his performance and, allegedly, found it wanting. Dominic was given the lowest possible rating, placed on probation, and soon after was terminated.

Ultimately, Dominic filed suit against Con Ed in federal court, alleging age discrimination and retaliation. Incredibly, despite the presence of more than sufficient evidence in support of the age discrimination charge, the jury rejected the claim, finding that age discrimination had not played a role in Dominic's discharge. However, the jury found in his favor on the retaliation charge, ruling that Con Ed had retaliated against him because he had asserted that age bias had been involved in the retroactive changes to his and Howe's performance ratings and also because he had filed a discrimination charge with the Division of Human Rights. An appellate court, later approving the jury's verdict, noted that the assignment of clerical functions to Dominic, the significantly lower performance ratings, and Dominic's dismissal all appeared to be acts of retaliation ordered by Con Ed in retaliation for Dominic's assertion of age discrimination and his filing of a charge against the company.[6]

Con Ed, like Jones's employer, overreacted to a claim of discrimination, then committed acts of retaliation, and ended up paying the price for its folly. When an employer unlawfully retaliates against a worker, it succeeds only in providing the worker with another weapon to bludgeon the employer.

"Bludgeon" is not too strong a word to describe what Catherine Malarkey and her employer, Texaco, did to each other over the course of a litigation that lasted more than ten years.

One of the judges involved in the case depicted Malarkey and Texaco as "two parties . . . locked in the destructive embrace of a bitterly contested employment discrimination case."

Malarkey began working for Texaco as a grade six secretary. When hired, Malarkey was just thirty and already had an impressive background, having served as a secretary to a high-ranking executive in another large corporation. By all accounts, she was a commendable employee at Texaco, rising quickly through the secretarial ranks and attaining a grade twelve position within ten years. At that point, Malarkey took a six-month unpaid leave of absence to care for an ailing family member. When she returned from her leave, no grade twelve secretarial positions were available. Texaco, however, offered her an administrative position in its employment office, and Malarkey accepted that position.

About a year later, Malarkey prepared a memorandum for her supervisor questioning Texaco's employment practices, alluding to possible acts of age and sex discrimination. Malarkey informed her supervisor that she found it very difficult to place older women in positions at Texaco since only young, physically attractive women generally were found acceptable by male supervisors. After she wrote this memo, Malarkey was demoted from grade twelve to grade eleven and forced out of the employment office.

Texaco then assigned Malarkey to a grade eleven secretarial position, working for one of the company's vice presidents. Malarkey later asserted that she accepted this assignment only because her supervisors had assured her that if her work proved satisfactory, her grade twelve rank would be restored. However, when the vice president for whom she was working was promoted to senior vice president, he selected another secretary to accompany him to the executive suite. Malarkey then filed discrimination charges with the EEOC, alleging that she had been the subject of age as well as sex discrimination. By the time her case reached trial in federal court, Malarkey had added to her lawsuit a claim for retaliation. She claimed that after she had filed the EEOC charges, Texaco had refused to assign her to any of the grade twelve secretarial positions that became avail-able and thus was guilty of retaliation.

Following an eight-day trial, the jury returned a verdict against Malarkey on her discrimination claims but sustained her allegation that Texaco had intentionally engaged in retaliatory conduct against her. This is another example of an employer's overreaction to a worker's charge of discrimination, a charge in this case, as in the Dominic case, that ultimately was rejected by the jury. In overreacting, Texaco committed acts of retalia-tion against Malarkey that the jury recognized as a basis for re-covery of damages for Malarkey.[7]

The reaction of an employer to a charge of discrimination does not vary that much from an employer's reaction to charges of fraud, theft, or other criminal activity. Employers are all too prone to strike back at a worker who even as much as utters the word "discrimination." It then becomes a violator of the law that bars acts of retaliation, whether or not it is guilty of acts of discrimination.

A worker who testifies on behalf of a fellow worker who has charged their employer with discrimination is engaged in a protected activity, and adverse actions later taken against the testifying worker may be retaliatory. Stephen Padilla found him-self in these circumstances.

Not long after Padilla began his employment with Metro-North Commuter Railroad in New York, he was promoted to superintendent of train operations. In this position, Padilla was in charge of Metro-North's operations control center and was responsible for the supervision of approximately thirty-five workers, including Metro-North train dispatchers. Padilla re-ported to Edmond Boni, who was in charge of the Transporta-tion Department.

One of Padilla's primary responsibilities was to ensure on-time departures and arrivals of Metro-North trains. Apparently, he was very good at his job, for his performance evaluation rat-ings were recorded as "above job expectations," and he was de-scribed as an excellent leader, having performed outstandingly in managing the train dispatchers.

One of the train dispatchers under Padilla's supervision was Michael Barletta, age sixty. Although Padilla believed Barletta performed his job functions well, Boni thought that Barletta was too old and too slow for the job, and he insisted that Barletta be demoted. Subsequent to his demotion, Barletta filed an age discrimination claim with the EEOC. At the request of an EEOC investigator, Padilla gave an affidavit supporting Barletta's charge, stating that "Boni had insisted that Barletta be removed from his job," that Boni had stated that "Barletta had old working habits" and that "some of these old guys can't stand the stress because the jobs are more pressurized than they ever were before."

When Boni learned about the affidavit, he accused Padilla of disloyalty and told Padilla he "was going to get [him] for co-operating [with Barletta]." When Padilla was soon thereafter suspended, he also filed a charge with the EEOC, alleging his suspension had been ordered in retaliation for his participation in the EEOC investigation of Barletta's charge. At that point, Padilla also was demoted, allegedly because of mismanagement. When Padilla's retaliation charge reached the trial stage, the jury had little difficulty in concluding that he had indeed been re-taliated against for participating in the Barletta EEOC investigation.[8]

A high proportion of retaliation charges are sustained, but not all of them, as Samuel Mesnick discovered. In 1974, Mesnick, a lawyer by training, was hired by Radio Corporation of America (RCA) as a senior contracts administrator at its plant in Burlington, Massachusetts. He was fifty-one at the time. RCA promoted Mesnick several times, eventually to manager of contracts administration. In 1986, the General Electric Company purchased RCA's business and installed new management at the Burlington facility. Subsequently, GE ordered Mesnick to report to a new supervisor. The initial evaluation of Mesnick's performance conducted by the new supervisor was largely negative, and Mesnick was given a smaller than expected salary increase. At this point, Mesnick complained to the Burlington plant manager that age discrimination may have influenced the poor performance evaluation and the small pay increase.

Later, GE reorganized the Burlington Contracts Department and created a new supervisory position that included some of Mesnick's former duties. Mesnick expressed an interest in the new position, but following a national search, GE assigned the position to a newly hired employee nine years younger than Mesnick. GE also designated a new title for Mesnick but deprived him of supervisory power over other employees. Mesnick was left, as a federal judge later noted, "an emperor without an empire." Mesnick then filed age discrimination charges with the EEOC.

A whole series of squabbles between Mesnick and his supervisor ensued that ultimately culminated in Mesnick's termination. Mesnick claimed that GE had retaliated against him for having initially complained to the plant manager about his suggestion that age discrimination had adversely affected the decisions made regarding his position with the company and, in addition, for having filed a charge with the EEOC.

The court later granted GE summary judgment, dismissing Mesnick's retaliation claim, on the ground that Mesnick had failed to establish a connection between his participation in protected activities and the adverse actions taken against him. Nine months had elapsed between Mesnick's complaint to the plant manager and GE's filling of the new supervisory position with a younger worker, and another nine months had passed between Mesnick's EEOC filing and his termination. As the court stated, "the very chronology of the case militates" against a finding in Mesnick's favor since the sequence of events suggests the absence of a causal connection between the protected activities (the complaining of age discrimination to the plant manager in the first instance and the EEOC filing in the second) and the adverse employment actions that followed (the failure to select Mesnick for the new supervisory position in the first instance and his termination in the second). In both instances, the passage of time was too great to prove that the adverse actions undertaken by GE were retaliatory.[9]

More often than not, retaliation is easier to prove than discrimination. Employers who discriminate generally conceal their discriminatory conduct, but they seem not to care who is aware of their acts of retaliation. When one of my clients complained to her supervisor about the discriminatory treatment she had experienced, she also informed him that she had consulted with the EEOC and had retained me as her attorney. She was fired on the spot. A clearer case of retaliation cannot be imagined.

Human resources personnel and company counsel are made aware through their training that acts of retaliation against any worker engaged in a protected activity are unlawful, but apparently this awareness is rarely assimilated by the management employees who order these acts of retaliation in response to claims of discrimination. Emotional responses made in retaliation only multiply the problems confronting an employer charged with employment discrimination.

9 | Women and Age Discrimination

The Equal Employment Opportunity Commission (EEOC) has jurisdiction over race, sex, national origin, religion, and disability employment discrimination claims, as well as claims based on age. In 1980, thirteen years after the enactment of the Age Discrimination in Employment Act (ADEA), 11,000 age claims were filed with the EEOC, representing nearly 19 percent of all employment discrimination claims filed that year. Thereafter, the annual filings of age claims steadily increased until they reached nearly 20,000 in 1993, about 23 percent of all discrimination claims filed.[1]

From the inception of the ADEA, most age discrimination claimants have been white males. Most often, they are between the ages of fifty and fifty-nine, have held professional or managerial positions, and are more likely than any other group of workers to file suits in connection with their terminations of employment. An early study showed that 86 percent of age claimants were male, 79 percent were white collar, 55 percent were between ages fifty and fifty-nine, and 76 percent were contesting their dismissals.[2] Another study disclosed that more than 50 percent of age discrimination claimants were professional or management employees, and although nearly 49 percent of

the labor force was then engaged in manual labor, only 17 percent of the age claims were filed by workers in that group.[3] Far
fewer blue-collar workers and women have appeared as age discrimination claimants.

The infrequency of blue-collar filings may be attributable
to the availability for many of these workers of collective bargaining grievance procedures and union-management arbitration. Seniority provisions of union agreements also afford older
workers protections not found outside unionized settings.

In one respect, this profile of the average age discrimination claimant is changing. Women are now far more likely than
in the past to be found in the courtroom prosecuting age claims.
In previous years, the small number of female claimants may
have been attributable, at least in part, to the common employer
practice of channeling women into lower-paying positions. The
average award granted to women who prevailed in EEOC age
claims filed between 1990 and 1995 was $12,115, whereas the
average award granted to successful male claimants during that
period was $25,479.[4] Having less at stake, women have been
less enthusiastic about becoming embroiled in litigious discrimination proceedings. Still, the proportion of age complaints filed
by women with the EEOC increased from 14 percent in the years
immediately following enactment of the ADEA to more than 30
percent during the five-year period between 1990 and 1995.[5]

In 1997, 19,000,000 women forty-five years of age and older
were in the labor force. Seventy-six percent of all women between the ages of forty-five and fifty-four were either employed
or looking for employment, and 50 percent of women in the
next oldest age group, that is, fifty-five through sixty-four, also
were so engaged. By 1997, women accounted for 46 percent of
the total workforce, and it is projected that by 2006, 48 percent
of the workforce will be female.[6]

A review of the cases reported in the Bureau of National
Affairs Labor Reports during the first six months of 1997 showed
that 36 percent of the age discrimination cases pending in the
federal courts throughout the country had been filed by women.
Thus, in parallel with the increase in the number of working

women, the courts have experienced a steady growth in the number of women willing to assert their legal rights under the ADEA. If this trend continues, we will soon witness an avalanche of women-initiated age discrimination cases descending upon our courts.

This trend is reflected in my own practice, since women now appear more inclined than men to initiate legal action once they have been victimized on the job. Long subjected to sex discrimination in the workplace, women are extremely sensitive to any form of animus exhibited by their supervisors and are more apt to attribute adverse job actions to the bias of their managers and supervisors. Middle-aged and older women identify that bias as associated with age, as well as with gender.

Men ordinarily do not experience the effects of age discrimination until they reach their mid-fifties. Women, however, become aware of age-biased actions by the time they reach their mid- to late forties. In the workplace, women get "old" at a younger age than men because youth is considered a more important qualification for women than for men.[7]

As some of the cases discussed in preceding chapters show, women are confronted with many of the same hazards as men in surviving RIFs and other types of corporate reorganizations, but women are vulnerable, where men are not, to age-related employment decisions affecting other areas of the employer-employee relationship. The combination of sex *and* age may culminate in a job loss for a woman, but not for a man. Although more women in the fifty to fifty-nine age group file age claims with the EEOC than any other age group, the same as for men, more women between ages forty and forty-nine simultaneously file *both* age and sex discrimination claims than any other age group of women.[8]

Joan Palmiero worked as a manufacturing supervisor for Weston Controls, a division of Schlumberger, Ltd. At age fifty-four, after Palmiero had spent thirty years on the job, Weston terminated her, and when she asked her supervisors the reason for her dismissal, she was told that her duties were to be assumed by two male workers, both of whom were much younger than she. Subsequently, Palmiero sued Weston for both age and sex discrimination. At the trial, Weston's executives testified to a number of issues that proved damaging to the company's defense. They testified that they had set out to re-plenish Weston's workforce and had maintained statistics on the average age of the workers on staff. In the hiring of new per-sonnel, they had been directed by Schlumberger to recruit in-dividuals "fresh out of college." Their goal was to keep the organization "lean and mean." Palmiero's male replacements were described as "young comers." This testimony left little doubt that age and sex discrimination paved the way for Palmiero's termination, and the jury awarded her more than half a million dollars in damages.[9]

In 1968, Merced Community College, located in Califor-nia, hired Edyna Sischo-Nownejad for the faculty of its art de-partment. The college generally based the assignment and scheduling of classes on the input of its faculty members, who customarily were consulted with regard both to their preferences and to their need for course materials and supplies. Senior faculty members who had developed particular courses were normally selected to teach them. The college followed these practices in connection with all faculty members other than Sischo-Nownejad, who was the only female member of the art department faculty and, moreover, one of its oldest. The col-lege declined to consult with Sischo-Nownejad concerning the courses she was assigned to teach, it assigned courses to her she would rather not have taught, and it failed to select her to teach the courses she had developed. Although other faculty members received all the supplies they requested, she received none. If all this were not enough for her to endure, for three years she was singled out among the art department faculty to have her classes closely monitored by her fellow teachers, all male.

For six years, Sischo-Nownejad was subjected to biased age and gender comments. She was referred to as "an old warhorse," and her students were characterized as "little old ladies." Her division chairperson sarcastically referred to her as a "women's libber" and on at least two occasions urged her to retire.

Sischo-Nownejad alleged that the college had discriminated against her on the basis of sex, in violation of Title VII, and on the basis of age, in violation of the ADEA. The college asked the court to dismiss her case, but the court refused, ruling that she had introduced sufficient evidence to give rise to inferences of both age and sex discrimination. As the only female and one of the oldest art department faculty members, she was subjected to treatment that differed substantially from that accorded all other faculty members. At the same time that her superiors were subjecting her to less favorable working conditions, she was made the butt of ageist and sexist stereotypical comments. Sischo-Nownejad presented a strong case for age as well as sex discrimination.[10]

What Sischo-Nownejad experienced in an academic community, Verna Turner encountered in the world of the blue-collar worker. Turner worked for Independent Stave Company (ISC), a manufacturer of wooden barrel staves. ISC purchased white-oak logs, debarked them, and then formed them into barrel staves and headings. ISC hired Turner in 1974 to work in its mill in Bunker, Missouri, and it assigned her the jobs of "strip catcher, stacker, and second edger." Turner, however, was unable to keep up with the mill's production demands, and ISC reassigned her to the position of "grader," a position she remained in for several years.

In 1985, when ISC confronted a diminished demand for bourbon barrels, one of its major products, it decided to combine some of the Bunker mill positions as a means of reducing its operating costs. It combined the jobs of grader and stacker and assigned the new position to Turner, but again she was unable to keep up with production. Not long after, ISC halted operations at the Bunker mill and it was shut down, and nine of the mill's thirteen workers, including Turner, were laid off. At the time the mill ceased operations, Turner was the only woman working at the mill and, at the age of fifty-four, was next to the oldest of the mill's workers. About seven months later, ISC recalled all the workers who had been laid off except for Turner, who was notified that she had been permanently laid off because the position of grader had been eliminated.

After the mill was reopened, the positions of grader and stacker were again combined, and several men, each younger than Turner, attempted to perform the operations of the combined positions. None, however, was successful, because none could keep up with production. Ultimately, ISC separated the positions of grader and stacker, as they had been when Turner filled the grader position, but Turner was not recalled to fill the reconstituted grader position. Turner then filed suit for age and sex discrimination.

Turner's case was tried before a court without a jury, and the court found in her favor, ruling that she had met her burden of proving that sex and age were determining factors in ISC's decision not to recall her after the mill reopened. The court was persuaded by the fact that Turner was the only female worker employed at the mill, that she was the oldest worker but one, and that she had satisfactorily filled the grader position for several years. The court was of the opinion that except for her age and sex, Turner would have been called on by ISC, on the mill's reopening, to fill the grader position.[11]

The replacement of an older woman by a younger man frequently establishes the basis for an age and sex suit, but sometimes the employer's discriminatory conduct is not as clearly apparent as in the cases we have just reviewed. After working for twelve years with the Defense Industrial Supply Center (DISC) as a computer specialist/instructor, Mary Arnett, who by then was forty-nine, sought to move on to a higher position. She responded to a job opportunity announcement for an equal employment specialist, a grade GS-7 position, but was notified that her experience was insufficient to qualify her for the position. About a month later, the same position was again advertised, this time as a GS-5 or a GS-7, and Arnett reapplied. Subsequently, the personnel office found that both Arnett and another woman, Kelly Williams, were qualified for the position on both the GS-5 and GS-7 levels, and that six other applicants had qualified at the GS-5 level only. DISC selected Williams, more than twenty years younger than Arnett, for the equal employment specialist position.

A short time later, another equal employment specialist position became available, and DISC considered Arnett and the six candidates who had qualified at the GS-5 level for the position. Again, DISC chose not to select Arnett for the position but instead assigned the position to a worker more than twenty years younger than she.

Arnett commenced an action in federal court alleging both age and sex discrimination. She claimed that DISC had denied her both of the equal employment specialist positions because she was a woman and because she was over forty, and that decisions pertaining to both positions had been infected with age as well as sex bias. The evidence gathered in support of her case showed that every woman ever selected for the position of equal employment specialist had been under the age of forty. On the other hand, every man selected for that position had been over forty. The evidence also established that every female candidate for the position who was over the age of forty had been rejected in favor of either a younger woman or a man over forty.

These circumstances presented a dilemma for Arnett and her attorneys. If Arnett were to charge DISC with sex discrimination alone, her case would be dismissed for the reason that women, albeit they were all young and under the age of forty, had been selected for these positions. On the other hand, if she alleged only age discrimination, her claim would also be subject to dismissal since men older than forty had been successful candidates for these positions. It was only because Arnett was a woman *and* over forty that she had been rejected. But neither Title VII nor the ADEA specifically grants protection against discrimination for "older women." The ADEA affords protection against discriminatory acts directed at workers age forty and older, and Title VII bars discrimination against women. But neither law, in and of itself, provides protection for a subgroup of workers composed of older women. Therefore, if Arnett's claim that she was discriminated against because she was an older woman were analyzed as two separate claims, one under Title VII and one under the ADEA, neither claim would survive.

In order to succeed, Arnett first had to convince the court that either Title VII or the ADEA entitled her to relief as an older woman. Her attorneys were able to accomplish this by persuading the court to consider Arnett's claim as a Title VII sex discrimination claim limited to a subgroup of women, namely, those over forty. In other words, in alleging sex discrimination, Arnett was not claiming that DISC had discriminated against all women but only against women over age forty.[12] This solution resolved Arnett's dilemma, and the court allowed her to proceed with her case.

Although Arnett was successful, other women have not been so fortunate. Some courts insist upon separating the statutes, thus requiring an older woman to prove that she was subjected to discriminatory acts either because she is a woman or because she is over forty.[13] In these circumstances, the courts require that sex and age claims be kept analytically separate. Arnett's claim would not survive in these courts. As we will consider in greater detail in chapter 19, the law should be amended to prevent this result.

Older women often face circumstances at the work site that men never have to confront. Some employers prefer attractive women on their staffs, and they largely equate attractiveness with youth. As we have seen, when Catherine Malarkey was assigned to Texaco's employment office, it was apparent to her that young attractive female workers were more readily hired and advanced than older women. If older women are held to a standard of attractiveness that differs from that for men and the basis of that standard is youth, then an employer implementing that standard is guilty of both age and sex discrimination.

Before being dismissed, Carolyn Proffitt worked as a salesperson for Anacomp, Inc., in Ohio. One of the reasons given the forty-one-year-old Proffitt for her discharge was that in order for women to do well in sales, they should be sexually attractive, and that Proffitt would not do well because, as she was told, she was no longer sexually attractive. After Proffitt was terminated, her accounts were assigned to a thirty-four-year-old female trainee whom management apparently found to be more

sexually attractive than Proffitt.[14] Waitresses and other workers whose positions require them to deal with the public are
frequently held to this standard of attractiveness, which clearly
violates the ADEA. Older men are spared this indignity.

Even though their life expectancy exceeds that of men by
seven years, women are expected to retire at the same age as
men. But continuing in the workforce may be a matter of necessity for a self-supporting widow, as it is for an increasing
number of older divorced women who seek to hold on to their
jobs well beyond the "normal" retirement age of sixty-five. Many
other women enter the workplace later in life, and still others
interrupt their work life to have children.[15] These women, if
self-supporting, will opt to remain in the workforce long after
the retirement dates suggested by their employers. Inevitably,
the increasing tension between these women and youth-oriented
employers will force greater numbers of women to assert their
rights under the ADEA.

10 The Employer's Motion for Summary Judgment

Employers abhor discrimination suits and are willing to spend vast sums in defending themselves against claims alleged by their workers. From the employer's perspective, it is money well spent if it achieves a positive result, since the dismissal of a discrimination suit may discourage other workers from initiating similar claims against the company. Thus, the suing worker must be prepared to confront the immense resources, financial and otherwise, the employer will place at the disposal of its attorneys to defeat the worker's claim.

Invariably, employers turn to the largest law firms to defend them against employment discrimination suits. The attorneys for the workers, on the other hand, are almost always solo practitioners or members of small law firms. Because the costs of pursuing a discrimination case to conclusion are beyond the means of most workers, their counsel will frequently find it necessary to enter into contingency fee relationships with their client-workers. Counsel fees, therefore, can be partly or wholly deferred until the end of the suit, but the other costs of the lawsuit cannot, and these costs can be and often are substantial. Deposition costs and experts' fees on occasion may reach

$15,000 to $20,000, even in a small case. But while the worker and counsel struggle with these costs and with preparations for a trial, the employer and its counsel have other matters in mind.

Jury trials in age discrimination cases present substantial risks for employers. Juries are generally sympathetic to the older dismissed worker who, because of his age, more than likely has been unable to find another job and probably will remain unemployed or underemployed for the remainder of his life. Thus, employers firmly believe they enter the courtroom at a distinct disadvantage. The employer's strategy, therefore, is to avoid that courtroom. While the worker and his counsel are devoting their efforts to preparing the case for trial, the employer and its counsel are directing their efforts to obtaining a dismissal of the worker's case before it reaches the trial stage. In its pretrial discovery and other pretrial preparations, the employer is primarily interested in developing a litigation record that will enhance its chances of securing a dismissal of the case before it reaches a jury. The pretrial discovery conducted by the worker's counsel, on the other hand, will focus on the development of a record of evidence that will appear persuasive to a jury. Thus, the jury factor stands as a significant ingredient in the strategy for both sides.

It is the motion for summary judgment that affords the employer the opportunity to procure an early dismissal of the worker's case, thus avoiding a trial before a jury. It is not surprising, therefore, that the employer's counsel often regard the motion for summary judgment as the most important aspect of the entire litigation. The purpose of the motion for summary judgment is to permit the court to assess the evidence that the employer and the worker intend to offer during the course of the trial to determine whether a genuine need for a trial actually exists.

Employers' counsel use several techniques in structuring a record in support of a motion for summary judgment. Typically, the worker will be forced to endure several days of deposition questioning, the primary purpose of which is to obtain admissions from the worker that then may be used to support the employer's reason for rendering a job-related decision adverse to the worker. As an example, if the employer intends to defend its discharge of the worker on the ground that the worker's performance had deteriorated, its counsel will attempt to elicit from the worker testimony admitting that in some respects his performance had indeed been deficient, thus buttressing the employer's case.

Another tactic used by company counsel is to attempt, during the course of the worker's extended deposition, to uncover inconsistencies in the worker's testimony. Variations, gaps, and disparities in testimony may persuade a court to dismiss the worker's testimony as not credible, which enhances the chances that the employer's position will be accepted by the court. Still another tactic is to try to demonstrate through the deposition testimony of the worker that little or no evidence exists to support his charge that the employer is guilty of age discrimination.

Even if the employer's counsel successfully weave a pattern of evidence supporting the company's position, a motion for summary judgment will fail unless the employer first demonstrates to the court's satisfaction that there are no unresolved issues of fact in the case. On a motion for summary judgment, the court is barred from deciding factual issues in favor of one side or the other. If the court is faced with issues of fact it considers material to a decision in the case, it must deny the motion for summary judgment and proceed to trial.

The employer and the worker almost always disagree on the basic fact issues in the case. For example, the employer argues that the worker was fired not because of advancing age but because of serious performance problems. The worker responds that his employment record shows an extended history of excellent performance evaluations, and that it was not until the employer decided to terminate the employment relationship that his performance was suddenly the object of severe criticism and his performance ratings were downgraded. A material issue of fact thus surfaces and cannot be decided by the court on a motion for summary judgment. It is an issue that must be deferred for the trial. The worker's basic strategy in defending against a motion for summary judgment is quite apparent: He must elaborate as many issues of fact as the circumstances permit.

One of the basic elements of the worker's burden of proof in an age discrimination case is proof that the employer intended or was motivated to discriminate against the worker because of his or her age. Because it is highly unlikely that any employer will ever freely admit to a discriminatory intent, proof establishing such an intent almost always depends on the inferences that may be drawn from the relevant facts in the case. This is discussed at length in chapter 11, but it is enough here to note that the question of the employer's intent almost always is dependent on issues of fact that must be reserved for the jury's consideration. The issue of intent is not one readily resolvable on a motion for summary judgment.

Even if the facts as presented by the parties are ambiguous, the law provides that all factual inferences must be drawn in favor of the party opposing the motion for summary judgment, in this case, the worker. Also, all the evidence must be viewed in the light most favorable to the worker. This places the employer at a tremendous disadvantage. As one court described it, twenty bishops testifying on behalf of the employer will not eliminate a genuine issue of fact.[1]

Flooded with fact issues, the court will turn aside the employer's attempt to obtain an early dismissal of the case. In order to avoid this result, the employer often uses another tactic: it eliminates issues of fact by assuming the worker's version of the facts to be true. The employer in effect says to the court, "We won't dispute the facts as the worker sees them. For the purpose of this motion, we will assume the worker's version of the facts is true. But even assuming the worker's factual contentions are accurate, his case still must be dismissed for the reason that the evidence fails to show that the worker's age was a factor in the decision to fire him." Accordingly, the employer argues, the case must be dismissed as a matter of law.

When confronted with this argument, the court must view

the factual assertions from the perspective of a typical jury. If the worker has failed to present any evidence of discriminatory motive on the part of the employer, then the motion for summary judgment may be granted. If the worker presents evidence sufficient at least to raise an inference of discriminatory intent on the part of the employer, then the motion must be denied, unless the court believes that no reasonable, fair-minded jury could find from the evidence on hand that the worker is entitled to a verdict.

In summary, if material facts are at issue, the case will not be dismissed at this stage of the proceedings. If the facts are not at issue and the evidence raises an inference of discriminatory conduct, the case will not be dismissed unless the worker's case is so weak that no jury could possibly rule in his favor. If you think this scenario favors the worker, you are absolutely correct. Because of the difficulties confronting the employer on a motion for summary judgment, few of these motions are successful. The worker more often than not defeats the motion, and the case proceeds to trial.

The picture presented here is somewhat oversimplified. The rules of law governing the granting and denying of motions for summary judgment differ from court to court. In addition, every case is different from every other, and lawyers and judges differ widely on the application of these rules in dissimilar conditions and contexts. But irrespective of the court and the attorneys involved, the employer always faces Herculean obstacles in attaining a successful outcome. Nonetheless, the employer invariably sets a litigation course requiring a motion for summary judgment and sometimes, but not often, wins.

The employer wins when the evidence shows that a dismissed worker is replaced not by a significantly younger worker but by a worker who is merely marginally younger. It wins when the worker's job performance record is so poor that no reasonable jury would question the employer's decision to fire him. It wins when it appears that the worker will fail to establish an essential element of his case. For example, at the trial, the worker has the burden of proving that the employer intended to discriminate against him on account of his age. This is an essential element of his case. To defeat a motion for summary judgment, however, the worker merely has to show that the facts pertaining to the employer's intent are in issue. But the worker will fail to defeat the motion if the employer is able to show that the worker has no evidence to support his claim that the employer intended to discriminate against him. In those circumstances, there are no issues of fact, and the case will be dismissed. We will examine a few cases to see how this works out in the courtroom.

At the time of his discharge by the Columbus & Greenville Railroad in Mississippi, Maud Lee Thornbrough was fifty-six years old and held the position of vice president of federal projects. He had worked in the railroad business for thirty-one years, the last five with C&G Railroad. During those five years, he held a variety of positions, including assistant chief engineer, vice president–chief engineer, vice president of transportation, and vice president of operations.

The C&G Railroad was established in 1975 and from its inception was plagued with financial concerns. Between 1975 and 1982, it experienced only one profitable year, and its net losses for that period were nearly $4 million. In 1982, it decided to cut its losses by reducing its workforce from 106 employees to 60. Thornbrough was one of those terminated.

No one replaced Thornbrough in his position of vice president of federal projects. Instead, the position was eliminated, and Thornbrough's duties were divided among the railroad's chief engineer (age forty-seven), accountant (age thirty), and general supervisor of maintenance (age fifty-four). The railroad also retained several younger workers and hired two new employees with little railroad experience.

Thornbrough sued for age discrimination, alleging that he was better qualified than the younger workers who were retained, including the three workers who assumed his duties, and those newly hired. According to Thornbrough, the fact that younger, less qualified workers were retained and hired in preference to him supported his contention that C&G had discriminated against him on account of his age. The railroad countered with claims that Thornbrough was less effective than the younger workers who were retained and, moreover, was unqualified for several of the positions held by these workers. C&G asked the court to grant it summary judgment, dismissing Thornbrough's claims.

In a reduction-in-force case like this one, the worker must show that the employer failed to treat age neutrally in the process of reducing staff. The only evidence Thornbrough could offer in this regard was that several younger, less qualified workers were retained on staff and two inexperienced workers were hired, while he was terminated in the workforce reduction. The question before the court was whether Thornbrough had raised a genuine issue of fact regarding C&G's explanation for selecting him, rather than one of the younger workers, for discharge.

The court stated that it would not second-guess C&G's decision that Thornbrough was less qualified than the younger workers who were retained and hired. But, based on the facts presented to it, the court felt that a jury hearing the case could very well conclude that the explanations offered by the railroad were not the reasons that resulted in Thornbrough's dismissal. The court opined that the facts of the case "exude that faint aroma of impropriety." Even if it is assumed that C&G simply made a mistake in rejecting Thornbrough rather than one of the others, if a "mistake is large enough, we may begin to wonder whether it was a mistake at all." Whether C&G allowed age to enter into the termination process was a factual issue that could be decided only by a jury. Thus, the court rejected C&G's attempt to dismiss and sent the case along to be decided by a jury.[2]

Mariano Colosi was not as fortunate as Thornbrough. Colosi was vice president in charge of manufacturing operations for Electri-Flex Company when, at the age of fifty-seven, he was terminated and his duties were assigned to two younger workers. When Colosi sued for age discrimination, Electri-Flex filed a motion for summary judgment and submitted to the court evidence that Colosi had been fired because he was irascible and irresponsible. For instance, when a worker had displeased Colosi by talking too much, Colosi offered him a choice between a three-day suspension and shouting at the top of his lungs for one hour outside the company's plant. (The worker decided to shout.) In addition, the company claimed that Colosi failed to learn and use a newly installed inventory control computer system.

Colosi had no direct evidence of age discrimination to offer the court, and thus in order to survive the company's motion for summary judgment, he had to demonstrate that disputed factual issues underlay the company's reasons for dismissing him. Colosi relied primarily upon the fact that the company's records failed to mention any of the shortcomings with which he was then being charged. The court, however, pointed out that Electri-Flex was a small, family-owned company, with no more than a hundred employees: "Family-owned companies of this size conduct their operations with less formality than large publicly owned corporations. Blizzards of paper are one of the symptoms of bureaucracy, and bureaucracy is the plague of large, not small, enterprises." The court held that in light of the dearth of evidence submitted in support of Colosi's age claim, there were no factual issues requiring a jury determination, and thus his suit was dismissed.[3]

Jack Spence's age discrimination suit against Maryland Casualty Company met a similar fate. Maryland Casualty was an insurance company headquartered in Baltimore. Spence began working with the company after graduating from college in 1950 and, except for a short period, continued as one of its employees for more than thirty-five years. In 1977, the company promoted Spence to manager of its office in Buffalo, where he proved to be very successful in that he succeeded in increasing the volume of policy premiums received by that office from $5 million in 1977 to $39 million ten years later. But all was not well with the Buffalo office.

In 1987, Spence, who was then fifty-eight, reported to William Loden, the branch manager supervisor of the company's Mid-Atlantic region, who in turn reported to Thomas Fitzsimmons, vice president for the region. In the spring of 1987, both Loden and Fitzsimmons criticized Spence's management of the Buffalo office. In June of that year, Loden visited the Buffalo office and harangued Spence and his staff. In a July meeting, Loden criticized Spence's management style "as unduly soft," and he told Spence he wanted him to "kick people in the ass, as I do it." Spence tried to explain that Loden's style was not his, and that he had been successfully motivating his staff for thirty-five years without resorting to the type of tactics advocated by Loden. Loden responded that if Spence wanted to remain with the company, he would have to change his management style.

Loden and Fitzsimmons continued throughout the remainder of 1987 and into the spring of 1988 to pressure Spence to alter his management style to conform with their perception of what was required to raise the level of proficiency of the Buffalo staff. Throughout all of this, Spence was placed under a great deal of stress, and his doctor later discovered he was suffering from a dangerously high blood pressure condition. His problems with Loden and Fitzsimmons worsened, and Spence elected to take sick leave in December 1988. Spence's lawyer later wrote to the company stating that Spence could return to work under normal conditions but not so long as he was required to work under the direction of Loden and Fitzsimmons. Thereafter, as a result of a complaint from another branch manager, both Loden and Fitzsimmons were demoted, and Spence was advised that he would no longer have to report to either of them. Since Spence was now relieved of the stress of dealing with Loden and Fitzsimmons, the company asked him to return to work. Spence refused to return, claiming that his doctor had advised against it. Spence, however, never informed his doctor that he no longer was required to report to Loden and Fitzsimmons.

Spence then commenced an age discrimination suit against Maryland Casualty, claiming that the company had abused him because of his age, ultimately forcing him into an early retirement. Spence's case was dismissed on the company's motion for summary judgment. The court questioned Spence's failure to register complaints against Loden and Fitzsimmons, especially in light of the fact that the company had acted promptly in relieving them of their responsibilities after another branch manager complained. The fact that the company asked Spence to return to the Buffalo office militated against the validity of his claim that he was forced into an early retirement because of his age. The facts were not in dispute. Summary judgment was appropriate; case dismissed.[4]

It may appear that the worker has little if anything to gain from a motion for summary judgment made by the employer. Unless reversed on appeal, a decision awarding the employer summary judgment constitutes total defeat for the worker. Conversely, a decision denying summary judgment to the employer leaves the employer and the worker in the same positions they held before the motion. Procedurally, the worker has nothing to gain other than the avoidance of total defeat, for he still must prove his case before a jury. But contrary to appearances, the employer's decision to move for summary judgment affords the worker advantages and opportunities otherwise not attainable.

Even though an employer may have been advised by its attorneys that the court is more likely than not to deny its motion for summary judgment, the impact of a defeat is no less devastating. No immediate appeal follows from the denial of a motion for summary judgment, and thus the employer at that point must confront the prospect of a jury trial, a prospect it has not even permitted itself to consider seriously until this point in the proceedings. After the motion is denied, employers generally appear psychologically unprepared to continue the battle. For the first time, settlement looks to be a more expedient option than continuing the litigation, and it is at this stage of the proceedings that many age discrimination cases are, in fact, settled.

In many of my cases, employers have resisted serious settlement negotiations until after the court denied their motions for summary judgment. Three cases in point—Elizabeth Brown, who was summarily dismissed after serving her employer bank for thirty-nine years, Virginia Green, the creator of television commercials and magazine advertisements, and Barbara Jones, who relied more on O. J. Simpson's lawyers than on me—were each awarded handsome settlements *after* their employers tried, but failed, to obtain summary judgment. Each of these cases was settled for an amount exceeding that which we would have been willing to accept before the motion was made. In each instance, the employer, because it chose to attempt a slam dunk of the worker's case by moving for summary judgment, a motion it should have known it would lose, actually increased the value of the worker's case. When a motion for summary judgment is filed against my clients, I often advise them that "this is the opportunity we have been looking for." This is not bravado; it is a fact of life.

I once had a law partner whom I look upon as the epitome of the eternal optimist. No matter what happened in the cases in which we were involved, inevitably he would announce, "This is the best thing that could have happened to us." On one occasion, a court dismissed our clients' case. "The best thing that could have happened," he informed us, and he was right. The dismissal was later reversed on appeal, and the appellate court's opinion regarding the law in question was so favorably stated in support of our legal position that we soon obtained a settlement for our clients that totaled in the millions.

Although a motion for summary judgment may not always be the best thing to happen to a worker-litigant alleging age discrimination, it more often than not presents opportunities for a conclusion favorable to the worker. I welcome these motions in my practice.

11 Proving Age Discrimination Using Indirect Evidence

Employers have learned to mask acts of age discrimination with the appearance of propriety. They neither admit discriminatory animus nor leave a paper trail disclosing it. Thus, few age cases turn on direct or "smoking gun" evidence of discrimination. Employers simply do not place memoranda in their files that openly admit that an older worker was fired because she was too old. Even the least sophisticated of employers are careful not to leave a trail of discriminatory conduct, and it is the rare corporate executive who will take the witness stand at trial and freely affirm that he was motivated to fire a worker because of her age.[1] How then does an older worker alleging age discrimination prove that discriminatory intent, rather than a legitimate business reason, motivated an employment decision adverse to the worker?

Typically, an unfairly treated older worker walks into a lawyer's office without a firm conviction that the unfair treatment she experienced was motivated by age. More likely, the worker has been told by a co-worker, friend, or family member to seek legal advice because age discrimination *may* have induced the unfair treatment.

While an older worker may feel unsure of an employer's

motivation, an African American is usually more willing to attribute unfair treatment to race discrimination; he has confronted discrimination in the past and knows it when he sees it. But because age is not a fixed attribute, the older worker does not necessarily perceive unfair treatment as discriminatory. He may not have previously experienced age discrimination and does not know it when he sees it.

When a new claim of age discrimination arrives at a lawyer's office, he must approach it with great caution. The conduct an older worker ascribes to her employer may very well have been motivated by her age, but the worker may have little evidence at hand to prove it. The lawyer's task in evaluating her claim is not an easy one and is made even more difficult by the lack of evidence immediately available to him. As we shall see shortly, age discrimination most frequently is established through circumstantial or indirect evidence. Circumstantial evidence is developed by first assembling all of the facts in the case, and generally this process is not completed until the attorney has progressed far into his preparations for trial. Because at the outset of the case the strength or weakness of this circumstantial evidence is unknown to the attorney, he is unable at that point to assess accurately the strength or weakness of a worker's claim.

In these circumstances, the lawyer's decision to proceed or not to proceed with the case must be based more on his evaluation of the worker, and less on the strength or weakness of her claim. The lawyer looks for a credible witness who will favorably impress a jury. If he finds the worker credible and persuasive, the jury will probably tend to believe her and identify with her, but if the lawyer doubts the worker's veracity or her ability to relate a convincing story, a jury probably will neither believe her nor identify with her. The credibility of the worker and her ability to tell her story convincingly are the two most important factors influencing the lawyer's decision to proceed with or to decline a case.

Once an attorney decides to proceed, what must he prove to win the case for his client? Except in certain instances to be discussed in the next chapter, he must establish, by a preponderance of the evidence, that his client's employer actually relied on her age in making a decision adverse to her—that is, if it were possible at the moment the employer made the adverse decision to ask the employer to tell us the reason for the decision, and the employer responded frankly and truthfully, the answer would be that "she was just too old."[2]

Proving that the employer *intended* to discriminate against the older worker is critical to establishing the employer's liability. The worker's lawyer must prove that age was a determining factor in the employer's decision adversely affecting his client—not necessarily the only factor, but a factor that made a difference in the decision.

In most age discrimination disputes, neither the employer nor the worker ever mentions the subject of age. On some occasions, however, an employer's loose tongue may provide some evidence of age discrimination. "We need a younger workforce," "People your age have little future with this company," "We want young blood," and "I feel more comfortable around younger people" are typical examples.[3] In one case, an employer was alleged to have said of an older worker who had been discharged that "older workers, like old dogs, won't hunt."[4] Rarely will statements of this ilk, standing alone, be sufficient to prove age discrimination, but added to the mix of other facts tending to establish age-related conduct, they may significantly advance the worker's case.

Verbal expressions of an employer's stereotypical, age-related assumptions also may afford assistance to the worker's attorney in establishing a case of age discrimination. An employer's description of an older worker as lacking in adaptability, wanting in versatility, or possessing a low energy level may be expressions of an age-biased corporate mindset. Statistical evidence also may be used on occasion to demonstrate a corporate or institutional prejudice or biased frame of mind. As an example, evidence that an employer generally hires younger workers and fires far more older than younger workers may prove decisive. In one case, a terminated older worker offered statistical evidence that his fellow employees over the age of fifty-five made up less than 20 percent of the employer's workforce but composed 42 percent of those laid off.[5] Statistical evidence, like verbal indiscretion, is usually submitted in combination with other evidence establishing a discriminatory motive.

Since direct evidence of age discrimination is almost always unavailable, the lawyer representing the older worker has no alternative but to search out indirect or circumstantial evidence of age bias. Soon after congressional enactment of the first laws barring discrimination in employment, the Supreme Court established ground rules for evaluating indirect evidence of discrimination. These rules were based on the Court's observation that an employer invariably responds to a charge of discriminatory behavior with the argument that the employment decision adversely affecting the worker was based on a legitimate, nondiscriminatory reason. If the worker establishes that the purported nondiscriminatory reason was not the actual reason motivating the employer, or that the employer's reason simply is not believable, the court may assume that the reason offered by the employer was a pretext to cover up an unlawful motive.[6] The Supreme Court explained why it was justified in making such an assumption:

> We are willing to presume this largely because we know from our experience that more often than not people do not act in a totally arbitrary manner, without any underlying reasons, especially in a business setting. Thus when all legitimate reasons for an [employer's decision] have been eliminated as possible reasons for [its] actions, it is more likely than not the employer, who we generally assume acts only with *some* reason, based [its] decision on an impermissible consideration such as race [or age].[7]

Recently, the Supreme Court expanded on this reasoning. Proof that an employer's explanation for a decision adversely affecting a worker (such as a decision to terminate him) is false constitutes one form of circumstantial evidence that is probative of intentional discrimination. A court or jury may infer from the falsity of the explanation that the employer is dissembling to cover up a discriminatory purpose. Once the employer's explanation is eliminated, discrimination may well be the most likely alternative explanation, especially since the employer is in the best position to put forth the actual reason for its decision. Thus, in some, if not most, circumstances, a court or jury may infer the ultimate fact of discrimination from the falsity of the employer's explanation.[8]

Another court stated it a bit more succinctly: "Resort to a pretextual explanation is like flight from the scene of a crime, evidence indicating consciousness of guilt, which is, of course, evidence of illegal conduct."[9]

Thus, the task of the older worker's attorney is to prove that the employer's stated reasons for its action were not its true reasons. He must prove that the employer's reasons are "pretextual" and are offered by the employer only to cover up its discriminatory intent.

Almost all age discrimination suits focus on the issue of pretext. Are the reasons expressed by the employer for its decision its actual reasons, or was the employer's decision motivated by an impermissible factor, such as age? Are the reasons advanced by the employer credible? Even if an employer's reasons did, in fact, serve as a basis for its decision that adversely affected the worker, was the employer also motivated to make that decision because of the worker's age? Are the reasons asserted by the employer merely pretexts proffered by the employer for the purpose of covering up the nature of its decision, namely, that it was discriminatory? These are the issues that typically confront juries hearing age discrimination cases.

Pretext may be established in a number of ways, including the following:

1. By showing that the employer's reasons for its decision adversely affecting the worker had no basis in fact. For instance, if an employer advances "poor job performance" as the basis for its decision to fire a worker, the worker may

be able to show that her performance was wholly accept-able during the entire period of her employment, and that it was not until *after* the decision to fire her was made that her job performance was placed at issue. In one case, an older worker was not notified of any performance problem, and her supervisors had commented favorably upon her per-formance until just prior to her termination, but the em-ployer nevertheless tried to justify the worker's termination on account of "poor job performance." There was no basis in fact for its position, and the employer lost the case.[10]

2. By showing that the employer's reasons for its decision were not the actual reasons that motivated it to act. You may recall the reasons advanced by the advertising agency to justify the termination of Virginia Green, the oldest of twenty-three associate creative directors (see chapter 3). The decision to terminate Green was based on the agency's contention that Green's productivity was not as great as that of her peers. But, in fact, as Green was able to establish, her rate of productivity was among the highest of all the associate cre-ative directors. Once this was established, the employer was left in the unenviable position of having asserted a rea-son for Green's termination that clearly was not its actual reason.

3. By showing that the reasons given by the employer are in-sufficient to have motivated it to act in the manner that it did. An older worker may establish this by offering evidence that younger workers exhibited the same shortcomings as those alleged to have caused the older worker's discharge, but while he was terminated, the younger workers were not. The courts label an employer's treatment of an older worker that is less favorable than that extended to younger work-ers "disparate treatment." Evidence of disparate treatment strongly suggests that the employer's explanation for its treat-ment of the older worker is pretextual.

4. By showing that the employer altered or manipulated its own rules and procedures to create the circumstances that pur-portedly justified the adverse action taken against the older

worker. Among the various reasons asserted by an employer for firing one of my clients was a highly critical performance appraisal it conducted *after* my client had been terminated. The company's internal procedures, however, did not provide for post-termination performance appraisals, and thus this deviation from normal procedures suggested a pretextual explanation for my client's discharge.

To gain a better understanding of how workers have succeeded in establishing pretext cases, we will examine several age discrimination cases in some depth.

A. N. George worked for Mobil Oil Corporation and its subsidiary, Mobil Europe, Inc., from 1969 until Mobil terminated him in 1986, when he was sixty-two. Four years after George was hired, Mobil promoted him to general manager of Mobil Europe's affiliate in Greece. Five years later he was promoted to area executive, the third highest position in Mobil Europe, and charged with supervising seven European affiliated companies. In this position, George reported to John Simpson, vice president of Mobil Europe, who in turn reported to its president, P. W. Wilson.

Each year, Mobil evaluated the performance of its employees, and throughout his tenure as area executive, George was rated "MR+," meaning that he exceeded the requirements of his position, a rating highly regarded by Mobil executive personnel.

In the mid-1980s, the oil industry experienced economic problems occasioned by falling oil prices. In response, Mobil Europe undertook a restructuring, ordering large cuts in staff and transferring some of its responsibilities to Mobil headquarters in New York. These changes affected George's area executive position in that he no longer could rely upon staff assistance to the extent that he had prior to the restructuring.

Early in 1986, Simpson completed George's 1985 performance appraisal, again rating him "MR+," describing him as a "results-oriented executive," and recommending that he remain in his position as area executive. At the time of the appraisal, the affiliates under George's supervision were profitable and were outperforming projections. The appraisal contained neither negative comments nor suggestions that George was experiencing any difficulty adjusting to the restructuring that had been put in place the previous year. Despite the positive tone of the appraisal, Simpson later testified that at the time he conducted the appraisal, he had begun to doubt George's effectiveness in the restructured organization.

Within a few weeks of the appraisal, Mobil Europe president Wilson recommended that George be replaced as area executive. Wilson's recommendation was accepted at Mobil headquarters, and he was directed to find a replacement. Subsequently, Mobil considered five high-ranking employees for the position, and Simpson was directed to review their employment histories to determine who was best qualified to assume the position. Simpson designed a ranking form, ostensibly free of age bias, that designated numerical values for various attributes necessary to perform the functions of the area executive position. For some reason never explained by Mobil, Simpson included George in this ranking exercise. Although George had satisfactorily performed as the area executive for eight years and had consistently been rated "MR+," Simpson gave him the lowest score of the six employees who were ranked, while he awarded a much younger employee, who was then working under George's supervision in a subordinate position, the highest ranking. This younger worker was selected by Mobil to replace George.

In June 1986, Mobil informed George that his term as the area executive would end that September and his employment with Mobil would be terminated at the end of the year. In November, after George had been relieved of the area executive position, Simpson prepared an appraisal of George's 1986 performance. This appraisal, totally negative in tone, rated George's performance "MR-," sharply attacked George's affiliate strategy and guidance, and noted his failure to adapt to the restructuring. This appraisal was entirely inconsistent with Simpson's assessment earlier that year of George's performance.

142 AGE DISCRIMINATION IN THE AMERICAN WORKPLACE

After his termination, George sued Mobil for age discrimination. Mobil later asked the court to grant it summary judgment dismissing George's case, and the primary issue then presented to the court was whether the reasons given by Mobil for George's termination were pretextual. The court first expressed doubt as to the validity of Mobil's assertion that George had failed to adjust to the restructuring. If he had failed, why did Simpson not note the failure in George's 1985 appraisal, since the restructuring had been fully implemented by the time of the appraisal? The court labeled the appraisal later conducted by Simpson in the fall of 1986 "suspect," not only because it was performed after George had been relieved of his position, but "because it reversed all of George's prior evaluations." The court also questioned the objectivity of Simpson's ranking procedure. "The inclusion of [George] in this exercise after the recommendation to separate him was adopted suggests that his dismal rating may have been a foregone conclusion." How was it possible for George to have received the lowest rating when he was the only one of the six candidates who had any experience as the area executive? The apparent lack of objectivity in this procedure supported George's position that the reasons given by Mobil for removing him from the area executive position were pretextual. The court rejected Mobil's bid to dismiss George's case, and his claims against Mobil were resolved soon thereafter.[11]

If George had not received consistently high performance appraisals over a period of several years, the court undoubtedly would have given Mobil's position greater credence. But Mobil's attack on George's performance was wholly inconsistent with his past appraisals. This is the type of evidence age discrimination claimants pray for. They also pray that the evidence will uncover employer manipulation of the performance evaluation process. We have already seen a retroactive alteration of a performance evaluation backfire on an employer (chapter 8, *Dominic v. Con Edison*), and Mobil's wholly negative performance appraisal, conducted after George had been relieved of the area executive position, was certainly ill-advised. Since

Mobil lacked a good business reason for conducting such an appraisal, it, at the very least, created the appearance of impropriety.

Other than the evidence that Mobil appeared to have perverted the performance appraisal and the ranking processes, George was unable to offer evidence suggesting that age discrimination was the reason for his termination. Although Mobil replaced George with a younger worker, he was sixty-two at the time, and any replacement selected by Mobil would likely have been younger than George. Thus, George relied solely upon proof of pretext to establish his case.

Employers frequently try to camouflage their attempts to force an employee into early retirement, and their attempts at camouflage often lead to worker assertions of pretext. Peter Sullivan's employment with ABC Manufacturing Company (both pseudonyms) ended when, at the age of sixty-four, he was forced into an earlier than planned retirement.[12] Sullivan had spent his entire thirty-six-year career with ABC as a sales representative and, like all ABC sales representatives, had been assigned annual sales quotas. Sullivan successfully met his annual quota on twenty-five occasions, a record achievement.

Two years prior to his forced retirement, Sullivan's annual quota provided for the sale of a large ABC machine to a customer located in his territory. Shortly after notification of his assigned quota, Sullivan learned that this particular customer had recently entered into a three-year lease of a competitor's machine. Inasmuch as the customer had no immediate plans for replacing the leased machinery, the possibility of a sale of an ABC machine to that customer simply did not exist. Since sales quotas supposedly were based on current marketing opportunities, Sullivan requested a quota reduction. In years past, Sullivan's quota had always been adjusted to reflect current marketing prospects, but this time, to his surprise, his managers insisted upon maintaining the quota as originally established. Sullivan was even more puzzled when he later learned that ABC had granted quota reductions to two other sales representatives in his sales unit, both of whom were considerably younger than he.

Sullivan was left with no alternative but to continue throughout the year trying to persuade the customer to purchase an ABC machine, but of course he was unsuccessful. Due to Sullivan's failure to achieve quota, at the end of the year, his supervisor reduced his performance evaluation from the previous level 2 to level 3. On the face of it, this was grossly unfair, but Sullivan was unsuccessful in having the rating changed.

At the beginning of the following year, ABC transferred Sullivan to another sales unit. His managers informed him that one of the new unit's major accounts was planning to purchase a top-of-the-line, water-cooled ABC machine, and that this sale would largely satisfy Sullivan's quota for the year. At his first meeting with this customer, Sullivan learned, much to his consternation, that it had no plans to purchase a water-cooled machine since it was unwilling to incur the cost of restructuring its building to accommodate this type of machine. The customer was interested, however, in purchasing an air-cooled machine. At the time, ABC did not manufacture such a machine, but it was in the process of designing one and expected to begin its manufacture soon. The customer advised Sullivan that it was willing to wait until ABC's air-cooled machine became available. Thus, Sullivan found himself in the same circumstances that existed the previous year; he had been given a quota without an available market opportunity.

ABC again denied Sullivan a quota adjustment, and his managers insisted that he persist in trying to sell the water-cooled machine, although it was clear that this customer had already decided to await the market arrival of the air-cooled machine. Sullivan persisted as directed but, as could be readily predicted, was unable to complete the sale. Toward the latter part of the year, Sullivan was demoted and replaced by a junior sales representative nearly twenty years younger than he. Within three weeks of his demotion and replacement, ABC publicly announced the availability of the newly designed air-cooled machine. The customer whom Sullivan had tried to persuade to make a purchase of the water-cooled model immediately placed an order for the new air-cooled model. ABC gave credit for the sale of the air-cooled model to Sullivan's younger replacement, and, as a result, Sullivan experienced a second consecutive year of failing to achieve quota.

Early the following year, Sullivan's manager advised him that his performance evaluation would be further reduced, this time to level 4, and on that account he was one step away from being placed on probation. When Sullivan protested and pointed out that in the past two years he had been assigned quotas that were unattainable, his manager told him that "it's going to get worse" and suggested that Sullivan consider the possibility of retirement.

Sullivan decided to retire, but shortly thereafter, he sued ABC for age discrimination. ABC moved for summary dismissal of the suit, but the court directed the case to proceed to trial for the reason that Sullivan had adduced more than sufficient evidence demonstrating ABC's awareness that Sullivan had been given highly unrealistic, if not impossible, sales quotas and that ABC's good faith in denying him quota reductions in these circumstances was, at the least, highly questionable. The court concluded that a jury could reasonably find that ABC's explanation for its denial of quota reductions for Sullivan was pretextual, and it actually had been engaged in a long-term plan to force Sullivan into retirement.

If ABC had elected to proceed to trial instead of resolving the case, Sullivan would have been in a position to present a strong case. ABC would have argued that Sullivan's failure to succeed in meeting quota in his final two years was attributable to his deteriorating job performance. But it could offer no rational basis for holding Sullivan to sales quotas he could not possibly have met. A jury would not find its position credible.

Sullivan had ample evidence to support his charge that ABC's real motive was to force him into retirement. Younger sales representatives were granted quota reductions when Sullivan was not. Even more telling, a younger employee replaced Sullivan just prior to the announcement of the availability of the air-cooled machine, and it was she, not Sullivan, who was given credit for the sale. Finally, when Sullivan complained to his manager, he was told it was only going to get worse. In other words, ABC intended to keep the pressure on Sullivan until he retired, and if he refused to accept retirement, his performance evaluation would be further downgraded and his annual earnings further diminished.

But in addition to this evidence of pretext, Sullivan submitted other evidence showing that the explanations proffered by ABC for its conduct failed to reflect its actual reasons. He provided the court with strong evidence that his employer tried to conceal its true motives, and he offered additional evidence showing that the real motive for its conduct was age bias. He was able to show that younger workers were more favorably treated by being granted quota adjustments when he was not, and by ABC's replacing him with a younger worker to prevent him from gaining credit for a substantial sale. It was not until retirement was suggested to him that it occurred to Sullivan that ABC had been striving to force him into retirement. Another worker might have realized this much sooner, but Sullivan had experienced such a fine career with ABC and was so overwhelmingly loyal to the company that he could not bring himself to believe that the company was acting adversely to his interests. When Sullivan finally realized he had been targeted for retirement and that ABC had spent two years trying to get rid of him, he was devastated.

Sullivan's case was resolved after both sides submitted the case for mediation. The mediator recommended a large settlement, and ABC finally acceded to making amends for its actions and agreed to a generous settlement. Unfortunately, Sullivan died a few months later and thus did not live long enough to enjoy the fruits of the settlement. He did, however, leave his wife and family in good financial circumstances.

Older workers must remain vigilant. They must remain alert to pressures, some subtle and others not so subtle, exerted by their employers to force them into earlier retirements than they had planned. The employer invariably denies that anything is amiss and blames the worker for any problems that occur on the job. "Deteriorating job performance" is the near universal explanation offered by employers. It is up to the worker to prove that such allegations are merely offered to cover up the employer's efforts to force an early retirement.

Because pretext appears in many different forms, it is often detected only because of the vigilance of an older worker. Take the case of Thomas Taggart. He not only detected a cover-up where others might not, but because he was convinced he was right, he was successful in acting as his own attorney in advancing his cause in the courts.

Taggart was hired by Preview Subscription Television, a subsidiary of Time, Inc., as a print production manager for Preview's magazine, *Guide*. Taggart had more than thirty years' experience in the printing industry and was fifty-eight years old at the time of his hire by Preview. About six months later, Time notified Preview employees that Preview was to be dissolved, but that they would be given special consideration for other positions at Time. Taggart thereupon applied for thirty-two positions with various Time divisions and subsidiaries, including HBO, *Sports Illustrated*, *People Magazine*, *Life Magazine*, *Money Magazine*, *Discover Magazine*, and *Cinemax Guide*. Taggart received no job offers. An angry Taggart claimed that the interview process for these jobs had been a farce, that he had been provided with courtesy interviews but had not been seriously considered for any of these positions. He also was angered when Time hired three younger Preview employees for positions for which he had applied, especially since those employees were less qualified for these positions than he.

Taggart later filed an age discrimination suit against Time, but he had little evidence to support his age claims. To no one's surprise, Time asked the court to dismiss his case. The question put to the court was whether Taggart had enough evidence of age discrimination to permit him to proceed to trial, or, in light of the little evidence he had to offer, whether his case should be dismissed without a trial.

With respect to thirty-one of the thirty-two positions he had applied for, Taggart did not have much of a case. The one exception was his application for a print purchaser position at

HBO. Time defended the decision not to hire Taggart for that position on the ground that his thirty years of experience in the printing industry "overqualified" him for the position. Time argued that it was reasonable for an employer to reject a worker whose qualifications were excessive and who would not be challenged by the position. According to Time, it also was reasonable to reject a worker who, if he were employed, would likely continue to seek other employment. The court rejected Time's position:

> An employer might reasonably believe that an overqualified candidate—where that term is applied to a younger person—will continue to seek employment more in keeping with his or her background and training. Yet, that rationale does not comfortably fit [older workers]; for them loss of employment late in life ordinarily is devastating economically as well as emotionally. Instead, an older applicant that is hired is quite unlikely to continue to seek other mostly nonexistent employment opportunities.

The court proceeded to rule that "overqualified" does not mean "unqualified," and that Time's use of the term "overqualified" might be nothing more than a "buzzword" for "too old." Denying employment to an older worker because he has too much experience may simply be "a euphemism to mask the real reason for refusal, namely, in the eyes of the employer the applicant is too old. . . . This constitutes circumstances from which a reasonable juror could infer discriminatory animus on the part of Time based upon a finding that the reason proffered was pretextual and unworthy of credence."[13]

The court refused to dismiss Taggart's case insofar as the HBO position was concerned. Since the Taggert case, older workers and their attorneys undoubtedly have been more alert to buzzwords masking an employer's discriminatory intentions. As noted, pretext comes in all forms. Another form confronted Eleanor Montana when she was terminated after devoting thirty-two years of service to her employer.

Montana began her long career with Knickerbocker Federal Savings and Loan Association at the age of twenty-four. Some thirty years later, Knickerbocker and three other savings and loan associations merged to create First Federal Savings and Loan Association of Rochester, New York. The merged company was then divided into four regions, one in New York City and three in upstate New York. After the merger, Montana, who had been vice president of personnel at Knickerbocker, was designated the personnel administrator of the New York City region. About eighteen months later, First Federal restructured its personnel reporting system, and soon after, the New York City region was relieved of all personnel functions, which First Federal then assigned to the Rochester office. First Federal then terminated Montana at the age of fifty-six and with thirty-two years of service with the company.

Until the time of her discharge, Montana had consistently received satisfactory-to-excellent performance ratings. Her supervisor described her as a "very capable personnel manager" and an "excellent personnel administrator." Nonetheless, after the restructuring, First Federal claimed it had no position Montana could fill.

Montana charged First Federal with age discrimination. The company centered its defense upon its contention that it had terminated Montana because her position had been eliminated in the restructuring and because her personnel functions had been transferred to the Rochester office. Montana responded that First Federal's explanation for her termination was pretextual. When First Federal later moved for summary judgment, the court listed a number of factors that, in combination, supported Montana's position on pretext:

1. At the time of her termination, Montana was the oldest nonclerical employee in the Personnel Department.
2. Montana's was the only position eliminated in the restructuring.
3. Although Montana was eminently qualified for a position in the Rochester office, First Federal failed to offer her the option to transfer to Rochester.

4. After her position was eliminated, most of Montana's responsibilities were assigned to a co-worker who was thirty years younger than she.
5. After Montana's termination, First Federal created three new positions in the Personnel Department, and although Montana was qualified to perform the responsibilities of each of the three positions, she was neither considered for nor offered any of them.

Montana presented a strong case. The main focus of First Federal's defense was the restructuring, but Montana's was the only job eliminated in this restructuring. While First Federal maintained that the restructuring required the elimination of Montana's position, three new positions were later created in Montana's old department. Thus, the legitimacy of the restructuring was placed in question. Was this truly a restructuring, or did First Federal create a facade to cover up its intention to get rid of one of its oldest employees? During the course of the trial, but before the case reached the jury, First Federal decided to settle with Montana.[14]

Employees like Montana who have a long history of excellent job performance are more apt to succeed in establishing pretext than a worker with a mediocre performance record. Older workers who have made mistakes or have not fulfilled their potential or have been content to coast along without really exerting themselves make easy prey for the employer determined to terminate them. Although these workers are protected by the Age Discrimination in Employment Act to the same extent as their better-performing peers, they confront a greater burden in proving pretext. An indifferent performance record renders it far easier for the employer to persuade a court and jury that the worker's termination was the consequence of poor performance and not of the worker's age. A record of mediocre performance also lends itself to distortion and exaggeration, and an unscrupulous employer has the means of manipulating its records to support its criticism of the worker's performance. But the same tactic used against the worker who is able to present an excellent performance record is likely to prove counterproductive for the employer.

The older worker always bears the burden of proving age discrimination. In most cases, evidence supporting an age claim is not as strong as the evidence in the George, Sullivan, and Montana cases. Older workers lose far more age discrimination cases at the trial stage than they win, and employers and their counsel are well aware that statistically they have a clear advantage over the complaining worker. Thus, it is highly likely that unlawful discriminatory conduct is often permitted because of the employer's awareness that even if a worker complains about age-related conduct, the odds favor an employer's victory in court. The difficulty confronting a worker in sustaining the burden of proof undoubtedly stands as a primary motivating factor in many employers' decisions to disregard the employment discrimination laws.

12 Proving Age Discrimination Using Other Evidentiary Procedures

In nearly all of the cases examined so far in this book, older workers have endeavored to prove age discrimination through indirect and circumstantial evidence of an employer's age-biased actions or conduct. Although the particular circumstances of a worker's case may require reliance on indirect evidence, primarily because no other evidence is available to the worker, in some circumstances, other options may be available.

Direct Evidence

Employers are rarely so cooperative as to indicate in a worker's personnel file "fired due to age," or to inform a terminated worker candidly that he is "just too old for the job." As one court expressed it, "Unless the employer is a latter-day George Washington, employment discrimination is as difficult to prove as who chopped down the cherry tree."[1]

It is the rare case, indeed, that discrimination is established solely through direct evidence of a discriminatory motive. Direct evidence establishes the employer's discriminatory intent without the need of inference or presumption, as is the case with circumstantial evidence. Courts often refer to direct evidence as "smoking gun" evidence—evidence that, in and of itself, leaves little if any doubt that the employer is guilty of age-biased conduct. The most common example of evidence of this type is the verbal enunciation of a company policy that obviously is infected with age bias: "We need a younger workforce in our business if we are to continue to grow, and thus there is no future in this company for a person as old as you." Less blatant ageist comments are generally rejected by the courts as insufficient, in and of themselves, to show age discrimination.[2] More commonly, ageist remarks are considered in conjunction with other evidence evincing age-related conduct, and not solely as direct evidence of age discrimination. On that account, the older worker is well advised not to rely solely upon this type of evidence.

Mixed-Motive Cases

Employer age-related comments are commonly used to support or buttress a pretext case, and at times, they may play another, perhaps more significant, role. As we have noted, at the trial of an age discrimination case, the burden of proving discrimination lies with the worker. There is one exception in which the burden of proof may shift to the employer. A shift in the burden of proof may occur only after evidence has been submitted demonstrating that age was a *substantial* motivating factor in the employer's decision. This is where the age-related verbal statements come into play.

Although an employer's ageist remark, standing alone without other evidence, may be insufficient to establish conclusively the presence of a discriminatory motive, such a remark may be sufficient to show that age was, at the very least, a substantial motivating factor in the employer's decision. If the court rules, by reason of the submission of evidence of this or some other type, that the worker has successfully presented substantial proof of an illicit motivating factor—in other words, the evidence strongly suggests that the employer has been guilty of age bias—

the employer, anticipating that it is about to lose the case, may opt to try to demonstrate to the court that it would have made the same decision affecting the worker regardless of its age bias. That is to say, the employer argues that even if it harbored an unlawful motive, it would have fired the worker in any event because it had a legitimate reason to fire him. But the employer must prove this.

At this point, the burden of proof shifts to the employer. If the employer succeeds in sustaining this burden of proof, the worker will be unable to claim that she was damaged as a consequence of the discriminatory conduct because the employer will have proved that the worker, in any event, would have been fired on account of a legitimate business reason. These cases that shift the burden of proof are referred to as mixed-motive cases; in them, an illegitimate motive (such as age bias) and a legitimate motive (such as the worker's poor performance) required the worker's dismissal. Both motives played a role in the employer's decision that adversely affected the worker.

In a mixed-motive case, the burden of proving that the employer would have made the same decision even if it had not taken the worker's age into account may be a burden the employer is incapable of sustaining. If this proves true, the employer's case will end in disaster. For example, Bethlehem Steel Corporation's failure to sustain its burden of proof in a mixed-motive case resulted in a large verdict for one of its former workers.

Alvin Joel Tyler began working for Bethlehem Steel when he was twenty-two. After twenty-six years of service, he was placed on "permanent layoff." A disgruntled Tyler then sued Bethlehem for age discrimination.

Prior to his layoff, Tyler had been serving as a general products salesman in Bethlehem's Buffalo office and had also worked one week each month in the company's Pittsburgh office. All of his performance evaluations over the years had been rated "good," "very good," or "outstanding." He was laid off when Bethlehem closed its Buffalo office for financial reasons. At that time, Tyler asked about a transfer to the Pittsburgh office, but he was informed there were no transfer possibilities. Two

months after Tyler's termination, Bethlehem filled a sales position in its Pittsburgh office with a twenty-six-year-old who had
only four years of service with the company. This young worker
had previously resigned from Bethlehem and then had been rehired, but even after his rehiring, he had remained generally
dissatisfied with his position. Thus, Bethlehem terminated Tyler
after denying his request for a transfer to a position in the Pittsburgh office, a position it then assigned to a much less experienced, discontented salesman barely half Tyler's age.

During the fifteen months following Tyler's termination,
Bethlehem transferred thirteen salespeople, each younger than
Tyler. In fact, the youth of the transferees was cited as one of
the factors in their selection for transfer. One of those transferred,
who was twenty-five at the time, was described in glowing
terms: "All indications point to a 'Young Tiger' classification.
We will continue to follow closely; feel we have a future 'High
Potential' individual here." Bethlehem also hired twelve new
sales representatives, ten of whom were recruited directly from
college campuses. Bethlehem's manager of sales and marketing
administration testified that it was necessary to recruit from the
colleges because the sales force was getting too old.

With this type of evidence available to him, it appeared
as if Tyler would have little difficulty in showing that age had
been a substantial motivating factor in Bethlehem's decision not
to transfer him but to fire him instead. Bethlehem then argued
that it would have terminated Tyler in any event, as tightening
economic conditions required it to make that decision. The burden of proof thus shifted to Bethlehem. Bethlehem failed to sustain its burden of proof, as the jury was not persuaded that the
company would have fired Tyler regardless of any illicit motivation it may have had. The jury ruled against Bethlehem and
in favor of Tyler.

Tyler established much more than a pretext case. His proof
consisted of compelling evidence that age had been a substantial factor in Bethlehem's decision to deny him a transfer and
also in the decision to terminate his employment. As the
appellate court that reviewed the case commented: "If there is

no 'smoking gun' in Tyler's case, . . . there is at the very least a thick cloud of smoke, which is certainly enough to require Bethlehem to [show] that, despite the smoke, there is no fire." Bethlehem was unable to do this, and the jury awarded Tyler damages totaling $995,000.[3]

In another mixed-motive case, a large jury verdict was awarded to John Starceski after he sued Westinghouse Electric for age discrimination. Starceski had been responsible for designing, building, and improving tools for use in repairing nuclear power plant reactor components, but Westinghouse terminated the sixty-four-year-old Starceski from his senior engineer position after he had spent thirty-six years on the job.

Starceski's troubles at Westinghouse began when his second-level manager received a directive from Westinghouse's executive offices to reduce his staff by eighteen workers. The second-level manager then directed the first-level managers in his department to transfer work from the older workers under their supervision to younger workers and then to rank all the workers in accordance with their value to the department. He also instructed Starceski's first-level manager to "doctor" Starceski's evaluations to reflect poor performance. Subsequently, Starceski was not given any new assignments, and work was taken away from others of his older colleagues. With little or no work assigned to them, the value of these older workers to Westinghouse quickly diminished. Three months later, Westinghouse terminated Starceski and four other engineers. Their average age was fifty-one, while the average age of the engineers remaining in the department following these firings was thirty-nine.

Some of the younger engineers who were not terminated ranked lower in performance than Starceski, and an incensed Starceski sued for age discrimination. Westinghouse defended the suit by arguing that Starceski's termination was part of a reduction in force occasioned by lack of work for employees of his experience and skills. The jury rejected Westinghouse's position and decided in favor of Starceski, awarding him more than $650,000 in damages.

Evidence that older Westinghouse workers were set up for

termination in the RIF together with the testimony that Starceski's evaluations were doctored were precisely the types of evidence required to show that Westinghouse relied upon an illegitimate criterion in deciding whom to terminate in the RIF. This evidence showed that age had been a substantial motivating factor in Westinghouse's decision to terminate Starceski. Once that evidence was offered by Starceski, the burden of proof shifted to Westinghouse. At this point, Westinghouse was required to prove that due to business reasons it was compelled to reduce its workforce, and thus it would have fired Starceski in any event, without regard to his age. The jury then had to decide whether Westinghouse sustained its burden of proof. The jury found that Westinghouse had failed to sustain that burden.[4]

On some occasions, a mixed-motive case may prove disadvantageous for the older worker. As we have seen, the mixed-motive concept does not come into play unless the worker is first able to offer evidence sufficient to show that the worker's age was a substantial factor in the employer's decision that adversely affected that worker. With that type of evidence available, the worker is more than likely to succeed in establishing that any other reason offered by the employer for the adverse decision is merely pretextual. The worker's evidence, therefore, probably will lead to a verdict for the worker.

But if the employer steps in at that point and argues to the effect that even if age had been a factor in its decision-making process, it still would have rendered the same decision, the employer will be provided with a second opportunity to defeat the worker's case. Although the burden of proof then shifts to the employer, thus making a jury verdict more difficult for it to obtain, the employer has nothing to lose—it was facing defeat in any event. The shifting of the burden of proof in effect provides the employer with another opportunity to undermine the worker's case and avoid liability by supplying a legitimate motive to supersede an illegitimate one.

An age discrimination case does not become a mixed-motive case unless the court determines that the case should proceed under that model rather than the pretext model, and a court will not ordinarily make that determination unless one of the parties makes a specific request that it do so. Whether to make that request is a decision fraught with hazards for either side of the litigation. Consequently, the mixed-motive case is a mixed blessing for both sides of the case.

Disparate Impact

The Starceski and Tyler cases, as well as almost all the other cases thus far discussed in this book, fall into a category of legal actions referred to by the courts as "disparate treatment" cases. Disparate treatment occurs when an employer treats some workers differently or less favorably than others because of their ages. Employers that allow age bias to infect the workplace generally treat their older workers differently from their younger workers, and as a result, the older workers are in some way disadvantaged, usually by losing their jobs.

Disparate treatment is not the only method of proving age discrimination. "Disparate impact," as distinguished from disparate treatment, occurs when an employment practice or decision that appears on its face to be nondiscriminatory falls more harshly upon older workers than upon younger workers. The situation that confronted Miriam Geller is a case in point.

Geller was a fifty-five-year-old teacher who sued the Bugbee School in West Hartford, Connecticut, for age discrimination. Before applying for a position at Bugbee, Geller had gained considerable teaching experience in New Jersey. After moving to Connecticut and filling some substitute teaching positions, she applied for a permanent position at Bugbee. After her interview, she was hired to fill a vacant position and was directed to report for work at the beginning of the school year. The school officials, however, continued to interview other candidates for the position. After ten days in the classroom, Geller was replaced by a twenty-five-year-old who had applied for the position and was interviewed *after* Geller had started teaching. The Bugbee School officials justified the replacement of Geller and her subsequent dismissal on the ground that the local school board had adopted a cost-cutting policy that limited the hiring of new teachers to those having fewer than five years' teaching experience. With her years of teaching in New Jersey and in Connecticut, Geller had far more than five years of experience.

At the trial of her age discrimination claim, Geller's attorneys placed in evidence statistical data showing that nearly 93 percent of Connecticut teachers who were over forty years old had in excess of five years of teaching experience, while only 62 percent of teachers under forty had taught more than five years. Thus, under the local school board's cost-cutting policy, the likelihood of the selection of a teacher over forty was substantially less than the selection of a teacher under forty. Although the purpose of the school board's policy was to economize by hiring less experienced teachers, it also opened more teaching opportunities to younger, less experienced applicants and substantially limited the opportunities for older, more experienced teachers.

This is a classic example of an employment policy that, although nondiscriminatory and appearing totally neutral on its face, disproportionately affected, or disparately impacted, older workers. Even if the school board had no intention of discriminating against older teachers, the direct result of its hiring policy was to make it impossible for almost all older teachers to obtain a job at the Bugbee School.

The school still could have defeated Geller's claim if it were able to establish that its cost-cutting policy was consistent with its business needs and that no other selection methods existed that less directly impacted older teachers, but it failed in that regard, and the jury ruled in Geller's favor.[5]

The older worker who has the disparate-impact approach available to her need not prove that the employer intentionally discriminated against her. The motivations of the employer are simply irrelevant in this type of case. If the worker is able to establish through statistics or other means that an employment policy disproportionately affected her because of her age, the employer will be confronted with proving that the policy was required by its business needs. But even if it succeeds in establishing this, the worker will nonetheless prevail if she can show that the employer also had available to it other policies that affected the older workers less disadvantageously.

The disparate-impact approach has proved a significant legal tool for older workers because it challenges systemic impediments to the hiring, advancement, and extension of employment of older workers. Unfortunately, the appropriateness of this approach to age discrimination cases currently is under heavy attack.

Several federal appellate courts have cast doubt on the viability of disparate-impact claims in age discrimination cases. It has been argued that the domain of the Age Discrimination in Employment Act (ADEA) is confined to employment policies and practices based on inaccurate stereotyping of older workers. In a disparate-impact case, the employer's policy in question is not motivated by unlawful stereotypes or by the ages of the workers. Neither an illicit motivation nor a discriminatory intent plays a role in these cases. Thus, some authorities have concluded that the disparate-impact approach falls outside the purview of the age statute.[6]

Even those courts that have approved of the disparate-impact approach in age discrimination cases have limited its applicability. The same appellate court that awarded Miriam Geller a victory denied it to two other teachers in a similar case

Annmarie Lowe and Marie Delisi were teachers in the Commack Union Free School District in New York. In 1976, the school district, facing a declining student enrollment, decided to abolish some teacher positions, and both Lowe and Delisi were "excessed." Under New York law, they were placed on a preferred eligibility list for vacancies that thereafter occurred. While Lowe and Delisi waited for vacancies to occur, they both accepted teacher assistant positions that paid substantially less than their former positions. No vacancies occurred, and after seven years, they were removed from the preferred list, as was required by law. Two years later, the school district adopted the New York State Retirement Incentive Program providing retirement incentives for teachers fifty-five and older. With the adoption of this plan, and the anticipated voluntary retirements of teachers age fifty-five and older, it was expected that vacancies for teacher positions in the district would soon become available. Lowe and Delisi, both fifty-two years old at the time, immediately submitted their applications for teacher positions.

As anticipated, some of the older teachers elected to accept retirement, and thirteen teaching positions became available the following year. But when neither Lowe nor Delisi was hired for any of those positions, they cried age bias and filed age discrimination suits. Basically, they claimed that the school district had decided not to replace the retiring fifty-five-year-old and older teachers with newly hired teachers close to the same age. The school district's defense centered around the procedures that were designed for the selection of the thirteen new teachers, and there was no evidence that these procedures were age biased. But Lowe and Delisi pointed out that those procedures disparately impacted applicants who were over the age of fifty. In essence, they claimed that the number of successful candidates age fifty and over was disproportionately low. The court rejected their position. The ADEA, the court reminded Lowe and Delisi, protects workers age forty and over, and eight of the thirteen newly hired teachers were over forty. When viewed from that perspective, there was no disproportionate impact.

The court's position, however, failed to recognize the validity of the argument that if the group of successful candidates over age fifty is compared with the group of successful candidates under age fifty, the group of older teachers was disproportionately disadvantaged by not being hired. The court, however, insisted that the only relevant age groups to be considered were those under forty and those over forty, and under these circumstances, the older group was not disadvantaged.[7]

The court's rationale in declining to accept the position espoused by Lowe and Delisi has been roundly criticized by other courts.[8] The disagreement on this issue is joined, as noted, by the failure of the courts to agree upon whether the disparate-impact approach is ever applicable to an age discrimination case. These issues will remain unresolved until the Supreme Court finally rules on them. In the meantime, older workers are well-advised to continue to use the disparate-impact approach whenever the circumstances of their cases make it available to them.

13 | Monetary Damages and Other Legal Remedies

After establishing the employer's liability for acts of age discrimination, the worker has the additional burden of proving the nature and amount of damages that accrued as a consequence of the employer's unlawful conduct. Surprisingly, many older workers underestimate the importance of this aspect of their cases. All too often, an older worker has marched into my office angrily demanding "justice," by which he means, "I want to nail my employer to the wall for what it has done to me." But a victim of age discrimination does not necessarily suffer monetary or other damages as a consequence of an employer's unlawful conduct, and unless the recovery of a monetary award is a likely prospect, workers are usually well-advised to refrain from suing.

If a worker fired on Monday obtains a better-paying job on Tuesday, he will not have suffered any losses of consequence. If he still wants "justice," he will have to pay for it from his own pocket without the prospect of a monetary recovery. On occasion, principle requires action regardless of the monetary outcome, but in the vast majority of cases, an aggrieved worker will attain retribution only through the recovery of monetary damages, whether by settlement before trial or by judgment after trial. Once the angry, justice-demanding worker cools off, the merits of his case may be evaluated with these facts fully in mind.

In determining the amount of damages an older worker is entitled to recover, the courts apply a fundamental principle common to all employment discrimination cases: The worker who proves discrimination is to be made "whole." This means that the worker should be placed in the circumstances she would have been in if the employer had not discriminated against her. The make-whole standard of relief requires the court to consider several areas of recovery, which in combination will make the worker whole.

Back Pay

Typically, workers suing for age discrimination receive higher jury awards than workers suing for race or sex discrimination. Age claimants also settle for more. This is attributable, at least in part, to the fact that age discrimination plaintiffs usually stand at the peak of their earning capacity at the time they fall victim to acts of age discrimination.

The basic form of relief awarded to a victim of age discrimination is back pay. Back pay is the monetary loss suffered by the worker between the time of the employer's act of discrimination and the trial of the worker's age discrimination suit. In the case of a terminated worker, back pay is computed by totaling the worker's loss of salary and the value of other lost employee benefits during that period of time, and subtracting from that total the salary and employee benefits received by the worker in subsequent employment during that same period. In the case of a failure to promote, back pay is computed as the difference between what the worker would have been paid in the new position if he had been promoted and the amount he actually was paid after being denied the promotion. In the case of a failure to hire, back pay is calculated by determining the difference between what the worker would have earned if he had been hired and what he actually earned in other employment. In view of the fact that a high percentage of age discrimination cases involve discharges, we will focus our attention on the measure of relief the terminated worker may expect to recover.

An award of back pay should reflect increases in salary the worker would have received had she not been terminated. The court may assume a worker's salary will continue to increase in the same proportion that it had historically. If the history discloses annual increases averaging 5 percent a year, that average may be used in the back-pay computation. Alternatively, the court may look to the salary history of the worker's replacement and assume that the terminated worker would have received the same increases as the replacement.

Other financial benefits that would have accrued to the worker also should be included in the back-pay award. Courts customarily increase the back-pay award to compensate the worker for reduced pension benefits and increased costs of health and medical benefits and life insurance premiums. In addition, the make-whole doctrine requires the court to examine all other circumstances that emerge from an unlawful act of discrimination.

Guy Foster was sixty years old when he was terminated by Excelsior Springs City Hospital and Convalescent Center in Missouri. Foster filed suit for age discrimination but died of a heart attack before his case reached trial. During his employment, premiums on his life insurance policy had been paid by the hospital, but payments ceased once he was terminated. Foster's medical history included a previous heart attack and open-heart bypass surgery, and this medical history, coupled with Foster's age, made procurement of a new life insurance policy after termination of employment next to impossible. Consequently, Foster died without any life insurance coverage.

After determining that the hospital indeed had been guilty of age discrimination, the court confronted a difficult damages issue. The court had to decide whether Foster's widow was limited to recovery of the insurance policy premiums that would have been paid by the hospital had her husband not been terminated, a matter of only a few hundred dollars, or whether she was entitled to recover an amount equal to the policy's death benefit, the sum of $60,000.

An age claimant has a general duty to minimize his damages (a matter we will examine shortly), and ordinarily a worker in Foster's circumstances would have been required, after his termination, to purchase another life insurance policy, and then to recover from his former employer, as an item of damages, any additional costs incurred in paying for such insurance. But Foster was uninsurable; he was unable to purchase another policy. In deciding that Foster's widow should recover the full $60,000, the court reasoned as follows:

> This court finds that the make-whole nature of the ADEA requires a remedy which puts the employee in the position he would have been had there been no discrimination. Had Guy Foster died while employed by defendant Hospital, [Foster's widow] would have received $60,000 in proceeds. Even though [Foster] is now deceased, when employed he had the expectation and security of knowing his spouse would be financially taken care of through life insurance. Clearly, it is the proceeds, not the premiums, that can make him whole in retrospect.[1]

This is a prime example of an enlightened court applying the make-whole doctrine in an equitable fashion. Any other decision would have constituted a second tragedy for the Foster family.

The make-whole doctrine also may require tax relief for the victorious age claimant. Back-pay awards are paid in one lump sum, the worker receiving all of her back pay in one year, while if she had remained employed, she would have received the same sum over a period of years. The back-pay award, therefore, may be subject to a higher income tax rate than would the periodic payments. Courts typically compensate the age claimant for these additional taxes.

Employers search for any means available to them to limit the back-pay period to the shortest possible time. A worker may justifiably claim recovery of back pay only for the period of time he was available to work or actually worked in another position. Thus, if an employer is able to show that after the worker was fired, he became disabled through illness or accident and no longer was able to work in any position, the back-pay period will end at the date of the commencement of the disability. But, as Trans World Airlines learned, the application of the make-whole doctrine may constrain the court to be guided by factors requiring a different result.

A jury decided that Trans World Airlines had been guilty of age discrimination in firing Theodore Grundman, and it was left to the court to compute his back-pay damages. Shortly after his termination by TWA, Grundman started working for Eastern Airlines, but within weeks, he was involved in a serious automobile accident and thereafter had been unable to work due to the injuries he suffered. TWA argued that since the accident disabled Grundman from further employment at Eastern, the court should assume that the accident also would have disabled him from working at TWA, and thus back pay should be limited to the short period of time between Grundman's termination at TWA and his accident a few weeks later. The court agreed that under ordinary circumstances the back-pay period should not extend beyond the date of the accident. Grundman's accident, however, occurred when he was returning home from his work at Eastern, and he testified that his work hours at Eastern were different from those worked at TWA, and as a result, he fell asleep at the wheel. The court ruled that the accident was associated with his work at Eastern, not his work at TWA, and there was no reason to believe that the accident would have occurred if he had remained at TWA. The court assumed that if Grundman had not been terminated, he would have continued to work at TWA until retirement, and it thus refused to consider the accident as a factor in limiting the back-pay award.[2]

An employer may argue that a worker, even if unlawfully terminated, would have lost his job in any event because his position was later eliminated in a companywide reduction in force (RIF). By proving such an occurrence or an event of a similar nature, such as a department or plant closing, employers have succeeded in limiting the back-pay period.

In some instances, it is the worker himself who is respon-sible for a shortened back-pay period. A worker claiming back pay must exercise reasonably diligent efforts to secure other em-ployment. He must act to minimize or "mitigate" his damages. What is considered a reasonably diligent effort to obtain other employment differs from case to case, but, generally, a termi-nated worker must undertake every action reasonably expected of any worker truly seeking other employment. In one case, a worker who had been involuntarily retired failed to attempt any significant job search. He did not apply for a single job or up-date a ten-year-old résumé. He neither sought job counseling nor contacted any employment agencies. As the court stated, the worker "pursued a retired lifestyle while on involuntary re-tirement." The court declined to award any back pay not be-cause the worker was unsuccessful in obtaining alternate employment, but simply because he had failed to look for other employment.[3]

An employer may also shorten the back-pay period by of-fering the terminated worker reinstatement to her former posi-tion. If the offer is rejected, the worker will be denied recovery of back pay from that point onward. The offer, however, must be made in good faith, and the worker is justified in rejecting the offer if it is conditioned upon her agreement to drop her age discrimination case. The offer may have the appearance of having been made in good faith, but if the worker has already obtained other employment, even if she is being paid less, she may be reluctant to return to a situation in which she may be subjected to acts of hostility or retaliation or to acts of discrimi-nation yet again. Although the courts seem to favor reinstate-ment as an appropriate form of relief, I have yet to have a client who actively sought reinstatement to his or her old position. The baggage accumulated during the course of a discrimination suit is just too great to allow the employment relationship to be reconstituted. Employers know this, and thus offers of rein-statement are not made with any expectation that they will be accepted by the worker. Rather, they are offered with the hope that a worker will refuse reinstatement and thus severely limit the damages the worker may then recover.

Front Pay

In addition to an award of back pay, a successful age claimant may apply to the court for an award of front pay. A claim for front pay seeks the recovery of the loss of salary and benefits the worker contends he will sustain in the future, after the trial. While an award of back pay is based on what already has happened, an award of front pay is based on what *may* happen in the future, and thus an element of uncertainty is innate to a claim for front pay.

If at the time of the trial, the terminated worker, despite a concerted effort, has yet to obtain new employment, the court must then determine, in light of all the circumstances, when it is likely the worker will become employed and at what salary. The court will then compute a front-pay award based on its inquiries. If the worker, on the other hand, has obtained new employment but at a lower salary, the court must determine when it is likely the worker will again be compensated on a scale comparable to that paid by the defendant employer. In either event, the court is dealing with uncertainties. Because the computation of front pay involves factors that may or may not occur, the court may be asked to make assumptions it is reluctant to make. Thus, the more facts a worker is able to furnish the court to reduce the degree of uncertainty, the more likely the court will agree to a front-pay recovery.

A jury found that Bear, Stearns and Company discriminated against Edith Wulach, one of its limited partners, on the basis of her age. After leaving Bear, Stearns, Wulach joined another brokerage firm and served, successively, as corporate vice president, senior vice president, and chief financial officer of one of its divisions. Even in these positions, she earned less than she would have earned had she continued at Bear, Stearns, and the court ruled that Wulach was thus entitled to an award of front pay. The court was then confronted with the task of determining how long it would take Wulach to find employment comparable to her job at Bear, Stearns. Given Wulach's impressive experience and her proven ability to attract offers of lucrative employment, the court concluded that it was reasonable to assume that she would find such employment within the two-year period following the trial. Thus, Wulach was granted a front-pay award in an amount equal to the difference between what she would earn in her current employment during the ensuing two years and what she would have earned during that period at Bear, Stearns had she not been terminated.[4]

Let us turn back a moment to Joseph Dominic's age discrimination and retaliation case against Consolidated Edison. After the jury heard that Con Ed had retaliated against Dominic by retroactively lowering his performance evaluation, it granted him a back-pay award and a huge front-pay award of $378,000. But the court rejected the jury's computation of the front-pay award because it was totally unreasonable and not supported by the facts of the case and thus was unduly speculative. The court decided that the award should be reduced to $34,000, an amount it felt sufficient to compensate Dominic for the length of time it would take him to find comparable employment.[5]

The amount of a front-pay award often turns on a worker's expected age of retirement. A worker fired while in his sixties will often argue that if he had not been terminated, he would have continued to work until age seventy; the employer, on the other hand, will try to show that it was more likely the worker would have retired at age sixty-five or even earlier. This issue arose in Morgan Doyne's age suit against Union Electric Company. Doyne testified that he had planned to work until he turned seventy and that he had so informed Union Electric. When this was later confirmed by one of his co-workers, a jury proceeded to provide Doyne with a large front-pay award computed on the basis of his anticipated year of retirement.[6]

One of the cases discussed earlier also culminated in a huge front-pay award. Stephen Padilla was demoted by Metro-North Commuter Railroad from his position as superintendent of train operations after he agreed to participate in an Equal Employment Opportunity Commission (EEOC) investigation of the demotion of one of Metro-North's older workers. A jury ultimately ruled that Padilla's demotion was ordered in retaliation for his participation in the EEOC investigation. The court then confronted a front-pay situation of major proportions.

Padilla claimed that his former position of superintendent of train operations was so specialized as to be virtually unique, and that no comparable position existed in any other industry. Moreover, it was highly unlikely that he could obtain a similar position in any of the other three railroads in the region. Padilla asked the court for reinstatement to his old position (a rare occasion when a worker has sought this relief), but the court felt reinstatement would be unworkable, since the relationship between Padilla and Metro-North had been irreparably damaged by the animosity associated with the litigation. Instead, the court ordered Metro-North to pay Padilla front pay computed as the difference between his salary in his demoted position and the salary he would have received as superintendent of train operations; these payments were to continue until Padilla reached the age of sixty-seven, when he would be entitled to a full pension. Since at the time Padilla was in his early forties, the front-pay award covers a period of more than twenty years.[7]

The uniqueness of Padilla's position eliminated all speculation or guesswork in the computation of the front-pay award. He was entitled to the maximum. Those of us who have jobs less unique in nature probably would not have fared as well.

Liquidated Damages

The Age Discrimination in Employment Act (ADEA) stands alone among the employment discrimination statutes in providing for the recovery of "liquidated damages," damages that are computed by doubling the back-pay award. Liquidated damages may be granted only if the court determines that the employer was guilty of a "willful" violation of the ADEA. The courts have long struggled with the definition of "willfulness," as well as with the identification of those circumstances that will allow a liquidated damage award.

Except in cases involving disparate impact, an employer may be found liable for age discriminatory conduct only if the worker proves that the employer "intended" to commit an act of discrimination. Proof of intentional conduct is crucial. But if an employer intended to discriminate, would not its conduct be willful? In that case, every proven act of age discrimination would be willful, and every successful worker-litigant would be entitled to liquidated damages. Congress obviously intended something different. Liquidated damages are to be awarded not in every case, but only in those cases that are in some way set apart from the ordinary.

This rationale led some courts to require a worker to show that the employer's conduct had been outrageous before they would declare it to be "willful." The Supreme Court rejected that test and defined an employer's conduct as willful if the employer "knew or showed reckless disregard for the matter of whether its conduct was prohibited by the ADEA."[8] Later, the court appeared to shift its rationale to favor employers: "If an employer acts reasonably in determining its legal obligation, its action cannot be deemed willful."[9] Even if an employer acts unreasonably in determining its legal obligations, courts have ruled that the employer's conduct will not be deemed willful unless it also acted "recklessly." It is not at all clear that Congress intended to place these limitations on awards of liquidated damages. In fact, it is not at all clear what Congress intended. Thus, the courts continue to struggle with the identification of those circumstances that will permit awards of this nature.

The question of the appropriateness of an award of liquidated damages was another issue that arose in the *Padilla v. Metro-North Commuter Railroad* case. Was Metro-North's demotion of Padilla for his cooperation with the EEOC investigation a "willful" act of retaliation? Padilla's supervisor made it easy for the court to decide this issue in favor of Padilla because he testified at the trial that he was aware of the federal laws prohibiting discrimination in employment. Moreover, he also admitted he was aware that it was a violation of those laws to retaliate against a worker for participating in an investigation of an alleged violation of those laws. Accordingly, the supervisor knew it was illegal for him to demote Padilla in retaliation for his participation in the EEOC investigation, but he did it anyway. His conduct clearly was "willful," and liquidated damages were awarded Padilla.

Retaliatory employer conduct is often defined by the courts as constituting a willful act. When a worker's complaint places the employer specifically on notice that it is violating the age discrimination statute, and the employer intentionally retaliates against the worker for having asserted such a complaint, a court may very well rule that the employer has shown reckless disregard for the illegality of its conduct and has therefore acted willfully.

The concept of willfulness clearly includes within its ambit the employer who knew it was acting in violation of the law. On the other hand, it clearly excludes the employer who *reasonably* believed it was not acting in violation of the law. But what about the employer who is simply careless with regard to the possibility that it might be violating the law?

Bobby Price was forty-five years old when hired as a salesperson for Marshall Erdman and Associates, and two years later he was fired under conditions a jury found to be discriminatory. Price's supervisor testified that he had fired Price without giving any thought to the ADEA, since he was under the impression that the statute protected only those who were fifty and over, and Price was not that old at the time. In affirming the jury's award of liquidated damages, the appellate court noted that if Marshall Erdman had mistakenly left its supervisor in ignorance of a basic tenet of the statute, namely, that its protections began with workers forty and over, not fifty and over, it was "an extraordinary mistake" for it to have made, and because Marshall Erdman was not "a mom and pop store" but a business with annual sales of $200 million, it was a mistake that connoted willfulness.

The court clearly distinguished between an employer's negligent mistake concerning the lawfulness of its conduct and an employer's reckless mistake or indifference to whether its conduct violated the law: "The jury was entitled to find that Erdman's conduct fell on the reckless side of the line. Erdman had so far neglected its responsibilities for compliance with the age discrimination laws as to allow a supervisory employee to whom it had delegated the power to hire and fire to remain ignorant of one of the most basic features of the law—namely the age at which workers are protected by it."[10] Mere carelessness would not have justified a liquidated-damage award for Price, but Marshall Erdman's conduct was more than just careless, it was reckless. The appellate court left intact the jury verdict doubling Price's back-pay award.

In the last chapter, we reviewed the age discrimination case pursued by John Starceski against Westinghouse Electric. The evidence showed that Starceski's performance evaluation had been altered to indicate a poor performance record, and that Starceski and other older employees had been set up for termination in a RIF. Westinghouse could not reasonably claim that this was inadvertent or negligent conduct, and thus the court awarded Starceski liquidated damages on the ground that Westinghouse either knew or showed reckless disregard for its statutory duty not to discriminate against Starceski because of his age.[11]

Just when it seems as if one is getting a grasp on this willfulness concept, along comes a case like *Blake v. J. C. Penney.* Euna Fay Blake worked in a J. C. Penney shoe department as a salesperson for seventeen years, had an excellent performance record, received the highest possible performance ratings, and just prior to her termination was rated among the top ten shoe salespersons for all J. C. Penney stores in the southeastern United States. At the time of her termination in 1986, she was fifty-six years old and was the oldest and most experienced shoe department employee in her store. Why was such a valued employee fired by J. C. Penney?

Two years before Blake's discharge, J. C.Penney had hired Daniel Hubbard, age twenty-five, as a salesperson in the shoe department where Blake worked. From the moment of his arrival in the shoe department, Hubbard subjected Blake to verbal harassment directed at her age. He repeatedly called Blake a "senile old woman," and worse, and repeatedly asked her, "Why don't you go home, you crazy old woman?" On numerous occasions, Blake complained of Hubbard's age harassment to J. C. Penney's supervisory and management staff, but no action was taken against Hubbard, and his contemptible behavior continued unabated. Blake's later requests for a transfer to another department—a transfer she sought because of Hubbard's harassment—were denied.

Some time later, Blake experienced a family health crisis, and she was working under considerable stress. Even though Hubbard was aware of Blake's problem, his behavior toward her worsened. Finally, Blake insisted on a transfer, even if it meant a reduction in compensation. While she was awaiting a decision on her request for transfer, Hubbard again verbally attacked her, telling her, "Get out of my way, you senile old thing," and this time Blake cracked. She slapped Hubbard across the face. The next day, Blake was fired, ostensibly for assaulting a coworker. In the months following Blake's termination, the shoe department hired three new salespersons, each significantly younger than Blake.

Blake's age discrimination suit was tried before a jury, which had little difficulty in arriving at a verdict for Blake. It also concluded that J. C. Penney had acted willfully. Incredibly, the appellate court reversed the jury's finding of willfulness. This was the appellate court's reasoning:

> Specifically, Blake failed to produce any credible evidence that Hubbard's misconduct came to the attention of the J. C. Penney management team at the time of the dismissal decision. Such notice seems to us especially important when an employee's conduct, e.g., striking a co-worker following what would appear to be an isolated instance of provocation, might ordinarily constitute legitimate grounds for dismissal. Hence Blake's evidence, while sufficient to establish that age factored into her termination, failed to show that the management team knew or acted with reckless disregard of the ADEA.[12]

I have struggled over this decision and have concluded that it cannot be justified under any interpretation of the underlying facts. The management team *was* informed of Hubbard's misconduct. It is inconceivable how the court could have concluded that Hubbard's action preceding the slap was "an isolated instance of provocation." The facts of the case simply fail to support the appellate court's opinion. It appears as if in some courts an award of liquidated damages is not a popular remedy, and to this appellate court, such an award appears to have been anathema.

A more sensible approach to the liquidated-damages issue appears in a case involving Peter Benjamin and his employer, United Merchants. Benjamin was in charge of international sales at United Merchants when these sales began to decline. United Merchants claimed that Benjamin had been demoted on two occasions and then finally terminated because of his poor sales record. Benjamin attributed the fall in sales to a weakening in the value of the U.S. dollar, which made it more difficult for United Merchants and other American companies to compete for foreign business. Benjamin, in his sixties, was fired after thirty-eight years with the company, and shortly thereafter, he was replaced by a forty-one-year-old employee.

After a trial of Benjamin's age claim, the jury agreed with him that United Merchants had terminated him on account of his age and that United Merchants' conduct had been willful. On appeal, the question of willfulness was hotly contested.

The appellate court began its analysis of the issue by stating that the concept of willfulness could most easily be understood if it were analyzed along a continuum. At one extreme of the continuum, no liability for liquidated damages exists when the employer acts negligently or inadvertently. At the opposite end of the continuum, liability exists when the employer deliberately acts from an evil motive. In the middle of the continuum, liability for liquidated damaged exists where the proof shows that the employer was indifferent to the requirements of the age statute and acted in a "purposeful, deliberate, or calculated fashion."

The court continued its analysis by distinguishing between an employer who makes a negligent attempt at complying with the dictates of the statute and an employer who is indifferent to the protection afforded older workers by the ADEA. The court offered this guideline: "An employer acting with indifference is one who acts without interest or concern for its employees' rights under the ADEA at the time it decides to discharge an employee; that is, without making any reasonable effort to determine whether the decision to discharge violates the law."

Applying this guideline to the facts at hand, the court ruled that United Merchants' conduct indeed had been willful. Its chief administrative officer responsible for establishing and implementing personnel policy knew that it was illegal to discharge an employee on account of age. Nonetheless, no steps were taken to determine whether Benjamin's dismissal was carried out on an impermissible basis. The omission of this officer to take these steps was particularly egregious given that he was responsible for seeing that United Merchants complied with the age law. Clearly, he was indifferent to the proscriptions of the age statute.[13]

The difficulties courts experience in applying the law, added to the reluctance of some courts to grant double damages—sometimes looked on as a windfall for the worker—frequently works to the disadvantage of the worker. As a result, unfortunately, liquidated damages are denied more often than granted.

Injunctive Relief

The primary goal for claimants in nearly all age discrimination cases is the recovery of monetary damages for past violations of the ADEA. Injunctive relief, on the other hand, because it is intended to prevent future violations of the statute, is less apt to be sought in a suit brought by an individual age complainant than in broad-based class actions and in cases initiated by the EEOC that relate to continuing employment practices.

The EEOC filed suit against the District of Columbia

Department of Human Services on behalf of Dr. Raymond Kielich, who had applied to the department for temporary as well as permanent dental officer positions. Dr. Kielich was certified by the American Board of Pedodontics, had conducted a private dentistry practice for thirty-seven years, and subsequently held appointments at the Children's Hospital National Medical Center in Washington, D.C., and at the Georgetown University School of Dentistry. At the time he applied for the Department of Human Services positions, he was sixty-three years old.

Although the department rated Dr. Kielich as "highly qualified," it failed to select him for any of the temporary or permanent positions. Instead, the department awarded the temporary positions to dentists ages thirty-one and twenty-eight, each with less than four years of experience. The two candidates selected by the department for the permanent positions were forty-six and thirty-four, one with less than four years' experience and the other with less than seven.

The department's defense in the EEOC suit centered on its position that it had not selected Dr. Kielich for any of the temporary or permanent positions because these positions entailed entry-level functions, and Dr. Kielich was simply overqualified. The court rejected this defense out of hand and turned to consideration of the appropriate relief to be granted Dr. Kielich. In addition to ordering the department to hire Dr. Kielich and reimburse him for his lost wages, it ordered injunctive relief that required the department to formulate and then implement appropriate procedures assuring that even entry-level positions were made available to experienced applicants, regardless of their ages.[14]

If the Department of Human Services had been able to convince the court that it had modified its practices and that the type of treatment Dr. Kielich received would not likely recur, the court probably would have denied any injunctive relief. Injunctions are more generally allowed where the employer has engaged in an unlawful employment practice and gives every indication that it intends to continue that practice. In those circumstances, injunctive relief is highly appropriate.

The First Federal Savings & Loan Association of Broward County, located in Florida, had six offices, and at any given time, it normally employed about thirty-five tellers, positions having a high turnover rate. Over a period of fourteen months, First Federal hired thirty-five tellers, all but three of whom were in their teens or twenties, and none as old as forty. During that fourteen-month period, Betty Hall, age forty-seven, applied for a position with First Federal. Hall did not specify in her application any particular position that she was seeking, and a personnel officer interviewed her with regard to all positions then available, including that of teller. The interviewer noted on Hall's application that she was "too old for teller." Hall was not hired for any position.

At the time, another applicant over forty also was rejected for a teller position because she was "too old." The U.S. secretary of labor (the EEOC had not yet been assigned jurisdiction over age complaints) brought suit on behalf of Hall against First Federal, seeking not only back pay for Hall but injunctive relief barring First Federal from discriminating against future job applicants over the age of forty.

The court had no difficulty in awarding Hall back pay, since the evidence clearly demonstrated the existence of a discriminatory hiring policy. Other evidence showed that this policy was not limited to the teller positions. Accordingly, the court also granted injunctive relief, enjoining First Federal from continuing to implement illegal employment practices with reference not only to the teller positions, but to all positions in First Federal's offices.[15]

Injunctive relief is not meant to be burdensome; it simply requires the employer to obey the law. An injunction, however, is an effective enforcement device for preventing future acts of discrimination against older workers.

Attorney's Fees

The successful ADEA claimant is entitled, pursuant to statute, to recover from the employer his or her reasonable attorney's fees. Absent such a statutory provision, many age claims would not be pursued because, as we have seen, a good many age discrimination complaints arise out of terminations of employment, and thus the prospective plaintiff is out of work and lacks the financial means to support a lawsuit. Lawyers, therefore, often agree to some form of contingency fee arrangement with these workers. In those instances where a large damage award is improbable, and hence a contingency arrangement is less meaningful, the statutory fee award may provide the only means for the lawyer to obtain adequate payment for her services.

The courts have consistently rejected the notion that an award of attorney's fees must be proportional to the amount of damages the worker recovers.[16] In fact, in some cases, the fee award has far exceeded the damages recovered by the worker. Rather than constituting a windfall for the attorney, such a fee award is a recognition that a worker's right not to be discriminated against commands the protection of the courts regardless of the amount of money involved. In a failure-to-promote case, for example, the worker's salary and other benefit losses may be quite small when measured against the cost of suing to protect the worker's rights. Without some means of recovering attorney's fees, failure-to-promote cases would often not be pressed.

The statutory provision for the recovery of attorney's fees by the successful age complainant has undoubtedly been instrumental in the development of a fairly large cadre of attorneys willing to take on employment discrimination cases. The greater portion of employment discrimination cases are complex in the factual issues underlying each case and complex in the variety of legal issues that frequently arise in these cases. Moreover, discrimination cases are vigorously defended by employers, and while the worker's counsel more likely than not is a sole practitioner or a small firm, the employer's counsel is likely to be one of the Goliath-sized law firms, with hundreds of lawyers and multitudinous support staff. In such circumstances, the worker's counsel needs all the assistance she can obtain. The fee award statute is Congress's recognition that the worker's attorney must be granted that assistance if the ADEA and the other employment discrimination statutes are to be adequately enforced.

Relief Not Obtainable

Despite the near universal application of the make-whole standard of relief, the remedies available to the worker are materially deficient in two respects. The worker is denied compensatory damages for pain and suffering, as well as punitive damages. Both types of damages are available to victims of race, sex, national origin, religious, and disability discrimination, but victims of age discrimination are barred from recovering these types of damages.

Pain and suffering correlate with discrimination, regardless of its nature. Anger, guilt, indignation, bitterness, frustration, humiliation, shame, depression, emotional distress, emotional instability, and massive loss of self-esteem are discrimination's natural consequences. A worker cannot be made whole if precluded from recovering damages for this type of injury. But the ADEA neither specifically provides for nor denies this type of recovery, and the courts have proved to be sorely lacking in courage and in plain common sense in failing to extend a worker's monetary recovery to damages for pain and suffering.

Although specific authority is lacking, the statute defines the relief obtainable in the broadest of terms: "In any action brought to enforce this Act the court shall have jurisdiction to grant such legal or equitable relief as may be appropriate to effectuate the purposes of this Act."[17] Early in the life of the ADEA, some courts did indeed interpret this broad statutory language to encompass recovery for pain and suffering.[18] But over time, the pendulum has swung to the other extreme, and the courts now generally conclude that pain and suffering damages are excluded from an age discrimination recovery.

Punitive damages stand in the same stead as compensatory damages for pain and suffering. The make-whole standard of relief requires an award of punitive damages when the discriminatory conduct of the employer is shown to have been outrageous. Again, the statute does not specifically authorize the recovery of punitive damages, but the broad authority granted to the courts by the statute allows them to order their recovery, if the courts were so inclined. Since they appear not to be so inclined, an amendment to the statute is required if age claimants are to be afforded all the relief necessary to make them "whole."

14 | The Roles of the EEOC and the Private Attorney

A reduction in the incidence of acts of employment discrimination and ultimately their eradication depend on the vigorous and effective enforcement of the statutes barring workplace discrimination. When Congress adopted the Civil Rights Act of 1964, barring discrimination in employment by reason of race, color, sex, national origin, and religion, it also assigned enforcement of the statute to the newly created Equal Employment Opportunity Commission (EEOC). From its outset, the EEOC has been burdened with a complaint load far in excess of that initially anticipated. By the time Congress adopted the Age Discrimination in Employment Act (ADEA) in 1967, the EEOC already was experiencing difficulty in performing its functions adequately, and a burgeoning backlog of race and sex discrimination cases threatened to undermine its effectiveness in enforcing the 1964 act. Congressional concern that this backlog would result in the subordination of age claims to race and sex discrimination claims eventually moved Congress to assign the enforcement of the ADEA to the Wage and Hour Division of the Department of Labor, an administrative agency that was particularly efficient in performing its functions. The Carter administration, however, later concluded that all the employment discrimination laws should by administered by a single federal agency, and in 1978, the enforcement of the ADEA was transferred to the EEOC. Since that time, the EEOC has been responsible for the enforcement of all federal employment discrimination laws.

Once a worker files an age discrimination charge under the provisions of the ADEA, the EEOC is required to "promptly notify all persons named in such charge as prospective defendants in the action and . . . promptly seek to eliminate any alleged unlawful practice by informal methods of conciliation, conference, and persuasion."[1] EEOC procedures call for it to investigate the allegations of the charge before engaging in the process of "conciliation, conference, and persuasion." But historically, a vast majority of these discrimination charges are dismissed by the EEOC before they reach that stage of the proceedings. Here lies the basic problem with the EEOC's efforts to enforce the ADEA and the other discrimination statutes.

An EEOC investigation of a discrimination charge generally culminates in one of two rulings: (1) a determination that reason exists to believe the worker has been subjected to discriminatory conduct (a "for cause" finding), or (2) a determination that no reason exists to believe the employer has engaged in such conduct (a "no cause" finding). A finding of no cause effectively terminates the EEOC's involvement in the charge. Conversely, a finding of for cause leads to further EEOC action, such as conciliation and settlement. However, between 50 and 60 percent of all charges filed with the EEOC are disposed of with a no-cause finding, and a large portion of the remainder of the charges are dismissed for other reasons or are withdrawn by workers grown weary of EEOC delays.[2] Thus, a relatively small number of charges reach the point at which the EEOC ventures to conciliate or settle the worker's claim against the employer. Statistics show that between 1994 and 1996, only 10 percent of the charges filed were settled by the EEOC.[3]

A matter of greater concern than the small number of settlements is the EEOC's apparent reluctance to conclude its investigations with affirmative for-cause findings. Of the nearly 72,000

charges resolved by the EEOC in 1994, approximately 1,900 received a for-cause finding, representing less than 3 percent of
the case resolutions that year.[4] Between 1994 and 1998, EEOC's
annual for-cause findings in age discrimination complaints varied from a high of just over 4 percent to a low of just over 2.5
percent of the age complaints filed with the agency during those
years (the percentage rose to 8.3 percent in 1999).[5] Typically,
the EEOC's for-cause findings amount to less than 5 percent of
the charges filed, creating the impression that the EEOC is engaged in discovering where discrimination does not exist rather
than where it does exist.

In addition to conciliation and settlement, the statute also
authorizes the EEOC to file lawsuits against employers in the
courts. During the twenty-year period between 1969 and 1989,
the EEOC filed court cases against employers in less than 4 percent of the discrimination charges filed by workers.[6] In more
recent years, the incidence of EEOC-initiated litigation has been
even more sparse. For its fiscal year ending September 30, 1996,
the EEOC processed 21,253 age claims but filed only twelve age
discrimination cases in the federal courts.[7] Perhaps even more
telling, with the exception of cases involving its own procedures,
the EEOC has rarely appeared as a participant in a Supreme
Court case involving employment discrimination.

From its creation, the EEOC has been underfunded and
understaffed, and the huge backlog of cases that first appeared
in the late 1960s exists to this day. An underfunded and overworked staff cannot competently and efficiently investigate the
thousands of charges filed each year, and many no-cause de-
terminations are attributable to inadequate EEOC investigations.
One of my cases graphically demonstrates the shortcomings of
a typical EEOC investigation.

Dr. Samuel Song studied medicine in his native Korea,
came to this country while still a young man, became a U.S.
citizen, and after several years in medical research, began employment with a pharmaceutical division of American Home
Products (AHP). After several years with AHP, Song was fired,
supposedly because of interpersonal problems with staff members,

but Song blamed his termination on his supervisor, who Song claimed was anti-Korean. After his termination, Song filed a discrimination charge with the EEOC, alleging national-origin discrimination. Following a time-consuming investigation, the EEOC found no cause to believe Song had been subjected to any discriminatory actions. At that point, Song visited my office and asked me to assume control of his case and to file a discrimination suit against AHP in the federal court.

My own investigation of the events related by Song quickly led to the impression that something had gone amiss at the EEOC, since it appeared that the no-cause determination was not warranted by the facts in the record. Eventually, after an extended period of discovery, the case came to trial before a jury in the federal court in New York City. After we presented our evidence of discrimination, AHP offered its defense, including the testimony of the EEOC investigator who had recommended the no-cause finding. Obviously, AHP hoped to persuade the jury that because the EEOC had found no reason to believe Song had been subjected to discriminatory acts, the jury should arrive at a similar conclusion.

At the point in the trial at which the EEOC investigator took the witness stand, the jury had already heard a great deal of testimony that appeared to substantiate Song's position. In fact, one of Song's witnesses had testified to being present at a meeting where Song's supervisor had made scurrilous anti-Korean comments about Song. On her direct examination, the EEOC investigator related the steps she had taken to investigate Song's charge and said that ultimately she had concluded that he had not been subjected to any discriminatory conduct by AHP. On her cross-examination, the investigator was asked whether her investigation had uncovered any of the evidence that the jury had heard at the trial, and she responded that it had not. More particularly, she knew nothing about the anti-Korean comments of Song's supervisor. By the time she left the witness stand, it was apparent that the EEOC had issued a no-cause finding without uncovering any of the evidence of anti-Korean bias that the jury had heard from other witnesses. The jury was thus made aware of the inadequacy of the EEOC investigation and its failure to discover evidence clearly supporting Song's charge. At the conclusion of the trial, the jury rendered its verdict in favor of Dr. Song.[8]

In recognition that its procedures have been less than adequate, the EEOC recently inaugurated new procedures designed to reduce its backlog of cases, and it also redirected its resources primarily to processing the cases that appear to have greater merit. Instead of the EEOC investigating every charge, the new procedures are intended to screen out the weaker cases and to focus the commission's investigative attention on the stronger ones. Under this procedure, approximately 20 percent of the charges are immediately dismissed. Historically, workers have filed charges having little or no merit, and thus summary dismissal of a relatively large segment of the charges filed may be justifiable, but the means of selecting the charges for dismissal are another matter.

Earlier, we discussed the issues that confront an attorney asked to represent a worker who has charged an employer with discrimination (see chapter 11). When an attorney is first introduced to a case, evidence of discrimination may not be immediately apparent, and a lengthy period of discovery often is required before it can be determined whether sufficient evidence exists to support the charge. If an attorney is required to make that kind of effort before she can definitively state one way or another whether her client has a viable claim, how is it possible for the EEOC to make such a determination without an investigation of any kind? True, at times an attorney with little information available must make a less than informed decision whether to proceed with a case. But she may make the decision not to represent the worker with the knowledge that even if she has erred, there are other lawyers with whom the worker may consult, and another lawyer may view the claim from a different perspective and agree to proceed with the case. When the EEOC rejects a worker's claim, however, no other governmental agency exists for further consultation. When the EEOC dismisses a charge, the opportunity to resolve the charge administratively ceases at that moment.

Although Congress intended the majority of employment discrimination claims to be resolved administratively, it also granted the EEOC the right to initiate judicial proceedings. Thus, the EEOC has the option of filing suit on behalf of a claimant, but it rarely does. If the EEOC elects not to proceed in the courts, a Title VII claimant has the right to demand from the EEOC a Right-to-Sue Notice, a document that divests the EEOC of jurisdiction over the worker's claim and gives the worker entry to the judicial system. Upon the worker's demand, the EEOC must issue the Right-to-Sue Notice, even if the EEOC has not completed its investigation or even if it has concluded its investigation with a no-cause determination. Under slightly different procedures, the age complainant has the same right to move his or her case to the judicial arena.

As a practical matter, an older worker who believes herself to be a victim of age discrimination will have to pursue the matter on her own behalf, with little or no assistance from the EEOC. As a result, more than 95 percent of the employment discrimination cases adjudicated in the federal courts are shepherded through the court system not by the EEOC, but by private attorneys retained by workers.[9]

Efforts to reshape or improve EEOC procedures will not diminish the role of the private attorney. Without funding adequate to its tasks, the EEOC cannot succeed. By default, private attorneys have assumed a major role in protecting U.S. workers from discrimination in employment, and in the years to come, the role of the private attorney will grow in parallel with the increase in the number of age complaints.

Private attorneys have been far more instrumental and far more successful than the EEOC in providing the American worker with broad protection against discrimination in the workplace. Because private attorneys have been involved in considerably more discrimination case decisions than has the EEOC, their cases have been far more significant in the judicial development of employment discrimination law.[10]

Because the EEOC has been successful in obtaining only limited relief for discrimination claimants, it has failed to attain the status of a major deterrent to discriminatory conduct. While a pending lawsuit threatens corporate tranquility, a pending EEOC administrative proceeding generally has minimum effect. On balance, the cost to an employer of defending against a discrimination claim in court, together with the substantial risk of an adverse jury determination, is far more likely to deter unlawful employer conduct. The private attorney is the instrument of the greater threat, and although employers and their attorneys may deny it, the deterrence value of the private attorney far exceeds that of the EEOC.

Even before enactment of the statutes requiring employers to pay the attorney's fees of prevailing discrimination complainants, a small group of dedicated lawyers assumed lead roles in protecting the American worker from employer discrimination. One of the effects of the fee statutes has been to increase the number of lawyers willing to specialize in this area of the law. Most of the attorneys representing workers are solo practitioners or members of small law firms, and their litigation contests with major corporations and their mammoth law firms are frequently fought in David and Goliath circumstances. To gain mutual support, lawyers representing workers have banded together to form the National Employment Lawyers Association, the only professional organization in the country composed exclusively of lawyers dedicated to representing workers in discrimination and other employment cases. Today, its membership numbers nearly four thousand, located in all fifty states and the District of Columbia.[11]

There are far easier ways to make a living than as a lawyer for discrimination complainants. The David and Goliath description applies to nearly every employment discrimination litigation. Employers take discrimination claims as seriously as they would charges of fraud, theft, or child molestation, and they rely for their defense on the best and most experienced counsel they are able to locate, usually in the country's largest law firms. Recently, I litigated an age discrimination claim against an employer and its successor company who were not satisfied with retaining the largest firm in New York City to conduct their defense; in addition, they retained another huge firm, one of the largest in the country, with branch offices in several large cities, including one in New York City.

As earlier noted, in 1996, the oldest of the boomer generation turned fifty. The number of workers age fifty and older in the workplace is increasing and will continue to increase until 2012. Unless employers alter their attitudes toward the continued presence of the older worker in the workplace, an increasing growth in the incidence of age discrimination cases is assured. Since a dramatic change in employer attitude appears unlikely, the private attorney will continue to play an increasingly greater role in protecting older workers from acts of age discrimination.

15

The Negative Attitude of the Courts and Enforcement of the ADEA

Age discrimination claimants have a courtroom advantage unavailable to workers complaining of race, sex, or other types of employment discrimination. Because of the jurors' natural fear of growing older and the prospect of being subjected to age discrimination themselves, jurors tend to identify with age claimants. When an older worker testifies in the courtroom, the young juror may see his mother or father sitting there, or perhaps his grandmother or grandfather, and an older juror may see himself. Clearly, the jurors' sympathies lie with the older worker. But this advantage of the age claimant is counterbalanced, in some courtrooms, by the negative attitude toward age discrimination cases exhibited by the judge presiding at the trial.

Reagan and Bush administration appointees to the federal bench are more conservative, are generally less sympathetic to the objectives of the employment discrimination laws, and appear less receptive to workers suing their employers than those judges appointed by earlier administrations and by the Clinton administration.[1] Some judges are well known to favor employers over workers. A federal judge once told me that when she is confronted with a serious employment discrimination legal issue, she refrains from considering the written opinions of certain of her judicial colleagues because their perception of the rights of workers is much narrower than hers.

Those judges who advocate this narrower perception are well known to lawyers representing workers since their success record before these judges is nearly nonexistent. For example, a review of the decisions rendered in employment discrimination cases by one federal judge sitting in New York shows that he ruled in favor of the employer in twelve of thirteen cases. Another judge's record is fourteen of sixteen cases in favor of the employer. This antipathy toward discrimination complainants is not concealed. One federal judge, highly critical of the number of age discrimination cases on his calendar, expressed the opinion that older workers are able to file these cases with no more evidence of age discrimination at hand "than a birth certificate and a pink slip."[2] Another judge stated that "no Federal District Court can ignore the wave of dubious and potentially extortionate discrimination cases currently flooding the Federal docket."[3]

Discrimination case filings have in fact clogged court dockets in recent years. Absent these cases, a judge's life would undoubtedly be a lot simpler. Thus, in this respect, antipathy toward discrimination cases is not surprising. Judges appear unaware that private attorneys dispose of discrimination cases lacking merit *before* these cases reach the court dockets. A very high percentage of discrimination claims do not survive an attorney's initial investigation; they never advance to the point where a formal complaint is filed with the court. Attorneys routinely advise prospective claimants not to sue, knowing they will be unable to sustain their burden of proving discrimination. In fact, some attorneys estimate that 90 percent or more of the workers conferring with them do not proceed beyond the initial investigation of their claims. My own experience confirms this.

Judges also appear unaware that the most meritorious discrimination cases are rarely seen in the trial courts since these are the cases most likely to be settled by the employer before trial. Thus, judges normally see only the weaker of the workers' cases in their courtrooms. One study showed that only 8 percent of employment discrimination cases filed in the federal courts actually proceed to the trial stage.[4] If 90 percent of age cases never proceed beyond the lawyers' offices, then the courts actually are confronted with trying only .008 percent of all potential employment discrimination cases.

Some judges appear unconvinced that older workers should be afforded protection from acts of age discrimination, and others appear less committed to ending age discrimination than to eradicating race and sex discrimination. These negative attitudes may explain the outcome of a review of jury verdicts rendered in favor of workers in age discrimination cases tried in 1996. This study disclosed that 42 percent of jury verdicts in favor of the worker were later reversed by the court.[5]

The negative attitude of the lower-court judiciary toward employment discrimination cases in general reflects the negative attitude of the justices of the Supreme Court. William P. Murphy of the University of North Carolina School of Law has expressed the opinion that not since the New Deal days has the Supreme Court treated laws passed by Congress with such hostility. He points to the Court's 1988–89 term in which it decided fourteen employment law cases, and thirteen of those cases were decided in favor of the employer. In all fourteen cases, Justices Rehnquist and Kennedy adopted positions advanced by the employer, and they were joined in thirteen of these cases by Justices White, O'Connor, and Scalia. Justices Brennan and Marshall, on the other hand, most frequently supported the worker's position. As Murphy observed: "It seems obvious that the determinant in employment law cases is something other than dispassionate and objective application of neutral principles. The majority and minority were clearly marching to different drummers."[6]

While marching to different drummers, members of our federal judiciary have created a whole host of problems for older workers striving to prove age discrimination. One of the most troublesome positions adopted by some judges is the rejection as evidence of age discrimination of age-biased remarks uttered by employers.

Some, but not all, age-biased or age-stereotypical comments or remarks are admissible as evidence in support of a worker's age discrimination claim. The rule of admissibility for these types of remarks and comments, as announced by the Supreme Court, is restrictive. The comment must have been made either by the person who made the decision adversely affecting the older worker or by a person who was in some way involved in making that decision. Remarks made by non–decision makers or persons not involved in the decision-making process are classified as "stray remarks," and remarks assigned to this category generally are not admissible as evidence against the employer.[7]

Some courts have excluded from evidence the ageist comments of a company CEO because he was not personally involved in the decision affecting the worker.[8] In one case, a senior vice president greeted a worker, just prior to his discharge, by remarking, "You've been around since the dinosaurs roamed the earth." The court excluded the remark because the decision to fire the worker was made by a managing director of the company and not by the senior vice president.[9]

To be admissible in evidence, the age-biased remark also must have been made fairly close in time to the adverse decision. An appellate court, in reversing a jury verdict in favor of an older worker, ruled that the trial court judge should have excluded evidence of age-biased remarks of the employer's president. Three or four years prior to the worker's termination, the president had referred to some of his older employees as "old ladies with balls." Even though the president made the decision to fire the worker, the court said his ageist comment was made too far in the past to be relevant.[10] Some courts have limited the admissibility of these types of statements to those made within one year of the adverse decision.[11]

Abstract comments are generally inadmissible. Facetious remarks, comments reflecting a favorable opinion of younger workers, and statements susceptible to both innocent and invidious interpretations are usually labeled "abstract" and thus incapable of raising an inference of discrimination. Comments that are merely condescending or inappropriate in the circumstances also are generally rejected by the courts. For instance, a worker who was about to be terminated asked the employer's personnel manager whether other positions were available to which he might transfer. The personnel manager responded that the worker would first have to take a physical examination and said he did not believe that the worker at his age could pass it. Although clearly an inappropriate comment, the court ruled that it was irrelevant to the decision to terminate.[12]

The negative attitude of certain members of the federal judiciary toward age bias cases has led them to even more restrictive rulings, leading to the rejection of nearly all ageist remarks on the ground that they are irrelevant and not probative. In the courts of these judges, an age-related comment rarely sees the light of day before it is banned from the courtroom. Just consider the iron curtain lowered by the court around James O'Connor's age suit against Consolidated Coin Caterers Corporation.

O'Connor was the general manager of Consolidated's sales region located in Charlotte, North Carolina. In 1990, the company was reorganized and O'Connor, age fifty-six, was terminated. Another general manager, age fifty-seven, was demoted, but two younger general managers, ages forty and thirty-five, retained their positions. O'Connor claimed age discrimination, relying heavily upon three ageist remarks made by his direct supervisor, who rendered the decision to terminate him. Two months before his termination, while O'Connor and his supervisor were watching a golf match on television, O'Connor remarked that he would have trouble playing eighteen holes of golf on consecutive days, and the supervisor agreed, commenting that O'Connor was just "too old" for that kind of an effort. Two weeks prior to O'Connor's discharge, the same supervisor remarked, "O'Connor, you are too damn old for this kind of work." Two days before O'Connor's termination, in reference to another employee about to turn fifty, the supervisor was heard to say, "It's about time we started to get some young blood in this company."

The court analyzed each comment separately and ruled in each instance that the supervisor's comment was merely a stray remark having no nexus to the decision to terminate O'Connor. The court failed to consider whether the comments, when examined in combination, disclosed an attitude or mindset of the supervisor or of the company's management. Even though the comments were made by the person who made the decision to terminate O'Connor, and each comment was made close in time to his termination, the court nevertheless ruled that the comments were not evidence that proved management's intention in ordering O'Connor's discharge.[13] Proving discrimination is always difficult; proving it under conditions in which evidence of age bias of this type is rejected as irrelevant is nearly impossible.

Alan Birkbeck and J. Richardson held supervisory positions at Marvel Lighting Corporation in South Carolina, and both were laid off, purportedly for economic reasons. At the time of their layoffs, Birkbeck was sixty-two and Richardson was fifty-five. One of the principal issues in their subsequent age discrimination case was the admissibility in evidence of an ageist remark made by a company vice president who was primarily responsible for the layoff decisions. Two years prior to the layoffs, this vice president had commented that "there comes a time when we have to make way for younger people." Initially, the vice president's comment was admitted into evidence, and the jury decided in favor of Birkbeck and Richardson. The trial judge then reversed the jury, ruling that the supervisor's comment was a simple "truism" and could not be considered evidence of age discrimination.

The appellate court that reviewed the case affirmed the lower court's reversal of the jury verdict, ruling that although the vice president's remark may appear to have been a declaration of company policy, it was nevertheless inadmissible. First, the remark was made too far in the past and was unconnected to the decisions to terminate Birkbeck and Richardson. Second, the statement was a simple truism and did not demonstrate a discriminatory intent. "Moreover," the court continued, "statements about age may well not carry the same animus as those about race or gender. Unlike race or gender differences, age does not create a true we/they situation—barring unfortunate events, everyone will enter the protected age group at some point in their lives."[14]

Excluding this type of evidence appears questionable on at least three accounts. First, whether the statement was too remote in time is a question that should have been left to the jury. The remoteness issue relates to the weight the jury should give the statement, not to its admissibility. Second, whether the remark reflected a discriminatory intent or was a mere truism is again an issue for the jury to determine. Third, contrary to congressional intent, the court appeared to attribute less importance and significance to acts of age discrimination than to acts of race or sex discrimination.

In another case, a company owner stated categorically that one of his older workers was "too old" to handle his supervisory duties and therefore had to be removed from his position, but because this was said some eight months before the worker's termination, the court ruled that the statement was too remote in time to be relevant to an age discrimination claim later asserted by the worker.[15] In another case, a supervisory employee said, "All you old bastards ought to be retired and let us young people run the company the right way." When a worker who was later terminated attempted to have this remark admitted into evidence in support of his case, the court ruled that the statement was irrelevant because the worker failed to show a nexus between the statement and his discharge. The court failed to perceive a nexus even though this supervisor participated in the decision to fire the worker.[16]

In order to understand how these courts appear to have gone astray, we must examine the legal standards that guide the courts in ruling on the admissibility of evidence, and for that guidance, we turn to the Federal Rules of Evidence. Rule 401 defines "relevant" evidence "as evidence having any tendency to make the existence of any fact that is of consequence to the determination of the action more probable or less probable than it would be without the evidence." The rule broadly defines "relevant evidence" to include any and all evidence "having any tendency" to prove or disprove the facts in issue. Relevant evidence can be excluded by the court only if it falls within the narrow limitations of Rule 403: "Although relevant, evidence may be excluded if its probative value is substantially outweighed by the danger of unfair prejudice, confusion of the issues, or misleading the jury." The important words here are "substantially outweighed." The rule places a severe limitation on the exclusion of relevant evidence. When these rules are applied as intended, a different result obtains, as the following cases clearly illustrate.

Charles Mitte began his career with Manville Sales Corporation in 1962, working as a sales representative selling fiberglass insulation products. In the early 1980s, Manville embarked on a series of cost-cutting measures, including the discharge of a large number of sales representatives. In 1982, the manager of the district that included Mitte's sales territory recommended that one of the three sales representative positions in his district be eliminated and that the responsibilities of the departing sales representative be divided between the two remaining sales representatives. He further suggested that Mitte be selected for termination, referring at the time to Mitte's age, fifty-five, and contrasting him with one of the other two representatives, who was thirty-two and described by the district manager as a "young aggressive sales rep." Not surprisingly, Mitte's position was later eliminated, and he was terminated.

During the trial of Mitte's age suit against Manville, the court refused to permit the jury to hear evidence of ageist comments made by the district manager. The excluded testimony included the remark that Mitte was incapable, old, and inflexible. The district manager had also bragged about "how he jumped that old man about smoking his pipe," and he had referred to Mitte, who apparently was accustomed to wearing a hat, as "old man hat." On the ground that the district manager's remarks were too remote, having been made over the four-year period he had served as Mitte's manager, the court barred Mitte's lawyer from presenting this evidence to the jury. An appellate court later reversed this ruling, stating that the lengthy period over which the remarks were made did not render them irrelevant: "To the contrary, the long time period may indicate a pattern of discriminatory comments and as such are directly relevant to showing the existence of discriminatory motive on the part of Manville."

Rather than excluding the comments from evidence because they were uttered sometime in the past, the appellate court ruled that the proper procedure was to allow the jury to hear these comments and then to permit the jurors to determine the weight to be given them in relation to all the other evidence presented. In contrast to the cases referred to earlier, the court properly assigned to the jury the responsibility of determining the effect these comments should have on the outcome of the case.[17]

Another case in point presents a scenario that may seem not entirely believable. Aaron Cooley worked for a theater chain for thirty-five years, moving up the ranks from "popcorn man" to manager of the chain's theaters in Chattanooga, Tennessee. Cooley supervised eighty-five employees and handled everything from auditing ticket sales to advertising to theater maintenance, and it was not unusual for him to work an eighty-hour week. Early in his career, when Cooley was asked to relocate to another city, he postponed his wedding to accommodate the relocation. Loyalty and dedication to his employer were at the top of Cooley's priority list.

In his position as manager of the Chattanooga theaters, Cooley reported to the theater chain's district manager, who in turn reported to the division chief. In December 1988, faced with increasing competition from other movie theaters in the Chattanooga area, the division chief ordered Cooley to run a full daily schedule of five screenings throughout the Christmas season, and contrary to past practice, he ordered the first matinee also to be shown on Christmas Day. Despite this directive, Cooley's direct supervisor, the district manager, decided not to present the first matinee show on Christmas, and Cooley proceeded to place advertising in the local newspaper that omitted the early matinee from the Christmas Day schedule.

A few days before Christmas, the district manager reversed himself and advised Cooley that management was insisting on the early Christmas showing. Cooley tried to reach his account representative at the newspaper to insert the additional Christmas show in the advertising, but the account representative was unavailable, and apparently he was the only one at the newspaper with authority to change the advertising. Cooley advised his district manager of the problem, and again the district manager reversed himself and directed that the first Christmas matinee be canceled. The early matinee was not screened on Christmas Day, and the division chief fired Cooley.

To his credit, the district manager informed management that the wrong person had been fired, that if anyone was to be relieved of his position, it should be he, not Cooley. Management refused to reconsider its decision, insisting that Cooley had been fired because of insubordination in failing to change the newspaper advertisement and in not screening the early Christmas show. Even before Cooley left the theater after being notified of his discharge, he was replaced by a newly hired younger employee. Cooley immediately charged his former employer with age discrimination.

Cooley's attorneys presented testimony at the trial that Michael Patrick, the president and chief executive officer of the theater chain, despised older people. One instance of this had been related to Cooley by his district manager some time prior to the trial, and the court permitted Cooley to repeat the conversation at the trial.

> On Thanksgiving [Michael Patrick] made the statement, "I got to go to my mom's and dad's and have lunch today with them. . . . I don't want to go."
>
> [The district manager] said, "Well, Mike, why? This is Thanksgiving."

And [Patrick's] words were, "Well, my grandmother is
over there, and I just don't . . . like to be around old people."

The court also permitted Cooley to testify to a conversation he had with Patrick some twenty years earlier. Patrick was
eighteen at the time and had just left a movie theater after seeing *Wild in the Streets,* and he said to Cooley, "Everybody over
thirty years old needs to be put in a pen. Yeah, if they don't
want to be put in a pen, they should be confined to a concen-
tration camp."

If the court had considered these two comments in isola-
tion, it might very well have barred the jury from hearing them
on the grounds that (1) they were abstract, (2) they were not
made by the person who made the decision to fire Cooley, and
(3) they were made at times too remote to be relevant. But the
appeliate court, in reviewing the trial court's acceptance of this
testimony, noted that "although those two quoted comments
were not made in the context of Cooley's termination, and they
had been made a long time before he was dismissed, they do
help to reveal [Patrick's] state of mind and reflect a deep-rooted,
on-going pattern that is anything but isolated." Other witnesses
substantiated Cooley's testimony by relating instances of
Patrick's deep-seated age bias; they said that he felt uncomfort-
able around older people, and that he expressed a desire for a
younger workforce. The district manager testified: "There was
hardly a meeting that I ever had with Mr. Patrick that something wasn't said about getting old. . . . [He] did not like older
people, he didn't like to be around them, and he never . . . made
any pretense about it. He just didn't like to be around older
people."

Patrick also often spoke of three older employees that he
kept on the payroll as his "token senior citizens" whose presence would protect him from age discrimination suits. Even
Cooley's replacement testified that Patrick made it clear that he
preferred younger workers in supervisory positions, such as the
position Cooley had held.

The jury accepted Cooley's contention that the reasons expressed by the theater chain for his Christmas dismissal were

"humbug," and that he had been fired as part of a corporate effort to clear out older workers. It then awarded Cooley more than $500,000 in damages.[18]

In affirming the trial court's decision to admit into evidence each of these age-biased remarks, the appellate court noted the "heavy evidentiary burden that Age Discrimination in Employment Act (ADEA) plaintiffs must bear" and noted that the ageist comments had been proffered to demonstrate a pattern of illicit behavior sufficient to meet that heavy burden. If the court had strictly limited the admissibility of ageist comments to those recently made by the person making the decision to fire Cooley, the jury would have heard none of this testimony. But the court's expansive interpretation of the provisions of the Federal Rules of Evidence permitted Cooley to establish a course of employer conduct that fully revealed the discriminatory motives underlying his termination.

Another case illustrating a court's more liberal approach to the admissibility of ageist comments involved John Ryder and Westinghouse Electric Corporation. Ryder, employed for eleven years as a staff assistant to the controller group for Westinghouse's Power Systems Group, was terminated at the age of fifty-two. Ryder sued for age discrimination, and a jury verdict in his favor was challenged by Westinghouse on the ground that the trial court should not have admitted into evidence a memorandum written by Westinghouse's CEO that referred to ageist comments by unidentified Westinghouse executives. These comments were made at a series of meetings that occurred after Ryder had been terminated. The memorandum recording the minutes of these meetings included these ageist remarks;

1. In many of our businesses we have an older workforce. As a result, that workforce gets a higher salary. Additionally, our low growth business can strain opportunities for younger workers. Somehow we must provide those opportunities. We have to get the "blockers" out of the way.
2. Westinghouse has been pretty paternalistic in the past and we've ended up with too much dead wood in the organization.

3. We don't have enough people in the organization ages thirty to forty.
4. What we need to do as the leadership of this organization is force ourselves to those standards so that the best persons get into the right positions. An eager high-energy person will get more done in a month than someone who has retired in place will do in one year.
5. We seem to be missing the people in the middle of the age range.

Westinghouse argued that the memorandum was largely irrelevant and highly prejudicial, and that on those accounts the trial court should have prohibited it from passing into evidence. Ryder's lawyers, on the other hand, argued that the memorandum was properly admitted as circumstantial evidence of the corporate culture that existed at Westinghouse at the time Ryder was terminated.

The appellate court first noted that, clearly, it is appropriate for a court to consider circumstantial proof of age discrimination, particularly if it is in the form of a supervisor's statements relating to managerial attitudes held by corporate executives. Such evidence becomes even more critical as sophisticated discriminators render their actions increasingly more subtle in circumventing the law.

After adopting Ryder's position that ageist statements of corporate executives are relevant to the company's culture and managerial policies, the court proceeded to set forth guidelines for evaluating such statements: "The court must . . . evaluate factors pertaining to the declarant's [that is, the person making the ageist remark] involvement in recognizing a formal or informal managerial attitude, including the declarant's position in the corporate hierarchy, the purpose and content of the statement, and the temporal connection between the statement and the challenged employment action."

Although the comments quoted in the memorandum did not relate directly to Ryder's termination and, in fact, were made about one year after his discharge and by persons not involved in making the termination decision, the court still held that the comments were relevant to that decision. These comments reflected past managerial viewpoints, and a jury might very well have concluded that they also reflected a managerial attitude toward older workers at the time of Ryder's discharge. The appellate court then affirmed the jury's verdict in favor of Ryder.[19]

The Mitte, Cooley, and Ryder decisions stand in clear contrast to the O'Connor and Birkbeck decisions and others like them. All too often, courts have failed fully to realize the very heavy burden of proof carried by workers claiming discrimination. Unless workers are given free rein to present all the evidence they are able to muster, it is unlikely they will be able to sustain that heavy burden, and acts of discrimination will remain unaddressed. A distressing number of unfriendly and overly restrictive courts continue to undermine the enforcement of the age discrimination laws. In fact, these courts may actually encourage acts of discrimination because an employer, perceiving that courts are unsympathetic to age discrimination complaints, may be more willing to risk litigation and, consequently, will focus less attention on adhering to the precepts of the ADEA.

16 | Judicial Limitations to Proving Age Discrimination

Congress quickly reacted to the Supreme Court's 1988–89 record of thirteen out of fourteen employment decisions in favor of the employer by adopting the Civil Rights Act of 1991. This legislation in effect reversed many of those decisions and added new rights for workers suing under the civil rights laws. Thus, Congress reaffirmed a strong national policy favoring the protection of the civil rights of workers.

Even with the adoption of the 1991 legislation, the Supreme Court, still dominated by conservative justices, on several occasions has made it more difficult for workers to prevail against employers who have discriminated against them. Two Supreme Court decisions, *St. Mary's Honor Center v. Hicks* and *Hazen Paper Company v. Biggins*, have made it substantially more difficult for workers to establish employer liability for acts of workplace discrimination.[1]

The Hicks Case

In 1973, soon after Congress enacted Title VII and the Age Discrimination in Employment Act (ADEA), the Supreme Court devised what it described as a "sensible, orderly way to evaluate the evidence" in employment discrimination cases, striking a balance between workers and employers by giving both fair opportunities to present their positions in a court of law. The Court established two procedures a worker may use to prove an employer's conduct was discriminatory: (1) directly persuading the court that the employer more likely than not was motivated by a discriminatory reason; and (2) showing that the reasons given by the employer for its conduct are false or not believable or, as more commonly expressed, pretextual.[2]

The first procedure comes into play less frequently than the second because direct evidence of discrimination generally is unavailable to a worker. Indirect evidence demonstrating that the employer has lied about its motivation in acting adversely to a worker's interests stands at the center of almost all employment discrimination cases. In nearly all cases, the basic factual issue to be decided is whether the employer's expressed reasons that purportedly justify its decision are true or false. According to early Supreme Court rulings, if the worker proved the employer's proffered reasons to be false or pretextual, she was entitled to a verdict in her favor. If the worker failed to sustain the burden of proving falsity or pretext, the employer was entitled to a verdict in its favor.

For twenty years, the Supreme Court repeatedly reaffirmed and refined this framework for proving workplace discrimination. In the *Hicks* case, decided in 1993, the Supreme Court abandoned this practical framework, subverting its previous sensible and balanced approach to proving discrimination.

Prior to the *Hicks* decision, the Supreme Court held fast to the rule that the falsity of the employer's explanation was alone sufficient to compel judgment for the worker. If the worker carried the burden of showing the employer lied, the court was required to decide in the worker's favor: "The worker] must have the opportunity to demonstrate that [the employer's] proffered reason was not the true reason for the employment decision. This burden . . . merges with the ultimate burden of persuading the court that [the worker] has been the victim of intentional discrimination."[3]

Proof of falsity was equated with proof of discrimination. But in the *Hicks* decision, the Supreme Court discarded this sensible rule and stated that the jury's rejection of the employer's reason for its action does not compel the jury to find in favor of the worker. In other words, it is not enough to disbelieve the employer; the jury still must find that the employer intentionally discriminated against the worker. This turned the concept of pretext on its head. What advantage does the worker gain by proving the employer lied if she still is required to prove that the employer's conduct was discriminatory?

The *Hicks* decision greatly disfavors the worker who has no direct evidence of discrimination to present to the court. In most instances, a worker relies upon evidence that her employer fabricated a defense to cover up its illicit motives, and prior to the *Hicks* case, workers were able to rely upon the presumption that the employer who lied about its reasons for acting adversely to a worker was simply trying to cover up the illegality of its conduct as alleged by the worker. The *Hicks* decision rejects this commonsense approach and, by placing an additional burden upon the worker, has made it substantially more difficult to prove that an employer's decision was motivated by a discriminatory intent.

The Supreme Court, however, attempted to ameliorate the full consequences of the *Hicks* decision. Although it ruled that proof of the falsity of the employer's position does not *compel* a verdict for the worker, the jury *may* nevertheless infer a discriminatory motive from the fact that the employer resorted to lying. Thus, if the only evidence offered in support of the worker's case is the falsity of the employer's position, a jury may decide that the employer's conduct was discriminatory, but it is no longer compelled to rule in that fashion.

The Hazen Case

While the ADEA affords workers protection against age-biased conduct, it also recognizes the reasonable business concerns of employers. In *Hazen*, also decided in 1993, the Supreme Court considered one of those employer concerns:

Does the ADEA permit an employer to terminate an older worker so as to reduces its costs?[4]

Before we analyze the action taken by the Supreme Court in the *Hazen* case, we first must review the law as it developed prior to 1993, and the earlier law is best exemplified by the age discrimination suit brought by Wayne Metz against his former employer, Transit Mix, Inc., of Plymouth, Indiana.

At age fifty-four, Metz was discharged after twenty-seven years of employment with Transit Mix, a company engaged in selling concrete to local construction contractors. At the time of his termination, Metz was the manager of Transit Mix's plant in Knox, Indiana. During the years just prior to Metz's termination, Transit Mix experienced financial problems due to the decline in the local construction business. In November 1983, Will Lawrence, president of Transit Mix, closed the Knox plant for the winter, and Metz was laid off. Early in 1984, Lawrence sent Donald Burzloff, assistant manager of one of Transit Mix's other plants, to inspect the plant at Knox and to arrange for any repairs necessary before the plant's reopening. Burzloff, who was forty-three and had been employed by Transit Mix for seventeen years, later requested that he be appointed manager of the Knox facility. Lawrence acceded to this request, and Metz was then fired. Metz sued for age discrimination.

At the time of his layoff, Metz was Transit Mix's second most senior employee and one of its highest paid. Metz's high salary was a product of his many years of employment with the company, owing to the fact that he received annual salary increases, even in those years that Transit Mix's operations were unprofitable. As Burzloff's salary was nearly one-half that paid Metz, Transit Mix relied on the cost saving as justification for Metz's termination. The trial court ruled that the reduction in its payroll was the determining factor in Transit Mix's decision to replace Metz with Burzloff, and although this cost savings factor "bore a relationship to Metz's age," Transit Mix had not violated the ADEA because its decision was motivated by cost savings rather than by Metz's age. Transit Mix, according to the court, had been motivated by financial reasons to terminate Metz and thus had acted on the basis of a reasonable factor other than age. In other words, Transit Mix had made a business decision unaffected by age bias. However, the appellate court that reviewed the lower court's decision rejected this reasoning.

The reviewing court first noted that Congress enacted the ADEA in response to the difficulties experienced by older workers in the job market, particularly the obstacles that long-term workers encounter when terminated at an older age. Long-term older workers develop firm-specific skills not readily transferable to other job settings. In fact, the long-term older worker's higher salary may lead to the very problem that ADEA was intended to address: the likelihood that the terminated older worker will be unemployable if forced into the job market. For this reason, the appellate court ruled, the ADEA must be interpreted to prohibit an employer from replacing higher-paid older workers with lower-paid younger workers solely to effect a cost savings. Because of the high correlation between age and salary, it would undermine the goals of the ADEA to recognize cost cutting achieved through the termination of older workers as a nondiscriminatory justification for an employment decision.

The court relied heavily on the fact that Metz's high salary resulted from a long series of annual increases, uninterrupted by Transit Mix operating losses in some years. Metz's salary reflected twenty-seven years of service; his salary directly correlated with his years of service, and his years of service directly correlated with his age. Thus, in these circumstances, salary may be considered a proxy for age, and a decision to terminate Metz because of his high salary was really a decision to terminate him because of his age.[5]

Anticipating that its rationale might be subjected to the criticism that the court was interfering with a legitimate business judgment made by an employer, the court relied on and quoted one of its earlier decisions:

> Although the ADEA does not hand federal courts a roving commission to review business judgments, the ADEA does create a [legal] cause of action against business decisions

that merge with age discrimination. Congress enacted the ADEA precisely because many employers . . . act as if they believe that there are good business reasons for discriminating against older employees. Retention of senior employees who can be replaced by younger, lower-paid persons frequently competes with other values, such as profits or conceptions of economic efficiency. The ADEA represents a choice among these values. It stands for the proposition that this is a better country for its willingness to pay the costs for treating older employees fairly.[6]

Regardless of his performance, Metz received a salary increase every year of his employment. In fact, no evidence was offered the court showing that he had ever been awarded a merit increase. Would the outcome of the case have differed if his high salary were a consequence of merit increases and promotions? Would a salary that reflected a worker's merit as well as longevity still be considered a proxy for age? We turn to Richard Holt's age discrimination case against Gamewell Corporation for the answer.

Due to large operating losses, Gamewell decided to reduce its payroll by $500,000, and Holt, the purchasing manager of Gamewell, was one of those selected for termination. Holt alleged that he was terminated because he was highly compensated, and since his rate of compensation was related to his seniority, he argued that his salary was actually a function of his age. But in contrast to Metz's salary, Holt's salary had increased primarily as the result of promotions and merit raises following excellent performance evaluations. Under these circumstances, the court rejected his contention that his high salary was a function of his age.[7]

Prior to the Supreme Court's *Hazen* decision, many federal courts across the country adopted the reasoning of the *Metz* decision as well as the limitations of the *Holt* ruling, recognizing that an employer's decision based on certain age-correlated factors may constitute the functional equivalent of an age-based decision. Among the factors the courts considered as age proxies were years of service and retirement eligibility, although most often the issue was raised by workers who contended their dismissals were directly related to their high rates of compensation. But not all courts considered a high salary as an age proxy, as Eugene Bay sadly discovered when he sued his former employer, Times Mirror Magazines, for age discrimination.

In 1975, Bay accepted the position of national marketing director for *Field & Stream* magazine, then owned by CBS Magazines. Four years later, he was promoted to associate publisher and two years after that, to vice president and publisher. In 1986, Diamandis Communications acquired CBS Magazines, and the following year it sold *Field & Stream* and three other magazines—*Yachting, Home Mechanix*, and *Skiing*—to Times Mirror. Times Mirror already owned four magazines—*Ski, Golf, Popular Science*, and *Outdoor Life*—and after the acquisition of the four publications from Diamandis, Times Mirror restructured its operations so that its eight magazines were organized into two groups based on reader demographics, advertising compatibility, and size of circulation. As a consequence of the restructuring, Bay's responsibility and authority were greatly diminished. At that point, Bay, who was fifty-four and earning nearly $200,000 a year, was replaced by a thirty-five-year-old earning $85,000 a year.

Bay's age discrimination suit was dismissed on Times Mirror's motion for summary judgment. In contrast to the reasoning of the Metz decision, the court ruled that

> there is nothing in the ADEA that prohibits an employer from making employment decisions that relate an employee's salary to contemporaneous market conditions and the responsibilities entailed in particular positions and concluding that a particular employee's salary is too high. To be sure, high salary and age may be related, but so long as the employer's decisions view each employee individually on the merits . . . and are based solely on financial considerations, its actions are not barred by the ADEA.[8]

The stage was now set for the Supreme Court's consideration of the issue, and this occurred in the *Hazen* case.

The Hazen Paper Company, owned by cousins Robert and Thomas Hazen, manufactured coated, laminated, and printed paper as well as paperboard. The company hired Walter Biggins as its technical director in 1977 but fired him in 1986, when he was sixty-two years old. The company's pension plan had a ten-year vesting period, and if Biggins had worked another few weeks he would have reached the ten-year mark. Biggins claimed that the Hazens were guilty of age discrimination by firing him to prevent his vesting in the pension plan. The issue presented to the court was whether an employer violates the ADEA by acting on a factor that correlates with a worker's age, such as pension status.

The Supreme Court began its analysis of the issue by first reiterating and emphasizing that the ADEA requires an employer to evaluate an older worker on the basis of his capabilities, not his age. An employer cannot rely on age as a proxy for evaluating a worker's capacity—it cannot, for example, assume that a reduction in productivity necessarily occurs with age. Rather the employer must focus on each individual worker's capacity to perform adequately. Stigmatizing stereotypes must be rejected; each worker's characteristics must be examined and evaluated individually.

But the Court pointed out that inaccurate age stereotypes do not come into play when the employer is wholly motivated by factors other than age, and this is true even if the motivating factors are correlated with age. Generally, an older worker, like Biggins, has had more years in the workforce than a younger worker, and he may have accumulated more years of service with a particular employer:

> Yet an employee's age is analytically distinct from his years of service. An employee who is younger than 40 . . . may have worked for a particular employer his entire career, while an older worker may have been newly-hired. Because age and years of service are analytically distinct, an em-

ployer can take account of one while ignoring the other, and thus it is incorrect to say that a decision based on years of service is necessarily "age-based."

The Court then applied this analysis to the situation confronting Biggins. Under the Hazen Paper pension plan, benefits vested after ten years of service. Although older workers are more likely to be close to vesting than are younger workers, a decision by the company to fire Biggins solely because he had nine-plus years of service and therefore was close to vesting does not constitute discriminatory treatment on the basis of age. The decision to terminate him was made not on the basis of inaccurate and denigrating generalizations about age, but rather on an accurate judgment about Biggins—that he, indeed, was close to vesting.[9] The Court did not preclude the possibility that an employer engages in age discrimination if it assumes that employees having a particular pension status are likely to be older and it then targets those employees for termination: "Pension status may be a proxy for age, not in the sense that the ADEA makes the two factors equivalent, . . . but in the sense that the employer may suppose a correlation between the two factors and act accordingly."

The Supreme Court thus reaffirmed prior court holdings that an employer who targets a worker for dismissal by using age-correlated characteristics violates the statute. Therefore, if an employer uses salary as a basis for eliminating its older workers, or if it is motivated to dismiss workers on account of both their ages and an age-correlated factor such as high salary, it would be guilty of age discrimination. But if an employer is motivated to reduce its staff solely by reason of cost, without regard to the ages of its workers, it would not be guilty of age discrimination.

Although the Supreme Court concluded that age is "analytically distinct" from years of service and other age-correlated factors, the typical employer decision makers sitting in the board room are not likely to make that fine a distinction. Within the confines of the board room, the decision to cut payroll costs is less likely to be distinct from a decision to fire higher-paid older workers.

Under the *Hazen* reasoning, Wayne Metz's age discrimination case against Transit Mix would fail because Metz now would be unable to rely solely on evidence that his termination was a product of his high salary and many years of service. Rather, he would have to prove that Transit Mix had been motivated to terminate him because of his age and not merely because of his high salary. The *Hazen* ruling has made the courts far less friendly to workers' cases cast in the age-proxy mold. Harold Johnson's travails with the Francis W. Parker School demonstrates this point.

Francis W. Parker School is a private school located in Chicago. Parker establishes teacher salaries in accordance with a step system that links salary to teaching experience; the salaries of newly hired teachers take into account prior teaching experience. When an opening occurred in Parker's drama department, its principal established a salary of no more than $28,000 for the replacement to be hired. Harold Johnson, sixty-three years old with thirty years of teaching experience, applied for the position but was rejected in favor of a much younger teacher whose experience qualified her for a $22,000 salary under the step system. One of the reasons given for Johnson's rejection was that he qualified for a salary that Parker could not afford.

The Equal Employment Opportunity Commission (EEOC) filed suit on Johnson's behalf against Parker. Parker later filed a motion with the court to dismiss the suit, but the motion was denied. In the meantime, the Supreme Court decided the *Hazen* case, and after that decision was published, Parker renewed its motion, and this time the court dismissed Johnson's suit.

The EEOC action was based on the premise that Parker's step system excluded a disproportionate number of older teacher applicants from consideration for teaching positions. Their longer experience placed these applicants higher up in the step system, but the school tended to hire those who placed lower in the system, and these were more likely to be younger applicants. The EEOC position was identical to that maintained by Miriam Geller in her suit against the Bugbee School (see chapter 12).

Because Parker had not offered any business justification for maintaining the step system, the EEOC contended it violated the ADEA. On Parker's second attempt at dismissal, the court ruled that a compensation policy such as the step system that links salary to experience is economically defensible, and even though it may be age correlated, it is not barred solely for that reason by the ADEA: "Though years of service may be age-correlated, *Hazen Paper* holds that 'it is incorrect to say that a decision based on years of service is necessarily age-based,' unless [the EEOC] can demonstrate that the reason given was a pretext for a stereotype-based rationale. . . . Ultimately, the EEOC must show that Parker's rationale is pretextual and that the salary system is predicated on some stereotype, conscious or unconscious."[10]

The existence of an age-correlated system of compensation was of no assistance to the EEOC in proving age discrimination in Parker's failure to hire Johnson. The EEOC could not prove pretext; it could not prove that Parker's step system was a subterfuge to conceal its belief that older teachers are less effective than younger teachers. Case dismissed.

The Aftermath of the Hicks and Hazen Decisions

As in the *Hicks* case, the Supreme Court's decision in the *Hazen* case has made it substantially more difficult for the older worker to establish an age discrimination claim.[11]

The *Hicks* decision fundamentally altered the direction the courts had followed from the beginning in regard to the employment discrimination laws. The courts early on recognized the difficulties confronting a worker who was trying to prove that an employer intentionally engaged in discriminatory conduct, and a system of proof was devised whereby a court would assume that an employer who lied about its reasons for treating a worker adversely was covering up illicit conduct.

Even prior to the *Hicks* case, some courts exhibited hostility to this approach of proving discrimination, and as a consequence, in those courts it became increasingly less likely that a worker would prevail, absent the submission of some direct evidence of discrimination. With the *Hicks* decision, the Supreme Court decided that a jury could assume that an employer lied to cover up its discriminatory conduct but that it was not compelled to make that assumption. As a practical matter, in most cases, the *Hicks* ruling requires the worker to submit more tangible evidence of discrimination, that is, some evidence in addition to disclosing the employer's untruthfulness in explaining its conduct.

Having made it more difficult through the *Hicks* ruling to establish pretext, the Supreme Court in the *Hazen* case materially narrowed the scope of the age proxy doctrine. Proof of age-correlated conduct is now generally insufficient to prove age discrimination. A worker is required to prove conscious or unconscious stereotype-based employer conduct, and without such proof, age-correlated conduct is generally of no relevance.

Another consequence of these Supreme Court rulings, particularly the *Hicks* ruling, has been a pronounced increase in the use of the summary judgment procedure to dismiss worker claims prior to trial.[12]

As related in chapter 10, if the employer is to prevail in its motion for summary judgment, it must first show that there are no material issues of fact for the court to decide. Because material issues of fact are nearly always in question, the employer is faced with a substantial barrier in obtaining an early dismissal of the worker's case. As we have seen, one means employers use to clear this barrier is to assume, for purposes of the motion, the accuracy of the worker's version of the facts. Even then, the motion may be granted by the court only if— upon reviewing the evidence in a light most favorable to the worker, and upon drawing all reasonable inferences in favor of the worker—the court still determines that no rational jury could find in favor of the worker's case.

At one time, this standard presented a formidable obstruction to a summary dismissal of a worker's case. In addition, since discrimination cases often turn on questions of credibility and intent, issues that generally must be decided by a jury, summary judgment was looked upon as inappropriate in most discrimination cases. However, since the *Hicks* and *Hazen* cases, and simultaneously with the appearance of a federal judiciary increasingly hostile to discrimination cases, summary judgment has become a more popular method of disposing of these cases. Cases that appear weak or unpersuasive fall victim to this trend. Ron McCoy's age discrimination case against WGN Continental Broadcasting met that fate.

WGN hired McCoy as director of creative services for WGN Television in Chicago. During his employment, McCoy received several performance awards, good performance evaluations, and several bonuses. Four years after hiring him, WGN transferred McCoy to a newly created position with substantially less responsibility and then replaced him with a newly hired younger employee who was paid substantially more. Within a month of his transfer, McCoy learned that his new position was not budgeted for the following year, and shortly thereafter, he was terminated. WGN maintained that McCoy's transfer and termination were required because of performance problems and a need to cut costs. McCoy was forty-six at the time.

McCoy filed suit for age discrimination, but his case was dismissed on WGN's motion for summary judgment. On McCoy's appeal, the appellate court started its review of the case by carefully outlining the principles a court must follow in deciding a motion for summary judgment. The court is required to draw all inferences in a light most favorable to McCoy, and summary judgment should not be ordered if the record discloses the existence of material issues of fact. The appellate court even indicated that these general standards should be applied "with added rigor" in a case such as McCoy's, where the intent of the employer is a central issue. The court then proceeded to slash at McCoy's case with even greater rigor.

McCoy argued that WGN's reasons for transferring and firing him were so implausible that they must be pretextual. First, the record showed that he had performed well, so performance was not a credible reason for transferring or firing him. Second, his replacement was paid more than he had been paid, and thus cost savings could not have been a factor. Despite this evidence, and even though the court purported to be guided by principles applicable to a summary judgment motion, it affirmed the dismissal of McCoy's case.[13]

This is a prime example of a case that should have been reserved for jury determination because material issues of fact underlie every aspect of the case. The determination of these issues was the province and responsibility of a jury, not of the court.

The recent trend favoring the summary dismissal of workers' cases and the rejection of jury verdicts has resulted in fewer successful conclusions to worker age claims. If this trend is allowed to continue, the employment discrimination laws will surely fail in their goal of banishing discrimination from the American workplace.

Michael C. Harper, professor of law at the Boston University School of Law, aptly describes the circumstances confronting the age discrimination plaintiff now that the Supreme Court has spoken in the *Hicks* and *Hazen* cases:

> An employer should feel confident that it can insulate itself from proof that its [supervisors] took age into account [in] making an employment decision, by constructing a plausible pretext that cannot be completely disproved, and by taking care that its decision-making [employees] do not comment directly on the age of the adversely affected employee. If [employers] take care not to provide direct evidence of discriminatory intent, plaintiffs will have to prove that the [employer] would not have made the same deci-

sion based on some plausible pretext. Judges, skeptical of
the existence of age discrimination and the policies underlying the ADEA, will be able to reject jury verdicts, based
on their conclusions that [proof of discrimination] has not
been established.[14]

If an employer feels confident that it can conceal its discriminatory intent, then it is more likely that it will continue to engage in illegal, discriminatory conduct The more difficult the
courts make it for a discrimination complainant to prove his
or her case, the more likely it is that the discrimination laws
will continue to be flouted.

17 | Arbitration of Age Discrimination Disputes

Juries that sit in employment discrimination cases appear most concerned with the element of fairness.[1] A jury tends to identify with the unfairly treated worker, especially if the employer has acted arbitrarily or harshly. Even the mere appearance of unfairness may prejudice a jury against an innocent employer. At the same time, if the jurors perceive that the employer has conducted itself fairly in its relations with its workers, they will give greater credence to the employer's positions on trial issues. The jury itself tends to act fairly. But in age discrimination cases, factors not present in other types of litigation may influence a juror's sense of fairness.

The fear of growing old, with the prospect of suffering through the aging process and eventual physical decline, is common to us all. Whether young, middle-aged, or old, jurors entering the jury box are influenced, at least to some degree, by such foreboding expectations. Jurors are prone to sympathize and identify with the older worker who is without a job and can expect to find few or no opportunities for other employment. This presents a unique problem for the employer charged with the commission of unlawful treatment of an older worker; "jurors find it difficult to close their hearts to the plight of the terminated older employee but easy to open the purse strings of his employer."[2] The hope of obtaining a jury verdict in these circumstances is not one an employer anticipates with any degree of sanguinity.

Another, potentially more troublesome factor confronts every employer upon entering the courtroom. Baby-boomer demographics portend an increase in the age of jurors as well as that of workers and the populace in general, and older jurors are even more apt than younger jurors to identify with the plight of a worker mistreated because of his or her age. It is no wonder then that employers consider age cases to be the most dangerous type of all employment discrimination litigation and will do almost anything to avoid trial before a jury.[3]

Undoubtedly, employers' fear of a jury trial has prompted management to alter its personnel practices—if not always to eliminate age-biased decisions, then at least to create the perception of fair dealing with older workers. These employers' fears, however, have left their greatest mark on the litigation process itself, profoundly influencing the strategies of lawyers for the employers as well as lawyers for the workers. The worker's counsel conducts pretrial discovery with the aim of developing a record of testimony and documentary evidence that will be viewed favorably by the jurors. Lawyers for the employer, on the other hand, do not want even to consider arguing before a jury, and as a consequence, they devote the greater part of their attention to developing a record that will enhance the prospect of a dismissal of the worker's case before it reaches the jury. As we have already seen in chapter 10, the motion for summary judgment is the employer's primary tool for avoiding a jury trial. Some employers, however, have available a far more effective method of evading a jury trial. In fact, they possess the means of excluding the judicial system from adjudicating any discrimination claims that are asserted against them. Securities brokerage firms were among the first to master this approach.

All securities firms require newly hired workers whose job functions include the buying and selling of securities to sign a document designated a "Form U-4." This document contains a provision requiring the workers to submit all future employment disputes to arbitration, and it reads in part: "I agree to arbitrate any dispute, claim or controversy that may arise between me and my firm . . . that is required to be arbitrated under the rules, constitutions, or by-laws of the organization with which I register." This provision of the Form U-4 is commonly referred to as a compulsory or predispute arbitration agreement.

Securities brokerage firms argue that a worker who signs a Form U-4 waives his or her right to a judicial forum and a trial by jury of any claims made by the worker against the firm. Accordingly, a worker who signs the form also waives her right to sue the employer for employment discrimination, and the worker may be compelled to arbitrate any discrimination claim she later alleges against the firm. If a worker violates this covenant not to sue and initiates litigation against the firm in the courts, the securities firm, with a signed Form U-4 in hand, may obtain a court order compelling the worker to move her discrimination claim to the arbitral forum, thus assuring the firm that no jury will ever hear the worker's case.

Workers argue that a compulsory or predispute agreement to arbitrate age discrimination claims is inconsistent with the statutory scheme contemplated by Congress when it enacted the Age Discrimination in Employment Act. The ADEA provides for a two-step resolution of discrimination claims, the first, an administrative process conducted by the Equal Employment Opportunity Commission (EEOC), and the second, a judicial process conducted before the courts. From the workers' viewpoint, arbitration should play no role in this process. Indeed, prior to 1991, the courts generally held that a worker could not waive his or her rights to litigate civil rights claims, but in that year, the Supreme Court declared that no inconsistency existed between the social issues fostered by the ADEA and predispute agreements to arbitrate age disputes.[4]

Once predispute arbitration agreements had Supreme Court approval, they spread to other industries, and the arbitration of employment discrimination claims quickly became the employers' most favored method of resolving these disputes. One writer has labeled this unfolding change "one of the most pernicious developments in employment law today."[5] Most workers' counsel would agree. Despite the many difficulties workers and their counsel have experienced with the courts, as outlined in the last two chapters, arbitration is not a viable alternative to judicial resolution of age complaints. Compulsory, predispute arbitration is unacceptable for a number of reasons.

The Worker Is Not Free to Reject Arbitration

A predispute arbitration agreement is basically not negotiable. The worker is required, as a condition of employment, or as a condition of remaining employed, to consent to the arbitration of all future employment disputes. These agreements appear in employment agreements, in employment application forms, in employee handbooks, and in other documents, such as the Form U-4. In all events, the worker is presented with a take-it-or-leave-it situation: "Agree to arbitration, or you don't get the job."

By agreeing to arbitration, the worker waives his statutory right to a judicial determination of any discrimination claim that the worker may later assert. But a waiver of a statutory right will be considered valid only if made voluntarily and knowingly. When the choice is between the acceptance of arbitration as a method of resolving future disputes and the relinquishment of a desirable position, the worker's agreement to arbitrate cannot be considered voluntary. An agreement to arbitrate disputes that have not yet occurred, the nature and identity of which are purely conjectural, cannot be considered to have been made knowingly. Yet these agreements to arbitrate future disputes are now routinely enforced by the courts.

Our experience and common sense tells us that an unemployed job applicant cannot afford to be overly concerned about problems that may never occur in the employment relationship. First and foremost, the worker needs a job, and he will agree to almost anything to get that job. Employers cannot justify the

enforcement of an arbitration agreement imposed upon workers as a condition of employment simply by arguing that the
worker voluntarily and knowingly agreed to arbitration. Nonetheless, employers, aided by the Supreme Court, have found a
near fail-proof method of avoiding jury decisions of discrimination claims.

Arbitral Forums Lack the Benefits and Protections of the Court System

In a lifetime, a worker may be involved in no
more than a single employment dispute requiring resolution by
a third party, such as a court or a panel of arbitrators. Employers, who require their workers to submit disputes to arbitration,
appear before the same panel of arbitrators time and again. While
the worker typically has only one experience with these arbitrators, the employer and the arbitrators know each other well.
Because they are paid for their services, the arbitrators want to
be selected for future arbitrations, and an employer is far more
likely to select arbitrators who have previously decided in its
favor. Furthermore, inasmuch as it is unlikely that the worker
will again appear before these particular arbitrators, the arbitrators have no concern about the worker's failure to select them in the
future. In these circumstances, the worker is justifiably concerned that the arbitrators may be biased in favor of the employer.

Even with the hostility exhibited by some members of the
federal bench toward age discrimination cases, workers favor
judges over arbitrators because judges have a great deal of experience in dealing with employment discrimination cases,
while arbitrators do not. Some years ago, when arbitration was
first offered as an alternative to judicial resolution of disputes,
arbitration was favored by the business community primarily
because it was commonly believed that business disputes could
be more readily resolved by arbitrators who were familiar with
the particular business giving rise to the dispute. The knowledge and experience of the arbitrator was the driving force
behind the arbitral concept. But arbitrators are totally inexperienced in the nuances of the civil rights laws. The basic, un-

derlying reason for the arbitration, therefore, is not present in discrimination cases.

When an arbitrator makes a mistake, the mistake probably will remain uncorrected, as the judicial review of arbitration decisions is severely limited by law. Recently, a panel of arbitrators ruled in favor of a worker but then failed to provide in their award for the payment of the worker's attorney's fees. When the worker complained to the court, the court refused to intervene to correct the mistake, even though the law clearly provides that a worker who prevails on a discrimination claim is entitled to recover his attorney's fees.[6]

Arbitration favors the employer in another respect. Prehearing discovery in arbitral proceedings is considerably more limited than the pretrial discovery available in court cases. As earlier noted, pretrial discovery is essential to the development of the worker's case, as these procedures allow the worker to obtain the deposition testimony of the employer's primary witnesses. In addition, they also provide the worker with access to relevant documents in the employer's files. Arbitral procedures generally allow only minimal discovery, while the Federal Rules of Civil Procedure call for very broad discovery. Although employers are often guilty of discovery abuse in court cases, the worker would rather suffer that abuse than be denied the discovery needed to develop the evidence required to support the worker's case. Discovery is particularly critical in an age case in which the discrimination may be of an unusually subtle character. To the extent that the worker's discovery is limited, the worker's chance of success is reduced.

Limited discovery that denies the worker access to the employer's documents and records may materially undermine the development of the worker's case. Under these circumstances, the employer will be free to use its documents to its own advantage, while preventing the worker from obtaining documents that may support her position. If these documents were available to the worker, they could provide the basis for showing statistical discrepancies in the treatment of workers in different age groups. Personnel records of other employees might establish the disparate treatment of older workers. In a judicial proceeding, the court would order these records be made available to the worker. In an arbitral proceeding, their availability to the worker is far less likely.

In the federal court system, the appointment of magistrate judges to oversee pretrial discovery assures both the worker and the employer that discovery will be conducted fairly, while affording both parties discovery broad enough in scope to develop their cases. Nothing of a similar nature exists in the arbitral system. Arbitrators, inexperienced in the area of employment discrimination and without the slightest inkling of what it takes in the way of discovery to construct a case around circumstantial evidence, are totally at sea when it comes to the discovery process. The inability of the arbitrator to serve a meaningful role in this process serves to benefit the employer and materially undermines the worker's ability to present a viable case.

The arbitral process, as it now exists, is governed by few rules and standards. Rules and standards serve the purpose of guaranteeing fairness to both sides of a dispute. Without meaningful rules of procedure, the potential for abuse by the stronger party is considerable. The arbitral process cannot substitute for the judicial process in guaranteeing fair procedures.[7]

Arbitration Does Not Adequately Further the Purposes of the ADEA

Civil rights cases involving major public policy issues that require the analysis of complex legal questions are better left to the courts. A federal judge in Massachusetts has said it best: "Whatever the competence of arbitrators to resolve disputes in a commercial setting, . . . the litigation of civil rights claims require[s] different sensibilities. Civil rights litigation . . . not only calls for 'dispute resolution,' but require[s] the articulation of public rights and obligations."[8]

A judge decides a case by writing an opinion, explaining the decision, and citing the precedents relied upon in support of the decision. An appellate court reviewing the determination of a lower court writes an opinion, detailing its reasons for upholding or reversing the lower court's decision. Arbitrators generally do not write opinions. The arbitration of age claims, therefore, retards development of the law inasmuch as it deprives courts of the opportunity of interpreting the statute in the light of differing fact situations. Court decisions and the precedents that develop through the judicial process guide employers with respect to distinguishing permissible from impermissible conduct. Unpublished, one-line decisions of an arbitrator accomplish nothing in that regard.

Since arbitration decisions are not reviewable on their merits by the courts, the entire process becomes privatized. If arbitration continues as the employers' most favored vehicle for resolving employment disputes, age discrimination will become more and more a private issue, and the perception may then develop that age discrimination is no longer a significant public issue.

How have workers fared under the arbitral process? At the time of the 1991 Supreme Court decision, when the court reversed previous rulings regarding the use of arbitration in employment discrimination disputes, compulsory arbitration was limited primarily to the securities industry. Five years after the Supreme Court decision, a prominent employer's lawyer surveyed decisions rendered in employment-related disputes by arbitrators sitting on New York Stock Exchange (NYSE) and National Association of Securities Dealers (NASD) arbitration panels. His survey disclosed that the securities firms prevailed in 76 percent of the cases heard by NASD arbitrators and in 59 percent of the cases heard by NYSE arbitrators. He concluded that employers experienced greater success in arbitration than in the courts, and even in those cases where the employers lost in arbitration, the size of the damage awards levied against the employers was smaller.[9]

It is no wonder, then, that an employer will do nearly anything to force a worker complainant into arbitration. The lengths to which an employer may extend itself to divert a case from a jury to an arbitration panel is well illustrated by the extreme measures recently undertaken against one of my clients.

Jennifer Maxwell was employed as an administrative assistant by a medium-sized New York City securities brokerage and investment banking firm.[10] After a few months on the job, Maxwell decided her career would be advanced if she were to study for and pass what is referred to in the securities industry as a Series 7 examination. Typically, a worker planning to take this examination first enrolls in a course specifically designed to prepare workers for the examination, and many securities firms reimburse their workers for the costs of this course. Maxwell approached management with her plan to prepare for the examination, and approval was given for her to proceed. However, she was advised that she would first be required to complete the necessary paperwork to initiate the process.

One of her supervisors provided Maxwell with a four-page form that she took back to her office to complete. It was a Form U-4 that included the arbitration clause quoted earlier. When Maxwell came to that portion of the form, she was puzzled by the presence of that provision. Maxwell had graduated from college the year before, and since this was her first full-time position in the business world, it was not surprising that the concept of arbitration of possible future employment disputes was a matter completely foreign to her. Rather than check off the box on the form indicating her agreement to the arbitration of "any dispute, claim or controversy that may arise between me and my firm," she left that portion of the form blank. Maxwell then signed the form, but before delivering it to management, she made a photocopy. This turned out to have been a very wise move.

A month or so later, her immediate boss began to sexually harass her. At first, she tried to ignore his conduct, but it steadily grew more offensive and more pervasive. She and her boss shared a small office, and there was no way she could avoid his sexual jokes, stories of his sex escapades, and sexual comments about Maxwell herself. She felt that she dare not complain about his treatment of her for fear she would lose her job. Maxwell was so disturbed by the harassment that she looked for advice from others and sought psychological counseling as well. Ultimately, she had to resign her position with the firm, and she then sued her boss and the brokerage firm for sexual harassment.

Immediately after the filing of her lawsuit, the brokerage firm filed a motion with the court asking it to dismiss Maxwell's case on the ground that she had agreed to the arbitration of all employment disputes. Attached to the firm's motion papers was a copy of the Form U-4 signed by Maxwell, but this copy showed that Maxwell had checked off the box indicating her agreement to arbitration. Unaware that Maxwell possessed a photocopy of the form she had signed, the brokerage firm had altered the form to indicate her acceptance of the provision for arbitration. Of course, we immediately brought this change to the court's attention. At that point, the brokerage firm and its lawyers were in deep trouble, since the court now knew they had submitted an altered document. But they were not yet prepared to give up. Their next step was to file with the court an affidavit signed by the supervisor who had presented the Form U-4 to Maxwell, and in that affidavit, he swore, under oath, that Maxwell had authorized him to complete the form by checking off the arbitration box. Maxwell responded with her own affidavit, advising the court that the subject of arbitration had not been discussed by her with anyone in the firm, that she had intentionally elected not to check off the arbitration box, and that she had not authorized anyone to alter the form she had signed. Ultimately, the court rejected the firm's attempt to divert the case to arbitration, and the case is now proceeding in the court. Rather than confront a jury, an employer will resort to almost anything to force a worker's discrimination complaint into arbitration.

Susan Desiderio decided to test the legality of the predispute arbitration provisions of the Form U-4. She was offered a position by SunTrust Bank in Florida as a registered securities representative. As a condition of her employment, SunTrust required her to sign the Form U-4. When she was presented with the form, Desiderio struck out the provision requiring the arbitration of future disputes and submitted the form to bank management. SunTrust then revoked its offer of employment. Desiderio sued the bank, claiming that it had violated her statutory and constitutional rights by requiring her to agree to the arbitration of future disputes as a condition of employment. The court dismissed her claim, and Desiderio joined the ranks of the unemployed.[11]

Following the 1991 Supreme Court decision, the use of predispute arbitration agreements by employers spread from the securities industry to other areas of the business world, the Form U-4 serving as a steppingstone to a variety of documents incorporating predispute arbitration provisions. One type of document employers have used with some frequency to require workers to resort to arbitration for the resolution of employment disputes is the employee handbook.

Sharon Kinnebrew, a claims administrative manager for Gulf Insurance Company in Texas, discovered she was being paid substantially less than the male manager who held the position before her had earned, and she sued Gulf for sex discrimination. After Kinnebrew had begun working for the company, Gulf instituted a predispute arbitration policy, and it mailed copies of its arbitration policy to all its workers, along with an explanatory memorandum. Gulf also outlined the arbitration policy in its employee handbook. The handbook entry included this provision: "Arbitration is an essential element of your employment relationship and is a condition of your employment. This policy makes arbitration required, and exclusive, for the resolution of all employment disputes which may arise." Rather than submit her sex discrimination claim to arbitration, Kinnebrew filed a discrimination claim with the EEOC and thereafter with the federal court.

When Gulf argued before the court that Kinnebrew's claim should be dismissed for the reason that she had agreed to the arbitration of all future employment disputes, Kinnebrew countered that she had never agreed to arbitration and that Gulf had unilaterally distributed copies of the new policy to its workers without adequately explaining the effect of the policy and without obtaining their acceptance or express agreement to the policy. The court rejected Kinnebrew's position, pointing out that she had received a copy of the newly initiated policy and had continued her employment with Gulf. In other words, according to the court, Kinnebrew had the option either of accepting the policy or quitting. Because she did not quit, she waived her statutory right to have her sex discrimination claims tried before a jury of her peers.

No evidence was submitted to the court showing that Kinnebrew understood the implications of the arbitration policy, that she specifically formulated an intent to accept the new policy, or that she consciously waived her statutory right to a jury trial for future disputes. No evidence of any kind was submitted showing that Kinnebrew actually agreed to arbitration. But the court ignored this lack of evidence and concluded that she must have assented to the new policy, else she would have resigned. The court ignored the legal requirement that a waiver of a statutory right must be made voluntarily and knowingly.[12]

Peter Nghiem was required to arbitrate an employment discrimination claim even though he had signed an employment contract that did not contain any provision for arbitration. Nghiem worked for NEC Electronics in California for nine years before being fired. At the outset of his employment, Nghiem and NEC entered into a written employment agreement that provided, among other things, that it could not be varied or modified except by another written agreement signed by both parties.

NEC's employee handbook provided for a "Problem Resolution Process" that culminated in arbitration. After he was dismissed, Nghiem abided by the terms of this process, including the arbitration. When the arbitrator ruled against him, Nghiem filed suit in court against NEC, arguing that the arbitrator's adverse decision was not binding on him since he had never signed an agreement to arbitrate. The court rejected Nghiem's position, holding that his participation in the arbitral process constituted his agreement to arbitrate. Thus, the court ruled that his participation served as a modification of his employment agreement, even though the agreement itself stated that it could not be modified except by another written agreement signed by both parties.[13]

Some commentators have suggested that the apparent readiness of the courts to uphold predispute arbitration provisions may result from overcrowded court calendars. It has been estimated that 10 percent of all cases filed in the federal courts are employment discrimination cases, and federal judges may be influenced by these circumstances to thin out their calendars by ordering arbitration in very questionable circumstances. But, as a prominent employment lawyer has said, "The constitutional and statutory rights of Americans should not be compromised by the logistical problems of overcrowded court dockets."[14]

In 1997, the EEOC announced that it was firmly opposed to the enforcement of arbitration agreements imposed on workers as a condition of employment. It felt compelled to announce this policy, publicly and formally, because it noted that an increasing number of employers were requiring workers, as a condition of gaining employment, to give up their rights to pursue employment discrimination claims in court, and to agree instead to the resolution of these disputes through arbitration. The use of these agreements, according to the EEOC, is no longer primarily limited to the securities industry; the practice has spread to retail, restaurant and hotel, health care, broadcasting, security services, and other areas of the business sector.

The EEOC prefaced its policy statement by reminding the public that federal civil rights laws, including the laws prohibiting discrimination in employment, have played a unique role in U.S. jurisprudence: "They flow directly from core Constitutional principles, and this nation's history testifies to their necessity and profound importance." The EEOC then stated that any analysis of mandatory arbitration of rights guaranteed by these laws must "be squarely based in an understanding of the history and purpose of these laws." While the EEOC is the primary federal agency responsible for the administrative enforcement of the employment discrimination laws, the courts have been vested with the final responsibility for statutory enforcement through the interpretation of the statutes while adjudicating claims. The EEOC then proceeded to explain why that responsibility must remain with the courts.

1. Many of the legal principles governing the application of these laws have been developed through judicial interpretations and case precedent. Without the courts, doctrines essential to free the workplace of unlawful discrimination would not have been developed.
2. The courts are public bodies; the exercise of judicial authority is subject to public scrutiny. When courts fail to apply these laws in accordance with public values, they are subject to correction by higher courts and by Congress.
3. The courts also play a critical role in preventing violations of the law. Court decisions give guidance to those covered by the laws, thus enhancing voluntary compliance with them. By issuing orders and decisions, later made known to the public, the courts identify violators of the law and their conduct. "As has been illustrated time and again, the risks of negative publicity and blemished business reputation can be powerful influences on behavior."
4. The courts cannot fulfill their enforcement responsibilities if workers do not have access to the courts. Individual workers act as "private attorneys general" in bringing claims to the courts, serving not only in their own private interest, but also as instruments of deterrence for would-be violators of the statutes.

The EEOC expressed its concern that predispute arbitration "privatizes" the enforcement of the employment discrimination laws, thus undermining public enforcement of these laws. The nature of the arbitral process allows for minimal public accountability of arbitrators or their decisions; the arbitrator answers only to the private parties to the dispute, not to the public. The arbitrator is part of a system of self-government created by and for the private parties. Because arbitrators' decisions are private, employers are not held publicly accountable for their violation of the law, and this lack of public disclosure weakens deterrence of further violations.

The commission also observed that the arbitral process does not allow for the development of the law. Arbitration decisions are usually not written and in any event are not made public. As a result, there is virtually no opportunity for the courts to correct errors of statutory interpretation.

The EEOC confirmed the long-held concerns of employment lawyers. Arbitrators are often biased in favor of the employer, discovery is overly limited, and arbitration is imposed on the worker simply because the employers stand a greater chance of success in arbitration than in a court before a jury.

In its policy statement, the EEOC concluded that further use of arbitration agreements as a condition of employment should be barred, because it harms both the civil rights of the claimant and the public interest in eradicating discrimination: "Those whom the law seeks to regulate should not be permitted to exempt themselves from federal enforcement of civil rights laws. No one should be permitted to deprive civil rights claimants of the choice to vindicate their statutory rights in the courts—an avenue of redress determined by Congress to be essential to enforcement."[15]

That is where the matter stands. On one side, employers, backed by the courts, continue to force arbitration on their workers. On the other side, workers, supported by the EEOC, adamantly hold that predispute arbitration agreements are basically flawed in that they are inconsistent with the country's employment discrimination laws. Ultimately, the issue will have to be decided by the Supreme Court. Based on its recent history, it appears likely that the Court will grant its approval to the mandatory arbitration of all employment discrimination claims. It will then remain for Congress to reintroduce reason to the process.

18 | The Role of the Worker in an Age Discrimination Suit

Workers can reduce the incidence of age-motivated workplace decisions. If older workers were fully committed to challenging age-based employment decisions, undoubtedly their employers would find it more cost effective to abide by the provisions of the Age Discrimination in Employment Act, since the costs of litigation incurred in defending against age claims in the courts would exceed those incurred in complying with the statute. But in challenging age-discriminatory conduct, older workers must be willing to accept responsibility for taking on the role necessary to such an undertaking. The role of the older worker, and the manner in which the worker fulfills that role, are vital to the successful use of the legal process in challenging employer age-biased conduct.

In fulfilling this role, older workers must first learn to recognize age-biased workplace actions. Of course, workers cannot be expected to make a definitive decision that an employment act is or is not age biased. Rather, workers must remain constantly alert to any workplace occurrence that may possibly signify illicit employer conduct. The cases presented in this book detail the diverse measures employers use to discriminate against older workers. A common thread runs through these cases. In almost every instance, age discriminatory conduct was detected by the worker simultaneously with an unexpected change in the work environment. As an example, take the case of Elizabeth Brown (chapter 3).

Brown was alerted to her department manager's age-discriminatory conduct through the occurrence of two incidents, each reflecting a major change in the treatment she had grown accustomed to over the thirty-nine years of her employment. Through all of those years, Brown had won a series of promotions accompanied by a continuous increase in responsibilities. Then, contrary to past procedures, she and other older workers in her department were no longer invited to attend staff meetings. This was the first sign that something was amiss—an unanticipated and unexplained change in procedure. Not long afterward, while Brown was on vacation, her department manager had Brown's desk moved from the private office she had occupied until that time to an open-floor area where workers very much her junior were located. Brown correctly interpreted these acts as age-motivated, and she thereafter remained especially alert to all conduct that might possibly be considered as motivated by age bias.

The changes in Brown's workplace environment were much too obvious not to be noticed. But even major changes in the workplace may remain unrecognized as age-motivated by a worker who has experienced a long, successful, and happy work career. This occurred in the case of Peter Sullivan (chapter 11). Sullivan was subjected to unrealistic sales quotas for two consecutive years before he realized that his employer was engaged in a scheme to force him into retirement. Because Sullivan had achieved much success as a salesperson, and because he was overwhelmingly loyal to his company, it simply did not occur to him that his employer had set out to force him into retirement.

The older worker should be especially alert to long-term patterns of employer conduct adversely affecting the worker. The state of affairs that confronted Joseph Bartek is a case in point (chapter 7). Sixty-two-year-old Bartek was repeatedly bypassed for promotion. Other than repeated denials of promotion in favor of younger, less qualified workers, Bartek had at hand no evidence of age discriminatory conduct on the part of his employer. But a pattern of employer behavior such as he experienced, occurring over an extended period of time, may prove, as in Bartek's case, to be motivated by unlawful age bias.

Contrary to the type of changes in workplace environment experienced by Brown, Sullivan, and Bartek, other changes may be difficult to detect as emanating from age bias. Small changes in the work environment that occur over a period of time are likely to be considered by an older worker more as irritants than as acts of discrimination in progress. Thus, as a worker grows older, he is well-advised to remain even more alert to changes in the workplace. I am not encouraging workers to poison the employment relationship with petty or unfounded complaints or to find conspiracies where none exist. Every decision adversely affecting an older worker is not necessarily discriminatory. Obviously, business considerations may require changes a worker may not prefer. But with advancing age, the older worker must carefully examine these adverse changes for evidence of age bias.

In some instances, small changes in the work environment may be insufficient to provide a basis for establishing a claim of discrimination. A worker is highly unlikely to succeed in establishing an age claim that is based on a single adverse action having little or no consequence for the worker. On hundreds of occasions, I have had to turn away would-be age claimants because they could point only to a relatively insignificant, isolated employer action in support of their claims. The majority of age-motivated employer acts, however, fall between those that are obviously discriminatory and those that are isolated, causing minimal harm for the worker.

Before a worker concludes that she has been the object of age-discriminatory conduct, she must be brutally honest with herself. An older worker's performance may, in fact, have deteriorated, and thus the worker herself is responsible for precipitating the adverse action taken against her. Thus, the worker must engage in a totally objective evaluation of her own performance. Has she slowed down? Has she slacked off in anticipation of retirement in a few years? Is she continuing to fulfill the reasonable expectations of her employer? The worker should undertake this self-examination before she runs off to a lawyer demanding the immediate filing of an age discrimination suit. Be assured, any experienced employment lawyer will demand such an examination before initiating any legal proceedings.

After conducting such an examination and concluding that she may have been the subject of discriminatory conduct, what should the worker do? She must turn to a lawyer. Workers, however, normally respond to these circumstances by deferring any direct action. This is usually a mistake. Even if a worker merely suspects the presence of age discrimination, she still should consult an attorney. The sooner the worker begins to act in accordance with the advice of counsel, the less likely it is that she will make a mistake that may seriously undermine her case. In addition, an early start to the collection of evidence may prove crucial to the successful prosecution of the worker's claim.

As a general rule of thumb, a worker should consult with an attorney if she has any intention of filing a claim against her employer. It is the rare worker indeed who successfully prosecutes an age discrimination claim without the advice and guidance of a lawyer. Thomas Taggart was successful in his age claim against Time, Inc. (chapter 11), but he stands as one among many thousands of age claimants who have proceeded without a lawyer only to confront total failure.

Not just any lawyer will do; the circumstances demand a lawyer experienced in employment discrimination matters. All employment discrimination cases are complex, and a lawyer inexperienced in these matters will suffer greatly at the hands of lawyers retained by the employer to defend it against age claims. The employer's lawyers will surely be well experienced in the law of employment discrimination and will be long accustomed to using tactics and strategies designed to undermine a worker's case.

An experienced employment discrimination lawyer will

nearly always enlist the services of his own client to assist in the preparation of an age claim. The worker stands in the unique position of knowing every aspect of his job better than anyone else. He has witnessed firsthand the conduct he claims was discriminatory. What better source of information does a lawyer have than his own client? The case of Virginia Green (chapter 3) is a prime example.

Green created television commercials for a large advertising agency and lost her position in a downsizing when she was the oldest of twenty-three associate creative directors working for the agency. The advertising agency defended her selection for the downsizing on the ground that she was less productive than her younger peers. Green could not believe the agency would rely on such a defense because she knew the agency's own records would show clearly that her productivity was equal to if not superior to that of nearly all the other associate creative directors. Green was able to identify for me the agency's documents that would demonstrate her superior productivity. Because the agency had made Green's productivity an issue—indeed, the major issue—in the case, we demanded and were able to obtain all the agency's production records for all twenty-three associate creative directors. Since Green was totally familiar with these documents, she was able to assemble the data we needed to prepare an evidentiary submission that graphically demonstrated her superior record of productivity.

Green played a crucial role in the preparation of her case for trial. But her involvement was not unusual. As previously noted, lawyers for workers almost always rely very heavily on their clients in preparing an employment discrimination case for trial, and a worker should anticipate that her assistance will be required. The worker must be prepared to remain very much involved in the litigation process.

At the first indication that the work environment has deviated from that experienced by the worker in the past, the worker should start keeping a diary, recording the details of any occurrence in the workplace that she conceives as possibly relevant to an age claim. In these circumstances, the worker should throw caution to the winds and record the details of any work-place incident that appears in the least bit out of the ordinary. It is far better to record too much information than not enough. The worker should not concern herself with the relevance of the information she is recording, as her lawyer will be able to sort through these data at a later time. Details are important. Dates, times, and the names of all persons who play any role in the events being recorded should be identified. Such a record will later prove invaluable in constructing a detailed chrono-logical analysis of all events underlying a worker's claim.

Elizabeth Brown kept a diary that strengthened her case immeasurably. When she ceased to be invited to departmental staff meetings and was deprived of her private office, Brown began to maintain a daily log of the work she was performing. When the bank later claimed that she was incapable of work-ing in high-volume situations, her daily log proved the contrary.

After detecting an unexplained change in the work envi-ronment, the worker should next focus on the issue of age. Is there any connection between the change in the work environ-ment and the worker's age? Has the employer been motivated to order these changes because of the worker's age? Inasmuch as certain aspects of illicit employer conduct commonly appear in age discrimination cases, the worker may review the cases in this book for assistance in answering these questions. The worker should examine these cases for occurrences similar to those he or she has experienced on the job. Some of the more common of these occurrences are the following:

1. An older worker is treated less advantageously than less-qualified younger workers, such as the promotion of younger workers with inferior qualifications instead of the better qualified older worker, or the dismissal of an older worker who is then replaced by a less-qualified or less-experienced younger worker.
2. The responsibilities of an older worker are reassigned to less-experienced younger workers, often leaving the older worker with little to do.
3. Younger supervisors—and sometimes even older supervi-

sors—use language that is either derogatory of the worker's age or indicates that the worker's age is a factor in the supervisor's workplace decisions.

4. An older worker is not provided with the same opportunities as younger workers for advanced training or for upgrading job skills.

5. An older worker's work life is manipulated with the intention of forcing him to elect retirement, or a middle-aged worker is compelled to agree to the terms of an early-retirement plan.

6. In the case of RIFs and other corporate reorganizations, it becomes readily apparent that older workers have been treated less advantageously than younger workers. For example, a greater proportion of older workers are selected for job elimination.

7. An older worker with a history of excellent performance appraisals is given a poor appraisal. This frequently occurs simultaneously with other adverse action against the worker.

8. The employer alters longstanding workplace procedures. In Peter Sullivan's case (chapter 11), his employer refused to adjust his sales quota to reflect existing market conditions, a practice the employer had followed until that time throughout Sullivan's thirty-six-year career with the company.

9. Despite a long history of adequate job performance, a worker is placed on probation, a move that inevitably leads to termination.

10. An employer finds fault with an older worker in circumstances where it had not found fault before.

11. An employer acts in a particularly cruel manner, as in Ann Hertz's interview with the Gap store or Richard Wilson's assignment to janitorial duties by Monarch Paper Company.

12. An employer resorts to altering its own documents or inexplicably deviates from its previous personnel procedures.

In light of the Supreme Court ruling in *St. Mary's Honor Center v. Hicks* (chapter 16), the worker is well-advised to remain constantly alert to the existence of any evidence that shows, in any respect, that age was a factor in the adverse decision affecting his employment. Proof that the employer out-and-out lied about the reason for making that decision is no longer enough to assure victory for the worker.[1]

At the trial of an age discrimination case, the employer invariably presents a plethora of witnesses, each testifying in contradiction to some portion of the worker's testimony. If the worker is unable to present witnesses of his own in corroboration of his testimony, the mere number of witnesses testifying for the employer and against the worker may persuade the jury to reject the worker's case. It is critical, therefore, that the facts related by the worker to the jury are affirmed by the testimony of other workers.

Workers currently in the employ of the employer may be subpoenaed to appear at the trial, but as these workers remain on the employer's payroll, it is probable, even if they testify truthfully, that they will slant their testimony in favor of the party who pays their salaries. The best sources of favorable testimony, therefore, are workers who have left the company. In addition to helpful trial testimony, these other workers may provide the worker's counsel with compelling data or other information that may not have been available to the worker himself.

By way of example, some time ago I was interviewing a prospective witness in preparing a sexual harassment case for trial. My client had informed me that on several occasions this witness had been present with her at the time the alleged harasser had made sexual comments. Not only did this worker affirm that she had been present and had heard these sexual comments, but she also proceeded to disclose to us other instances in which the harasser had sexually harassed her and other young female workers as well. Until this point in the proceedings, we understood that the harasser had focused his obnoxious conduct solely on my client, but now we learned that his sexual harassment extended to several other young women. This unforeseen testimony strengthened our case immeasurably.

Earlier, we discussed the case of Dr. Samuel Song, a Korean American who accused his employer of national-origin discrimination (chapter 14). In preparing his case for trial, attorneys in my office interviewed one of Song's fellow workers who had since left the company, and to our total surprise, he described a staff meeting he had attended at which Song's supervisor had excoriated Song, referring in extremely negative terms to his Korean nationality and disparaging and maligning Koreans in general.

In each of these cases, my client had retained friendly relationships with former co-workers and thus was able to call upon them to present corroborating testimony. Since every worker alleging employment discrimination requires the assistance of other workers to support his case, he must remain in communication with former employees of the company and preserve good relations with them.

Following the initial signs that something is amiss in the employment relationship, another matter that the worker should address is the preservation of her personnel file. She should arrange with the human resources department to review her personnel file, and if company policy permits it, she should photocopy its entire contents. If photocopying is not permitted, the worker should prepare an index of the contents of the file, noting significant entries in performance evaluation ratings and letters or memoranda of praise or criticism. As we have seen, employers are known to have altered a worker's performance evaluations, for example in Joseph Dominic's case against Con Edison (chapter 8) and John Starceski's case against Westinghouse Electric (chapter 12). Thus it is not inconceivable that a desperate employer may resort to altering other aspects of the contents of a worker's personnel file.

Workers who have charged their employers with age discrimination but who still remain on the job often ask whether they should photocopy their employer's documents that may contain information pertinent to the worker's case. The worker is concerned, of course, that if not copied, these documents may disappear. This is certainly a valid concern. But employers frequently adopt rules barring employees from photocopying documents that do not directly relate to the worker's job functions, and a violation of the rule may culminate in dismissal. If the worker ignores the rule, and the employer later discovers that the worker has engaged in photocopying its documents, the employer may then claim that if it had known about the photocopying at the time, it would have fired the worker. If the employer can demonstrate to the court that, historically, it has dealt forcefully with workers who have violated the rule and that such violators as a matter of practice have been dismissed, the court may order a limitation in the amount of damages the worker may ultimately recover. Thus, a worker's violation of the rule may have a devastating effect upon the value of his case.

On occasion, a worker has come into my office on her first visit with a file folder full of documents photocopied from her employer's files. Rarely are these documents of any use. Sooner or later, the employer discovers that the photocopying has occurred, and then the worker is placed in the embarrassing position of endeavoring to explain why she had engaged in the photocopying. One of my clients turned over to me highly confidential payroll and commission payment records that she had photocopied just before she was terminated. These documents were of no use to us because they had no relevance to her claim. Later in the litigation, her employer demanded that we turn over any documents that my client had removed from its office. As a matter of course, nearly all employers make this demand. Since my client had not disclosed any of this confidential payroll and commission information to anyone, the employer could not show that the company had been damaged by reason of my client's conduct. However, ultimately she had to admit she had surreptitiously photocopied documents from company files. None of this helped our case one iota.

Workers are also prone to tape-record conversations they believe may prove helpful to their cases. They almost always tape the wrong conversations. The employer always ultimately discovers that office conversations have been secretly recorded, and it uses this information to disparage the worker's honesty and integrity in the eyes of the jurors. In more than thirty years,

I have never been presented with a tape recording that proved helpful to my client's case. In one instance, when I first met my client, I asked her, as I ordinarily ask all clients early in the proceedings, whether she had taped any conversations while on the job. She said she had not, and I promptly turned to other matters. Later in the litigation, during the course of my client's deposition, she was questioned by opposing counsel about a conversation she had with her supervisor, a conversation that appeared to be particularly pertinent to the outcome of the case. My client testified at length about the conversation, seeming to have near total recall as to what she and the supervisor had said on that occasion, and, of course, her testimony very much favored our position in the case. Indeed, her testimony was directly contrary to the testimony given by the supervisor during the course of his deposition, taken a few weeks earlier.

During a break in the deposition, while my client and I were talking in the hallway, she informed me that she had taped the conversation that she had just been questioned about. In total disbelief, I asked her, "But didn't you tell me that you had not taped any conversations?" "Yes," she said, "but I lost this tape, and I had forgotten that I had made it." She then proceeded to inform me that after she had been fired, she had moved to Florida, and once there she could not locate the tape. She assumed she had lost it during the move.

We proceeded with the deposition, and after it was concluded, I directed my client to search her apartment upon her return to Florida to determine whether the tape still existed. About a week later, I received the tape in the mail. When I listened to the tape, I realized that its contents did not support my client's version of the conversation with her supervisor, but rather, it reflected her supervisor's version in nearly every detail. It made a liar out of my client. Of course, I was duty bound to provide opposing counsel with a copy of the tape. It all but destroyed our case. I was forced to agree to a settlement that amounted to a fraction of what I thought the case was worth before I heard that tape.

The answer to the question of whether documents should

be photocopied or whether conversations should be tape-recorded is quite simple. The worker should never photocopy any document and never tape any conversation unless her lawyer directs her to do so.

The worker's primary contribution to the advancement of her case does not lie in illicit photocopying or covert tape-recording, but rather in the gathering of information pursuant to the directions of her lawyer. The more involved the worker becomes in her case, the more likely it is she will be able to furnish her lawyer with information relevant to the presentation of her case and to the defenses proffered by the employer. In nearly all cases, these contributions of the worker are invaluable. The worker who commits herself to challenging age-discriminatory conduct, and who then participates with her lawyer in a knowledgeable and orderly fashion in developing her claim for presentation in the courtroom, will play a major role in the elimination of age discrimination from the workplace.

19 | Recommendations for Changes in the ADEA and Its Enforcement

It was not until more than ten years after its enactment that the Age Discrimination in Employment Act achieved recognition as something more than a relatively obscure piece of legislation. In the late 1970s, the act began to gain a more prominent position in the American workplace, and subsequently the filing of age discrimination complaints with the Equal Employment Opportunity Commission (EEOC) rapidly grew to more than 20,000 a year. Since one of the primary purposes of the ADEA was to elicit a change in the public perception of the capabilities of older workers, the continued filings of thousands of age complaints demonstrate, rather forcefully, the near total failure of the ADEA to achieve a meaningful change in the public's attitude toward the older worker. On the other hand, the ADEA has been hugely successful in affording older workers procedures for the recovery of monetary damages flowing from illicit age-motivated conduct by employers.

The age discrimination cases discussed in this book demonstrate both the strengths and weaknesses of the ADEA. Although the statute surely should be strengthened, more serious problems have arisen in connection with its enforcement by the courts. Some of those enforcement problem areas may require congressional action, but others may be resolved through a change in the disposition of the courts toward the goals of the statute.

Following is a listing of those aspects of the statute that require strengthening and the problem areas in enforcement that demand a change in focus.

The Hiring of Older Workers

For older workers who have lost their jobs and have sought substitute employment, the ADEA has been pretty much a total failure. In fact, the ADEA may actually exacerbate the plight of unemployed older workers by discouraging employers from hiring them. Because a newly hired older worker may later be fired and, as a consequence, file an age suit, an employer may decide to avoid that risk in the first instance by not hiring the older worker. The anticipated costs of defending against an age claim may be a factor the employer considers before hiring an older worker. For this reason, the very existence of the ADEA stands as a barrier to the hiring of older workers.

Except for the expense incurred in defending against a failure-to-hire lawsuit, an employer has little reason to fear a claim made by a rejected older job applicant since the pattern of proof devised by the courts for establishing an act of discrimination does not readily lend itself to a hiring case. The nature of the hiring process is highly subjective, allowing the employer to conceal its discriminatory motives behind its protestations that, for this particular position, another applicant was better qualified than the rejected older worker. As a consequence, most rejected older job applicants do not sue, and those who do sue generally lose. If an employer is unlikely to find itself in court on account of its hiring practices, and if it is sued, it is more apt to prevail, then the employer will be far less inclined to comply with the provisions of the ADEA when it comes to the hiring of older workers. Opening the hiring process to greater public scrutiny, however, may induce the employer to be more compliant.

Broader record-keeping requirements, including the maintenance of hiring records for public inspection, would constitute a step in the right direction. Currently, EEOC regulations require employers to preserve for one year all job applications, résumés, advertisements, and notices relating to job openings. Employers having a hundred or more workers are also required to file each year with the EEOC a report designated "EEO-1," which lists by job categories the number of the company's male and female employees and their races. By reviewing this report, one may determine, for example, how many female African Americans are working for the employer as managers, or how many male Hispanics are employed as skilled workers. These reports may then form the basis for statistical studies of the distribution of workers by job category, sex, and race—but not by age.[1]

The EEOC should require employers to file annual reports similar to the EEO-1 that identify by age category the number of persons applying for positions, the number of applicants in each age category interviewed, and the number in each age category hired. A review of these data may disclose the rejection, either for interview or for hire, of a disproportionate number of older workers. But even if these data fail to establish age-discriminatory conduct, the public scrutiny of employer hiring records would strongly motivate employers to remain more alert to the appropriateness of their hiring procedures and their treatment of older job applicants.

Class Actions

Unlike Title VII, from its inception the ADEA has not permitted the use of the class action in the enforcement of its provisions. Class actions have been particularly successful in dealing with systemic, discriminatory employment policies and practices. Race, sex, and sexual harassment class action cases have been instrumental in obtaining legal relief for tens of thousands of workers. The class action, if available to older workers, would constitute a particularly useful tool in dealing with longstanding and undeviating discriminatory hiring practices.

An unsuccessful older worker job candidate may be completely unaware of any age bias involved in his rejection by an employer. That employer may similarly reject all other older worker applicants, without any of them realizing their applications were rejected because of their ages. Along comes an older worker applicant who, unlike his predecessors, suspects his age entered into the employer's decision to deny him a position. He retains a lawyer, who investigates, and the illicit hiring system is revealed. These circumstances cry out for a class action. If these workers all had been women and the employer had refused to hire them on that account, Title VII would permit the last of the rejected applicants to file a sex discrimination class action on behalf of all the women rejected before her. But the ADEA does not make this procedure available to older workers discriminated against because of age.

In addition to its use as a powerful tool for obtaining relief for a group of older workers, the class action would serve another purpose. The mere threat of a class action suit undoubtedly would raise the concerns of an employer about to engage in illicit conduct and thus make it more likely to desist from engaging in such conduct. Congress should amend the ADEA to provide for class action suits.

The Employer with Fewer Than Twenty Workers

The ADEA, as originally drafted, applied to all employers having twenty-five or more workers. In 1974, the act was amended to reduce the number to twenty workers, and there it has remained. Title VII, however, is binding on all employers of fifteen or more workers. There appears to be no rational basis for excluding from ADEA coverage employers who employ between fifteen and twenty workers. Age discrimination laws adopted by the states are generally applicable to employers having as few as fifteen workers, and many state statutes cover employers with even fewer employees. For instance, the New York statute begins coverage with employers of four workers, and California's statute begins at five.[2]

Twenty-five percent of all workers are employed by employers with fewer than twenty workers.[3] Small companies also are the primary sources of new jobs. Therefore, the number of companies falling within the fifteen-to-twenty employee category employ a significant number of older workers, all of whom are denied the protection of the ADEA. Coverage of the ADEA should be extended to employers having fifteen or more workers on their payrolls, and consideration should be given to extending coverage to employers of even fewer workers.

The Statute of Limitations

If a worker fails to file her charge of age discrimination promptly, she may be denied the opportunity of proceeding with her claim. A worker generally is required to file a charge of discrimination with the EEOC within three hundred days of the incident she claims to have been discriminatory. This is an unusually short period of limitations, and it originally was thought to be justified on the ground that the prompt processing of claims should be encouraged. A continuous EEOC case backlog of huge proportions has made the prompt processing of claims wishful thinking. Consequently, the three-hundred-day filing period serves little purpose. Nevertheless, the short period of limitations continues to remain applicable, and not a few workers have been denied relief from acts of age discrimination even though the late filing of their charges resulted from the disingenuous conduct of their employers.

In 1994, Gary Gastineau was interviewed for a sales position by the regional sales director of Austin Nichols & Company. Shortly after the interview, the regional sales director informed Gastineau that he would not be offered a position because the company's New York office had not granted its approval to hire him. When Gastineau asked whether his age had been a factor in his not being hired, the regional sales director assured him that age had not entered into the decision.

Two years later, while attending a trade show, Gastineau had the occasion to meet and talk with the regional sales director again. At that time, contrary to his previous representations, the regional sales director disclosed to Gastineau that he had not been hired two years earlier because he was indeed considered too old for the job. Gastineau immediately filed a charge of age discrimination with the EEOC and later filed suit in the federal court. Gastineau's case was dismissed by the court on the ground that his charge had not been filed with the EEOC within three hundred days of notification that he would not be hired. It made no difference to the court that at the time Gastineau first learned he would not be hired, he had no reason to believe his rejection was based on age. In fact, an official of the company specifically stated that age had not been a factor. Moreover, the court was singularly unimpressed by Gastineau's prompt filing of a charge once he learned that age had been a factor.[4]

John Thelen had a similar experience. Nearly a year after he had been fired by Marc's Big Boy Corporation, Thelen learned from his former supervisor that the person who had replaced him was thirty-three years younger than he, not six years younger as he had been informed at the time of his termination. Again, the court held that the employer's misrepresentation of the facts did not excuse Thelen's late filing of his EEOC charge.[5]

In each case, the employer lied to the worker and thereby successfully concealed its discriminatory motive. In each case, the fabrications of the employer led to a late EEOC filing and, ultimately, to a dismissal of the worker's case. In each case, the employer directly benefited from its concealment of acts of age discrimination. In each case, justice was denied.

It is not uncommon for a worker to learn sometime after her discharge that unlawful conduct was involved in her termination. For those workers, the short period of limitations nearly always leads to a dismissal of their claims. The statute of limitations for employment discrimination claims in many states is three years. It is reasonable and equitable to establish a similar period of limitation for the filing of an EEOC charge of discrimination. Alternatively, an age complainant should be permitted to file an EEOC charge within three hundred days of discovering he had been subjected to an act of age discrimination. Under such a rule, both Gastineau and Thelen would have been permitted to proceed with their claims.

Damages for Pain and Suffering

When Congress enacted the ADEA, it inexcusably failed to provide for the recovery of damages for pain and mental distress suffered by victims of age discrimination. Studies have shown that older workers who have been terminated find the resulting loss of self-esteem even more devastating than the loss of income, and the impact is felt not only by the person fired but also by the worker's entire family.[6]

When an employer terminates the employment of an older worker, the worker suffers mental distress in two areas. First, he suffers in the loss of employment, the same as would a worker subjected to any other type of discrimination, such as race, national origin, or sex discrimination. Second, he suffers in his inability to find new employment. This second category of suffering is unique to victims of age discrimination. For this reason, the employer who commits an act of age discrimination is doubly culpable.

Psychologists identify eleven types of mental suffering a victim of age discrimination may experience: stress; feelings of helplessness; disillusionment; feelings of hopelessness; guilt and self-blame; loss of self-esteem and self-confidence; a sense of loss of self-identity; decreased ability to cope and function, both at work and in other areas of life; compromised ability to think clearly, with poor judgment and decision making; passivity; and the feeling of being trapped. To this list, I would add anger.

The loss of self-identity appears to be an especially troublesome aspect of a job loss late in life. A person's self-identity and self-worth are often anchored in his work, and the loss of work leads inevitably to the loss of identity. Many of my clients have told me that their loss of identity and self-esteem made it far more difficult for them to engage in a search for other employment, with some workers taking as long as a year to regain the confidence they required to reenter the job market. The inability of an older worker to find another position, a common experience among these workers, only increases the pain.

The ADEA must be amended specifically to provide for the recovery of mental and emotional distress damages suffered as a consequence of acts of age discrimination. The make-whole doctrine of damages demands nothing less.

Punitive Damages

The ADEA provides for the recovery of liquidated damages but not punitive damages. Although liquidated damages are sometimes considered punitive in nature, they are recoverable only on account of willful conduct, not outrageous conduct. Unlike punitive damages, the amount of a liquidated damage award is a result of an arithmetic calculation; it is precisely equal to the back-pay award. Thus, the liquidated-damage award is very much limited, while an award of punitive damages is open-ended, so that the greater the outrage committed by the defendant, the greater the punitive damage award.

In other areas of the law, punitive damages are recoverable for outrageous conduct. No rational basis exists for excluding the recovery of these damages from the area of age discrimination.

Arbitration of Age Claims as a Condition of Employment

Little more need be said on this account. Congress should amend the ADEA to put an end to the pernicious practice of requiring consent to the arbitration of age claims as a condition of employment. The imposition of predispute arbitration as a condition of employment is itself a victimization of the worker and is antithetical to the very concept of civil rights in the workplace. Congress has in the past acted to reverse actions taken by the Supreme Court that appeared not in the public interest, and clearly now is the time for Congress to return to the worker the right to elect to have a claim of discrimination litigated in a court of law and before a jury of his or her peers.

Older Women

A recent study by the Women's Legal Defense Fund, sponsored by the AARP, found that older women face discrimination in the workplace on account of age, sex, and age and sex in combination.[7] Employment discrimination against older women does not always fall neatly into the narrow categories specified by the ADEA and Title VII of the Civil Rights Act of 1964. Consequently, the courts will need to become more sensitive to the plight of the older woman in the workplace.

An older woman may be held to a standard of physical attractiveness never demanded of her fellow male workers, and on that account she may be subjected to both sex *and* age discrimination. A court that approaches this type of case by analyzing it under the rubric of the ADEA to determine whether the claimant was discriminated against because of her age, and separately analyzing it under Title VII to determine whether she was discriminated against because of her sex, undoubtedly will fail to grasp the totality of the circumstances that confronted the claimant. In such circumstances, the older woman is subjected to workplace discrimination not solely because of her age, or solely because of her sex, but rather because of a combination of her age and her sex. An employer who may not have violated Title VII or the ADEA when the two statutes are considered separately would be guilty of violating both statutes if they were viewed in combination. Unless the courts prove willing to undertake this type of analysis, amendments to Title VII and the ADEA may be necessary.

The courts also will need to become more alert to the occurrence of acts of discrimination against older women who return to the workplace after an extended absence to raise a family. Upon their return to employment, these women often find their fellow male workers of a similar age further advanced in their careers, but this should not serve as an excuse for employers to treat these older women as second-class citizens.

Because the life expectancy of women exceeds that of men, and because women are becoming more and more economically independent, an increasing share of the workforce consists of older women. Financial independence also motivates older women to remain in the workplace, delaying retirement for as long as possible. This inevitably will lead to a dramatic increase in the incidence of acts of age discrimination against older women. The ADEA must be vigorously enforced by the courts to protect older women who become targets of unscrupulous employers.

Mixed-Motive Cases

As the law has developed, even if an employer is clearly guilty of age discrimination, the court may nevertheless afford it the opportunity of proving that its conduct was motivated by a legitimate as well as an illegitimate reason. The mixed-motive case theory permits an employer to discriminate without penalty. Howard C. Eglit, Chicago-Kent College of Law professor, in his three-volume work on age discrimination cites the basis for rejecting this theory:

> There is, however, a policy argument to be made that if an employer is found to have engaged in an act of wrongful discrimination, it should not be absolved of all liability just because it would have made the same decision even had it not taken into account the [worker's age]. This argument is premised on the perception that the ultimate aim of employment discrimination statutes is to eradicate bias from the workplace. As long as that bias is operative in a given work setting, it should not matter, so the argument goes, that the biased employer would have made the same decision anyway. Rather, what does matter is that it made the wrong decision in the first instance.[8]

The mixed-motive theory should be abolished. It is inconsistent with a basic tenet of the employment discrimination statutes: Acts of employment discrimination are always wrong and always unlawful.

The Hicks and Hazen Decisions

Although the Supreme Court's decision in the *Hicks* case reaffirmed earlier decisions that disbelief of the employer's reasons for its adverse action against a worker is sufficient to prove that the employer was guilty of discrimination, the Court also changed the law by ruling that disbelief of the employer's reasons no longer compels such a finding. A court or jury may or may not draw an inference of discrimination from the fact that the employer lied about its reasons. Thus, proving pretext may not be enough for the worker to prevail. Additional direct evidence—in almost all cases, a scarce commodity—may be needed to establish unlawful employer conduct. This change in approach to proving discrimination increases the burden placed on the worker and has made it easier for employers to gain dismissals of workers' cases through the summary judgment procedure. To make matters worse for workers, the *Hazen* case all but eliminated the age-proxy concept from the courtroom.

Congressional action reversing this trend toward making it more difficult to prove discrimination appears unlikely. One can only hope that the Supreme Court's future approach to proving discriminatory conduct becomes more balanced, placing the rights of employers and workers on an equal footing. Fortunately, the most recent Supreme Court decision appears to point in that direction.[9]

Contingent Workers

As much as 25 percent of the American workforce now consists of contingent workers—temporary, part-time, and leased workers, as well as independent contractors.[10] Typically, these workers are not considered to be employees of the company for whom they provide services. But the ADEA applies only to acts of age discrimination committed by employers against their employees. If contingent workers continue to maintain the status of nonemployees, they will be denied the protections of the statute. The definition of "employee" will have to be broadened to include these types of workers, else they will continue to be without any protection from unlawful acts of age discrimination.

Hostility of the Courts

Despite Congress's declared interest in banning age discrimination from the workplace, some courts appear less than enthusiastic about enforcing the provisions of the ADEA. As one law review commentator put it: "There is an ambivalence toward the notion that older workers should be protected from discrimination. . . . This ambivalence, on many occasions, has resulted in judicial opinions that strain to reach a dubious result, or that frankly admit that the nation's commitment to end age discrimination is not as strong as its commitment to other public policy ends, such as race and sex discrimination."[11]

In the end, forceful application of the age discrimination protections depends on a judiciary committed to eradicating age discrimination from the workplace. Without that commitment, all is for naught.

The Attitude of the Employer

Even with a committed judiciary, the law is not perfect, and justice will not prevail on every occasion. Certain workplace problems may only be resolved through the goodwill of the employer. As an example, an employer's decision pertaining to a particular worker may not be discriminatory but may nevertheless be wholly unfair. In such an instance, we rightly demand more of the employer than just compliance with the law. Witness the case of Betty Moses and Falstaff Brewing Corporation.

Moses was employed by Falstaff for twenty-two years, and during that time she served as secretary to Joseph Griesedieck, who steadily advanced up the corporate ladder from assistant to the president, to president, and finally to chairman of the board. Falstaff had a longstanding policy that secretaries for executive officers remained secretaries for those persons when they changed positions within the organization, and when an executive officer's job was eliminated, the policy also required the elimination of the secretary's position. When Griesedieck retired, Moses was terminated, purportedly in accordance with the company's stated policy. As one commentator noted, "This smacks a little of burning a widow on her husband's funeral pyre."[12]

Moses sued for age discrimination. The court said her case bordered on the frivolous, since it found no evidence that her age was a factor in the decision to terminate her. She was not replaced by a younger person; no statistical evidence was submitted showing a pattern or practice of age discrimination; Falstaff's reasons for terminating Moses were not pretextual; and the evidence failed to disclose that any Falstaff officer made any statements indicating that age had been a factor in the termination decision. In short, Moses could offer no evidence of age discrimination, and because she had been terminated for "sound business reasons," her case was dismissed.[13]

Even though Falstaff's decision to terminate Moses appears to be totally unfair, the decision may not have been discriminatory, at least insofar as age discrimination is defined by the statute. Hence it can be argued that from the perspective of the law, Moses met with a just end. But who among us would disagree with the proposition that a worker who has devoted twenty-two years of her life to her employer is entitled to better treatment than the loss of her job merely because her boss retires? But the solution to Moses's dilemma did not lie with the age discrimination law; rather, the solution could only have been provided by the Falstaff Brewing Corporation.

There will always be cases that fall between the cracks of the ADEA's provisions. The law is not perfect, and the courts that enforce the law are surely less than perfect. The Moses case never should have reached the stage of litigation. It should have been resolved by Falstaff in some fair and equitable manner. Employer-employee relations often call for more than the exercise of sound business judgment. They also call for compassion.

Conclusion

Hope for the Older Worker in the Future

Some years ago, a young boy was sitting on a bridge that crossed over a narrow but deep and swiftly flowing stream. He had been fishing for some time when a horse-drawn wagon approached along the road, and as it neared the bridge, the boy saw that it was his father who held the reins. It was the back of the wagon, however, that caught the boy's attention, because there stood a large wooden cage, and inside it, his grandfather was sitting on a stool. As the wagon neared the crest of the bridge, it stopped, and the boy's father jumped down beside him. "Dad, why is Granddad in the cage?" The father hesitated before answering. "Well, son, your grandfather has grown quite old, and he is not much use around the farm anymore. So I am going to lower the cage into the stream and let nature take its course." The boy considered this for a moment. "I understand," he said, "but Dad, make sure you save the cage. I am going to need it for you."

What goes around comes around.

As noted earlier, we all must remain alert to the legal rights of our older citizens, if for no other reason than that we ourselves will soon grow old. Older workers especially must remain alert, since they have an obligation to themselves as well as to other older workers to challenge age discrimination in the workplace. Effective enforcement of the Age Discrimination in Employment Act depends on the willingness of workers to uncover and challenge discriminatory practices they experience. If, on the other hand, older workers refrain from resisting acts of discrimination, employers will lack any incentive to alter their conduct.

With the passage of time, age stereotypes have not become any less prevalent. Older workers are still looked upon as less productive, less adaptable, more rigid, and looking forward only to retirement. The facts are to the contrary. Aging has no effect on productivity, except in physically demanding occupations. In fact, intellectual performance may improve with age, especially if the worker remains active and involved. Teachers, professors, doctors, writers, lawyers, and judges, among others, remain productive and highly motivated with advancing age and adapt to new technologies. Despite the corporate trend toward early retirement, increasing numbers of older workers want to remain in the workforce past the age of sixty-five, unfortunately still looked upon as the "normal" age of retirement.

Much more now than in the past, older workers tend to shun early retirement. This attitude, of course, clashes with prevalent corporate attitudes, thus generating age disputes. More enlightened thinking directed to retirement issues could lead to more contented older workers and less costly litigation for employers.

For the older worker, few options are available other than full retirement, but employers could introduce a degree of flexibility into their retirement programs by offering some or all of the following:

1. Part-time employment or a reduced work week
2. Retraining of obsolescent employees for lateral transfer
3. Flexible work scheduling
4. Reduction of wages to reflect reduced capacity

The last suggestion may be the most productive but also the most difficult to initiate.

An employer's offer of continued employment in return for a reduction in wages may or may not violate the provisions of the ADEA. If an older worker's capacity to continue in his present position has truly diminished, a proposal to maintain the worker on the job in return for a concession in compensation is an appropriate alternative for the worker who would rather not retire. Such an offer would not be appropriate, however, if the worker's capacity has not diminished or if the proposal is used merely to induce retirement.

Unfortunately, as matters now stand, employers are unlikely to take the approach of offering less compensation for continued employment for fear that the worker will claim the offer is age related. A well-designed retirement program that makes such a proposal an intricate part of the program could well insulate the employer from suit on the part of the worker. The entire process of retirement has to be rethought.

Is it likely that Americans will soon eliminate age discrimination from the workplace? I would not be too quick to say no. In 1986, most Americans were totally unfamiliar with the concept of sexual harassment. In that year, the Supreme Court ruled that sexual harassment is a form of sex discrimination, barred by Title VII. Since that time, a number of high-profile sexual harassment cases, some culminating in the payment of millions of dollars to the harassed victims, have made the public very much aware that sexual harassment has no legitimate place in the world of employment. An entire industry has now developed devoted to advising employers on the measures to be undertaken to minimize sexual harassment in the workplace and the ways in which to address it effectively when it does appear. It is conceivable, with the attention devoted to it, that sexual harassment will sharply diminish in importance as a workplace problem.

Unfortunately, age discrimination cases generally do not culminate in the payment of millions of dollars to prevailing older workers, and thus age cases have not engendered the high profile that has occurred in the area of sexual harassment. But someday soon, a particularly egregious case of age discrimination will awaken the American conscience to the problems confronting the older worker. At that time, perhaps, age discrimination also will begin to pass from the American workplace.

I started this book by stating, "Discrimination against middle-aged and older workers has long been a common practice of American business firms." Halfway through the writing of the book, an article appeared in the *New York Times* that caught my attention: "A Company Where Retirement Is a Dirty Word." The company, the Vita Needle Company of Needham, Massachusetts, has been in existence for sixty-five years, and most of its thirty-five current employees joined the company after retiring from positions in other companies. Their average age is seventy-three. It was reported in the article that the owner of the company recruits older workers because he finds them loyal, responsible, and eager to get to the job every day. His experience with older workers confirms the 1993 Commonwealth Fund survey that workers over fifty-five have better work attitudes and less turnover and absenteeism than their younger colleagues.[1]

Less than a month later, an article appeared on the op-ed page of the *New York Times* entitled "Now Hiring! If You're Young." The article reported rampant age discrimination in the hiring practices of computer companies:

> High-tech companies save money by shunning most mid-career programmers and focus their hiring on new or recent college graduates, who are cheaper. . . . As a result, careers in the programming field tend to be short lived. According to a survey conducted by the National Science Foundation and the Census Bureau, 6 years after finishing college, 57 percent of computer science graduates are working as programmers; at 15 years the figure drops to 34 percent, and at 20 years—when most are still only in the early 40's—it is down to 19 percent.[2]

These two articles represent the extremes in current employment practice. I can still state, without fear of contradiction, that age discrimination continues to be a common practice of American business firms. However, isolated instances of enlightened thinking on the subject may be a harbinger of better times in the future.

I end this book by repeating—an eminently worthwhile repetition—a quote from a decision issued by the U.S. Court of Appeals sitting in Chicago:

> Congress enacted the ADEA precisely because many employers and younger business executives act as if they believe that there are good business reasons for discriminating against older employees. Retention of senior employees who can be replaced by younger, lower paid persons frequently competes with other values, such as profits or conceptions of economic efficiency. The ADEA represents a choice among these values. It stands for the proposition that this is a better country for its willingness to pay the costs for treating older employees fairly.[3]

America will be an even better country once age discrimination in the workplace is eliminated.

Notes

Chapter 1 *The Baby-Boomer Generation at Middle Age*

1. 29 U.S.C. Sections 621–634.
2. *Congressional Record*, 13 Cong. Rec. 31,256.
3. *Complete Auto Transit, Inc. v. Reis*, 451 U.S. 401 (1981); also quoted in *Metz v. Transit Mix, Inc.*, 828 F.2d 1202 (7th Cir. 1987).
4. *Payne v. Western & Atlantic R.R.*, 81 Tenn. 507 (1884).
5. Montana Wrongful Discharge from Employment Act of 1987. Mont. Code Ann. Sections 39–2–906 to 39–2–914.
6. Richard W. Judy and Carol D'Amico, *Work Force 2020* (Indianapolis: Hudson Institute, 1997), 38.
7. Ken Dychtwald and Joe Flower, *Age Wave* (Los Angeles: Tarcher, 1989), 8, 21, referring to the Population Reference Bureau.
8. *Statistical Abstract of the United States 1998* (Washington, D.C.: U.S. Department of Commerce, 1998), 15, 21.
9. Peter G. Peterson, *Will America Grow Up before It Grows Old?* (New York: Random House, 1996), 15–20.
10. Sara E. Rix, ed., *Older Workers: How Do They Measure Up? An Overview of Age Differences in Employee Costs and Performance* (Washington D.C.: Public Policy Institute of the AARP, 1994), 21.
11. Judy and D'Amico, *Work Force 2020*, 103.
12. *Statistical Abstract 1998*, table 645 at p. 403.
13. Judy and D'Amico, *Work Force 2020*, 95.
14. Robert Coulson, *Empowered at Forty* (New York: Harper Collins, 1990), 12.
15. Peterson, *Will America Grow Up*, 137.
16. *Americans over 55 at Work Program, Research Reports 1, 2* (New York: Commonwealth Fund, 1990).
17. AARP, *Valuing Older Workers: A Study of Costs and Productivity* (Washington. D.C.: AARP, n.d.).

Chapter 2   Age Stereotypes

1. *New York University Law Review* 41 (1966): 288.
2. Lawrence M. Friedman, *Your Time Will Come: The Law of Age Discrimination and Mandatory Retirement* (New York: Russell Sage Foundation, 1984), 11.
3. Title VII of the Civil Rights Act of 1964, 42 U.S.C. Section 2000e and those following.
4. Department of Labor, Secretary of Labor, *The Older American Worker: Age Discrimination in Employment* (Washington, D.C., 1965).
5. Daniel P. O'Meara, *Protecting the Growing Number of Older Workers: The Age Discrimination in Employment Act* (Philadelphia: University of Pennsylvania, Wharton School, Industrial Research Unit, 1989), 13.
6. House Committee on Education and Labor, General Subcommittee on Labor, hearings on H.R. 3651, H.R. 3768, and H.R. 4221, 90th Cong., 1967, 7, referred to in Samuel Issacharoff and Erica Worth Harris, "Is Age Discrimination Really Age Discrimination?: The ADEA's Unnatural Solution," *New York University Law Review* 72, 4 (1997): 781–785.
7. *McKennon v. Nashville Banner Publishing Co.*, 513 U.S. 352 (1995).
8. Age Discrimination in Employment Act of 1967, 29 U.S.C. Section 623.
9. Ibid., Sec. 623 (f).
10. Senate Special Committee on Aging, *Improving the Age Discrimination Law*, 93d Cong., 1st sess., *Congressional Record: Legislative History* 14 (1973), 215.
11. A Louis Harris poll conducted for the National Council on Aging showed that 90 percent of those interviewed felt that workers should not be forced into retirement if they were capable of performing on the job. Reported by Lex K. Larson, *Employment Discrimination*, vol. 8 (New York: Matthew Bender, 2000), 123–3.
12. *Visser v. Packer Engineering Associates, Inc.*, 924 F.2d 655 (7th Cir. 1991).
13. Department of Labor, *Older American Worker*.
14. *Hazen Paper Co. v. Biggins*, 507 U.S. 604 (1993).
15. Richard A. Posner, *Aging and Old Age* (Chicago: University of Chicago Press, 1995), 19.
16. Robert N. Butler, *Why Survive? Being Old in America* (New York: Harper and Row, 1975), 6.
17. *Americans over 55 at Work*.
18. AARP, *Valuing Older Workers*, 7.
19. Rix, *Older Workers*, v.
20. Posner, *Aging and Old Age*, 20.
21. *Hazen Paper Co. v. Biggins*, 507 U.S. 604, 610 (1993).
22. A 1975 survey conducted by Louis Harris and Associates, referred to by Betty Friedan, *The Fountain of Age* (New York: Simon and Schuster, 1993), 36.
23. The 1990 Department of Health and Human Services study is referred to in Rix, *Older Workers*, 41.
24. Butler, *Why Survive?*, 12. Butler is quoted in Paul H. Brietzke and Linda S. Whitton, "An Old(er) Master Stands on the Shoulders of Ageism to Stake Another Claim for Law and Economics," *Valparaiso University Law Review* 31 (1996): 105, fn. 93.
25. Ibid.

Chapter 3 Reductions in Force

1. Coulson, *Empowered at Forty*, 1.
2. Rix, *Older Workers*, iv.
3. Stewart J. Schwab, "Life Cycle Justice: Accommodating Just Cause and Employment at Will," *Michigan Law Review* 92, 1 (1993): 10–11, 43.
4. *Goldman v. First National Bank of Boston*, 985 F.2d 1113 (1st Cir. 1999).
5. Alfred W. Blumrosen, "The EEOC at the End of the First Clinton Administration," in Citizens' Commission on Civil Rights, *The Continuing Struggle: Civil Rights and the Clinton Administration* (Washington, D.C.: Citizens' Commission on Civil Rights, 1997), 72.
6. *EEOC v. Doremus & Company*, 69 FEP Cases 449 (S.D.N.Y. 1995).
7. *Palmer v. The Reader's Digest Association, Inc.*, 1992 WL 73468 (S.D.N.Y. 1992).
8. *Maresco v. Evans Chemetics, Division of W. R. Grace & Co.*, 963 F.2d 520 (2d Cir. 1992).
9. Blumrosen, EEOC, 84–85.
10. Brian W. Bulger and Carolyn Curtis Gessner, "Sign of the Times: Implementing Reductions in Force," *Employee Relations Law Journal* 17, 3 (winter 1991–92): 431.
11. *Gallo v. Prudential Residential Services*, 22 F.3d 1219 (2d Cir. 1994).
12. *Viola v. Philips Medical Systems*, 42 F.3d 712 (2d Cir. 1994).

Chapter 4 Early-Retirement Plans

1. Richard G. Kass, "Early Retirement Incentives and the Age Discrimination in Employment Act," *Hofstra Law Review* 4 (1986): 63; Michael C. Harper, "Age-Based Exit Incentives, Coercion, and the Prospective Waiver of ADEA Rights: The Failure of the Older Workers Benefit Protection Act," *Virginia Law Review* 79 (1993): 1271; Niall A. Paul, "Reduction in Force, Early Retirement Incentives, and the Age Discrimination in Employment Act," *Detroit College of Law Review* 3 (1989): 387.
2. *Raskin v. The Wyatt Co.*, 125 F.3d 55 (2d Cir.1997).
3. Lisa E. Meyer, "A Proposal to Use a 'Knowing and Voluntary' Standard to Evaluate the 'Voluntariness' of Early Retirement Plans," *Fordham Urban Law Journal* 16 (1988): 703.
4. *Henn v. National Geographic Society*, 819 F.2d 824 (7th Cir. 1987).
5. *Smith v. World Insurance Co.*, 38 F.3d 1456 (8th Cir.1994).
6. *Hebert v. The Mohawk Rubber Co.*, 872 F.2d 1184 (1st Cir.1989).
7. *Cazzola v. Codman & Shurtleff*, 751 F.2d 53 (1st Cir. 1984).
8. *Moylan v. National Westminster Bank*, 687 F.Supp. 54 (E.D.N.Y. 1988).
9. See discussion by Posner in *Aging and Old Age*, 342.
10. *James v. Sears, Roebuck & Co.*, 21 F.3d 989 (10th Cir. 1994).
11. *Anderson v. Montgomery Ward & Co. Inc.*, 650 F.Supp. 1480 (D.C. Ill. 1987).
12. *Calhoun v. Acme Cleveland Corp.*, 798 F.2d 559 (1st Cir.1986).
13. *Stamey v. Southern Bell Telephone & Telegraph Co.*, 859 F.2d 855 (11th Cir. 1988).

Chapter 5 Waivers of Claims

1. The use of a pseudonym is necessary because of the confidentiality provisions of a settlement agreement requiring nondisclosure of material aspects of the case.

2. Blumrosen, "EEOC," 84.
3. Older Workers Benefit Protection Act, 29 U.S.C. Section 626(f).
4. *Grillet v. Sears, Roebuck & Co.*, 927 F.2d 217 (5th Cir. 1991).
5. *Oberg v. Allied Van Lines*, 11 F.3d 679 (7th Cir. 1993).
6. *Forbus v. Sears, Roebuck & Co.*, 958 F.2d 1036 (11th Cir. 1992).
7. *Reid v. IBM*, 74 FEP Cases 332 (S.D.N.Y. 1997).
8. *Kristoferson v. Otis Spunkmeyer, Inc.*, 965 F.Supp. 545 (S.D.N.Y. 1997). The law reports do not show that this case has been concluded.
9. *Oubre v. Entergy Operations, Inc.*, 118 S.Ct. 838 (1998).
10. Blumrosen, "EEOC," 84–85.

Chapter 6 Hiring of Older Workers

1. O'Meara, *Protecting Older Workers*, 1.
2. Walter K. Olson, *The Excuse Factory* (New York: Free Press, 1997), 145.
3. Lyndon B. Johnson, *Public Papers of the Presidents of the United States: Lyndon B. Johnson, 1967,* bk. 1 (Washington, D.C.: GPO, 1968), 32, 37, referred to in Larson, *Employment Discrimination*, 8:120–12.
4. H.R. Rep. No. 805, 90th Cong., 1st sess. 4 (1967), reprinted in *EEOC Legislative History of the Age Discrimination in Employment Act* (1981), 74, 77; and S. Rep. No. 723, reprinted at pp. 105, 108 (1981), referred to in O'Meara, *Protecting Older Workers*, 14–15.
5. O'Meara, *Protecting Older Workers*, 15.
6. John J. Donohue and Peter Siegelman, "The Changing Nature of Employment Discrimination Litigation," *Stanford Law Review* 43 (1991): 983, 984.
7. *McDermott v. Lehman*, 594 F.Supp.1315 (D.C. Me. 1984).
8. *Punahele v. United Airlines, Inc.*, 756 F.Supp. 487 (D.C. Colo. 1986).
9. *Reed v. Signode Corp.*, 652 F.Supp. 129 (D.C. Conn. 1986).
10. *Senner v. Northcentral Technical College*, 113 F.3d 750 (7th Cir. 1997).
11. *Hertz v. The Gap*, 75 FEP Cases 1883 (S.D.N.Y. 1997).

Chapter 7 Promotions, Demotions, Transfers

1. *Bartek v. Urban Redevelopment Authority of Pittsburgh*, 882 F.2d 739 (3d Cir. 1989).
2. *Lindsey v. American Cast Iron Pipe Co.*, 772 F.2d 799 (11th Cir.1985).
3. *Weihaupt v. American Medical Association*, 874 F.2d 419 (7th Cir. 1989).
4. *Jackson v. Shell Oil Co.*, 702 F.2d 197 (9th Cir. 1983).
5. *Curto v. Sears, Roebuck & Co.*, 38 FEP Cases 547 (D.C. Ill. 1984).
6. *Haimovitz v. United States Department of Justice*, 720 F.Supp. 516 (W.D. Pa. 1989).
7. *D'Aquino v. Citicorp/Diner's Club, Inc*, 755 F.Supp. 218 (D.C. Ill. 1991).
8. *Wilson v. Monarch Paper Co.*, 939 F.2d 1138 (5th Cir.1991).
9. Examples of constructive discharge cases: *Mitchell v. Mobil Oil Corp.*, 896 F.2d 463 (10th Cir. 1990); *Minetos v. City University of New York*, 875 F.Supp. 1046 (S.D.N.Y. 1995).
10. *Cazzola v. Codman & Shurtleff, Inc.*, 751 F.2d 53 (1st Cir.1984).
11. *Jacobson v. American Home Products Corp.*, 36 FEP Cases 559 (D.C. Ill. 1982).
12. *Greenberg v. Union Camp Corp.*, 48 F.3d 22 (1st Cir. 1995).
13. See *Garner v. Wal-Mart Stores*, 807 F.2d 1536 (4th Cir. 1987).

Chapter 8   Employer Retaliation

1. Because of contractual obligations to maintain confidentiality, the use of a pseudonym is necessary.
2. 29 U.S.C. Section 623 (d). "It shall be unlawful for an employer to discriminate against any of his employees or applicants for employment . . . because such individual . . . has opposed any practice made unlawful by this section, or because such individual . . . has made a charge, testified, assisted, or participated in any manner in an investigation, proceeding, or litigation under this chapter."
3. *Robinson v. Shell Oil Co.*, 167 S.Ct. 843, 72 FEP Cases 1856 (1997).
4. Because Jones was unemployed at the time that her lawsuit was filed, I had agreed to represent her on a contingent-fee basis. With this huge settlement, my fee also was large. At that point, I had to concede that Jones had been quite right in not trying too hard to find alternate counsel.
5. The filing of a charge of discrimination is a protected activity, whether the charge is filed with the EEOC or a state fair-practices agency, such as the New York State Division of Human Rights.
6. *Dominic v. Consolidated Edison Co. of New York*, 822 F.2d 1249 (2d Cir. 1987).
7. *Malarkey v. Texaco, Co.*, 983 F.2d 1204 (2d Cir. 1993).
8. *Padilla v. Metro-North Commuter RR.*, 92 F.3d 117 (2d Cir. 1996).
9. *Mesnick v. General Electric Co.*, 950 F.2d 816. (1st. Cir. 1991).

Chapter 9   Women and Age Discrimination

1. James Walsh, *Mastering Diversity* (Santa Monica, Calif.: Merritt, 1995), 94; Bimal Patel and Brian H. Kleiner, "New Developments in Age Discrimination," *Labor Law Journal* 45 (1994): 709, 712.
2. O'Meara, *Protecting Older Workers*, 24–26.
3. Posner, *Aging and Old Age*, 45.
4. AARP, *Employment Discrimination against Midlife and Older Women: An Analysis of Discrimination Charges Filed with the EEOC*, vol. 1 (Washington, D.C.: AARP Women's Initiative, 1997), 29.
5. Ibid., 2:13.
6. Statistical Abstract 1998, table 645, at p. 403.
7. Marilyn Webb, "How Old Is Too Old?" *New York Magazine*, March 29, 1993, 66.
8. AARP, *Employment Discrimination against Women*, 2:13.
9. *Palmiero v. Western Controls*, 809 F.Supp. 341 (M.D. Pa.1992); affirmed 8 F.3d 812 (3d Cir. 1993).
10. *Sischo-Nownejad v. Merced Community College*, 934 F.2d 1104 (9th Cir. 1991).
11. *EEOC v. Independent Stave Co., Inc.*, 754 F.Supp. 713 (E. D. Mo. 1991).
12. *Arnett v. Aspin*, 846 F.Supp. 1234 (E.D. Pa. 1994).
13. *Rollins v. TechSouth, Inc.*, 833 F.2d 1525 (11th Cir. 1987).
14. *Proffitt v. Anacomp, Inc.*, 747 F.Supp. 421 (S.D. Ohio 1990).
15. Betty Friedan, *The Fountain of Age* (New York: Simon and Schuster, 1993), 197.

Chapter 10   Motion for Summary Judgment

1. *Gannon v. Narragansett Electric Co.*, 777 F.Supp. 167, (D.C. R.I. 1991).
2. *Thornbrough v. Columbus & Greenville R.R. Co.*, 760 F.2d 633 (5th Cir. 1985).

3. *Colosi v. Electri-Flex*, 965 F.2d 500 (7th Cir. 1992).
4. *Spence v. Maryland Casualty Co.*, 995 F.2d 1147 (2d Cir. 1993).

Chapter 11   Indirect Evidence

1. *U.S. Postal Service Board of Governors v. Aikins*, 400 U.S. 711 (1983).
2. *Price Waterhouse v. Hopkins*, 490 U.S. 228 (1989).
3. Robert J. Gregory, "There Is Life in That Old (I Mean, More 'Senior') Dog Yet: The Age-Proxy Theory after Hazen Paper Co. v. Biggins," *Hofstra Labor Law Journal* 11 (1994): 397–398.
4. *Siegel v. Alpha Wire Corp.*, 894 F.2d 50 (3d Cir. 1990).
5. *Barnes v. Gencorp*, 896 F.2d 1457 (6th Cir. 1990).
6. *McDonnell Douglas Corp. v. Green*, 411 U.S. 792 (1973).
7. *Furnco Construction Corp. v. Waters*, 438 U.S. 567, 577 (1978).
8. *Reeves v. Sanderson Plumbing Products, Inc.,* No. 99–536 (June 12, 2000), 2000 WL 743663.
9. *Binder v. Long Island Lighting Co.*, 57 F.3d 193 (2d Cir. 1995).
10. *Kraus v. Sobel Corrugated Containers, Inc.*, 915 F.2d 227 (6th Cir. 1990).
11. *George v. Mobil Oil Corp.*, 739 F.Supp. 1577 (S.D.N.Y. 1990)
12. A confidentiality agreement requires me not to disclose the identities of the parties in this case.
13. *Taggart v. Time, Inc.*, 924 F.2d 43 (2d Cir. 1991).
14. *Montana v. First Federal Savings & Loan Association of Rochester*, 869 F.2d 100 (2d Cir. 1989).

Chapter 12   Evidentiary Procedures

1. *Thornbrough v. Columbus and Greenville RR Co.,* 760 F.2d 633 (5th Cir. 1985).
2. *Williamson v. Owen-Illinois, Inc.*, 589 F.Supp. 1051 (N.D. Ohio 1984).
3. *Tyler v. Bethlehem Steel Corp.*, 958 F.2d 1176 (2d Cir. 1992).
4. *Starceski v. Westinghouse Electric Corp.*, 54 F.3d 1089 (3d Cir. 1995).
5. *Geller v, Markham*, 635 F.2d 1027 (2d Cir. 1980).
6. Jeffrey S. Klein and Rose E. Morrison, "Courts Rethink ADEA Disparate-Impact Claims," *National Law Journal*, June 20, 1997, B-10.
7. *Lowe v. Commack Union School District*, 886 F.2d 1364 (2d Cir. 1989).
8. *Graffam v. Scott Paper Co.*, 848 F.Supp.1 (D.C. Me. 1994).

Chapter 13   Monetary Damages and Other Remedies

1. *Foster v. Excelsior Springs City Hospital and Convalescent Center*, 631 F.Supp. 174 (W.D. Mo. 1986).
2. *Grundman v. Trans World Airlines, Inc.*, 54 FEP Cases 224 (S.D.N.Y. 1990).
3. *Logan v. Pena*, 61 FEP Cases 564 (D.C. Kan. 1993).
4. *Wulach v. Bear, Stearns & Co.*, 52 FEP Cases 1022 (S.D.N.Y. 1990).
5. *Dominic v. Consolidated Edison Co. of New York*, 822 F.2d 1249 (2d Cir. 1987).
6. *Doyne v. Union Electric Co.*, 953 F.2d 447 (8th Cir. 1992).
7. *Padilla v. Metro-North Commuter RR.*, 92 F.3d 117 (2d Cir. 1996).
8. *Trans World Airlines, Inc. v. Thurston*, 469 U.S. 111 (1985).
9. *McLaughlin v. Richland Shoe Co.*, 486 U.S. 128 (1988).
10. *Price v. Marshall Erdman & Associates*, 966 F.2d 320 (7th Cir. 1992).
11. *Starceski v. Westinghouse Electric Corp.,* 54 F.3d 1089 (3d Cir. 1995).
12. *Blake v. J. C. Penney Co., Inc.*, 894 F.2d 274 (8th Cir. 1990).

13. *Benjamin v. United Merchants & Manufacturers, Inc.*, 873 F.2d 41 (2d Cir. 1989).
14. *EEOC v. District of Columbia, Department of Human Services*, 729 F.Supp. 907 (D.C. Cir. 1990).
15. The Hall case was reported along with *Hodgson v. First Federal Savings & Loan Association of Broward County, Florida*, 455 F.2d 818 (5th Cir. 1972).
16. *City of Riverside v. Rivera*, 477 U.S. 561 (1986).
17. 29 U.S.C. Section 626(b).
18. *Wise v. Olan Mills Incorporated of Texas*, 485 F.Supp. 542 (D.C. Colo. 1980).

Chapter 14   Roles of the EEOC and the Private Attorney

1. 29 U.S.C. Section 626 (d).
2. For the percentages, see Blumrosen, "EEOC," 74.
3. Ibid.
4. Ibid., 74–75.
5. EEOC record of ADEA charge filings: http://www.eeoc.gov.
6. Donohue and Siegelman, "Nature of Employment Discrimination Litigation."
7. Robert Lewis, "ADEA Draws Flak, but Marches Forward," *AARP Bulletin*, July/August, 1997, 1, 13; also, National Employment Lawyers Association's *Employee Advocate*, spring 1997, 3.
8. The jury's verdict was later overturned by the court, thus making it necessary to try the case a second time. On the second trial, AHP did not even bother to offer the testimony of the EEOC investigator.
9. Michael Selmi, "The Value of the EEOC: Reexamining the Agency's Role in Employment Discrimination Law," *Ohio State Law Journal* 57, pt. 1 (1996): 6, fn. 17.
10. Ibid., 50.
11. National Employment Lawyers Association: http://www.nela.org.

Chapter 15   Negative Attitude of the Courts

1. Blumrosen, "EEOC," 81.
2. *Ferriol v. Brink's Incorporated*, 841 F.Supp. 411 (S.D. Fla.1994).
3. *Kristoferson v. Otis Spunkmeyer, Inc.*, 965 F.Supp. 545 (S.D.N.Y. 1997).
4. Reported by Howard C. Eglit, "The Age Discrimination in Employment Act at Thirty: Where It's Been, Where It Is Today, Where It's Going," *University of Richmond Law Review* 31, 3 (1997): 591, fn. 47.
5. Ibid., 651.
6. William P. Murphy, "Meandering Musings about Discrimination Law," *Labor Lawyer* 10, 4 (1994): 649.
7. *Price Waterhouse v. Hopkins*, 490 U.S. 228 (1989).
8. *Aungst v. Westinghouse Electric Corp.*, 937 F.2d 1216 (7th Cir. 1991).
9. *Berkowitz v. Allied Stores of Penn-Ohio, Inc.*, 541 F.Supp. 1209 (E.D. Pa. 1982).
10. *Haskell v. Kaman Corp.*, 743 F.2d 113 (2d Cir. 1984).
11. *Atkin v. Lincoln Property Co.*, 991 F.2d 268 (5th Cir. 1993).
12. *Barnes v. Southwest Forest Industries, Inc.*, 814 F.2d 607 (11th Cir. 1987).
13. *O'Connor v. Consolidated Coin Caterers Corp.*, 56 F.3d 542 (4th Cir. 1995); reversed on other grounds, 116 S.Ct. 1307 (1996).
14. *Birkbeck v. Marvel Lighting Corp.*, 30 F.3d 507 (4th Cir.1994).

15. *Mulero Rodriguez v. Ponte, Inc.*, 891 F.Supp 680 (D.C.P.R. 1995); reversed 98 F.3d 670 (1st Cir. 1996).
16. *Duart v. FMC Wyoming Corp.*, 859 F.Supp. 1447 (D.C. Wy. 1994).
17. *EEOC v. Manville Sales Corp.*, 27 F.3d 1089 (5th Cir. 1994).
18. *Cooley v. Carmike Cinemas*, 25 F.3d 1325 (6th Cir. 1994).
19. *Ryder v. Westinghouse Electric Corp.*, 74 FEP Cases 1867 (3d Cir. 1997).

Chapter 16 Judicial Limitations

1. *St. Mary's Honor Center v. Hicks*, 509 U.S. 502 (1993); *Hazen Paper Co. v. Biggins*, 507 U.S. 604 (1993).
2. *Texas Department of Community Affairs v. Burdine*, 450 U.S. 248 (1973); *McDonnell Douglas Corp. v. Green*, 411 U.S. 792 (1973).
3. *Texas Department of Community Affairs v. Burdine*, 255–256.
4. *Hazen Paper Co. v. Biggins,* 507 U.S. 604 (1993).
5. *Metz v. Transit Mix, Inc.*, 828 F.2d 1202 (7th Cir. 1987).
6. *Graefenhain v. Pabst Brewing Co.*, 827 F.2d 13 (7th Cir. 1987).
7. *Holt v. The Gamewell Corp.*, 797 F.2d 36 (1st Cir. 1986).
8. *Bay v. Times Mirror Magazines, Inc.*, 936 F.2d 112 (2d Cir. 1991).
9. The Court was careful to note that its decision did not mean that an employer could, under the circumstances, lawfully fire a worker solely in order to prevent his pension rights from vesting. An employer so motivated would violate ERISA.
10. *EEOC v. Francis W. Parker School*, 61 FEP Cases 967 (N.D. Ill. 1993).
11. "A Rose by Any Other Name No Longer Smells As Sweet: Disparate Treatment Discrimination and the Age Proxy Doctrine after Hazen Paper Co. v Biggins," *Cornell Law Review* 81 (1996): 530, 553–555.
12. "Credulous Courts and the Tortured Trilogy: The Improper Use of Summary Judgment in Title VII and ADEA Cases," *Boston College Law Review* 34, 2 (1993): 203.
13. *McCoy v. WGN Continental Broadcasting Co.*, 957 F.2d 368 (7th Cir. 1992).
14. Michael C. Harper, "ADEA Doctrinal Impediments to the Fulfillment of the Wirtz Report Agenda," *University of Richmond Law Review* 31, 3 (1997): 757, 776.

Chapter 17 Arbitration of Discrimination Disputes

1. Lisa Stansky, "New Age Woes," *American Bar Association Journal*, January 1997, 66.
2. *Visser v. Packer Engineering Associates, Inc.*, 924 F.2d 655, 656 (7th Cir. 1991).
3. Thomas J. Piskorski, "The Growing Judicial Acceptance of Summary Judgment in Age Discrimination Cases," *Employee Relations Law Journal*, 18, 2 (autumn 1992): 245.
4. *Gilmer v. Interstate/Johnson Lane Corp.*, 500 U.S. 20 (1991).
5. Pearl Zuchlewski, *Employee Rights Litigation: Pleading and Practice*, vol. 3 (New York: Matthew Bender, 2000), 16–2.
6. *DiRussa v. Dean Witter Reynolds, Inc.*, 121 F.3d 818 (2nd Cir. 1997).
7. For a general discussion of the lack of benefits and protections in the arbitral system, see Robert Layton, Glen D. Nager, and Deena B. Jenab, "Using Compulsory Arbitration to Resolve EEO Disputes," *New York Law Journal*, July 14, 1992, 1.
8. The quoted material is from federal judge Nancy Gertner's opinion in

Rosenberg v. Merrill Lynch, 965 F.Supp. 190 (D.C. Mass. 1997). Judge Gertner's decision, barring arbitration in that case, was later reversed by an appellate court. 170 F.3d 1 (1st Cir.1999).

9. Stuart H. Bompey and Michael P. Pappas, "Is There a Better Way? Compulsory Arbitration of Employment Discrimination Claims after Gilmer," *Employee Relations Law Journal*, 19, 3 (winter 1993–94): 197. Also, Stuart H. Bompey and Andrea H. Stempe, "Four Years Later: A Look at Compulsory Arbitration of Employment Discrimination Claims after Gilmer v. Interstate/Johnson Lane Corp.," *Employee Relations Law Journal*, 21, 2 (autumn 1995): 21.

10. Her real name cannot be used, as her case is pending.

11. *Desiderio v. National Association of Securities Dealers, Inc.*, 1998 WL 195271 (S.D.N.Y. 1998).

12. *Kinnebrew v. Gulf Insurance Co.*, 1994 WL 803508 (N.D. Tex. 1994).

13. *Nghiem v. NEC Electronics, Inc.*, 25 F.3d 1437 (9th Cir. 1994).

14. Janis Goodman, "Mandatory Arbitration Is Not an Alternative for Employees," prepared for the National Employment Lawyers Association (manuscript).

15. "EEOC Policy Statement on Mandatory Arbitration," EEOC Notice No. 915.002 (July 10, 1997), reprinted in Bureau of National Affairs, *Employment Discrimination Report* (July 16, 1997), 166.

Chapter 18   The Role of the Worker

1. *St. Mary's Honor Center v. Hicks*, 509 U.S. 502 (1993).

Chapter 19   Recommendations for Changes

1. Bureau of National Affairs, *Fair Employment Practices Manual*, 8 (Washington, D.C., 2000), EEOC Regulations, part 1602, p. 403.55.

2. The AARP, in *Age Discrimination on the Job* (Washington, D.C.: AARP, 1996), reports that "at least forty-five states apply their state age discrimination laws to employers with fewer than twenty employees" (2).

3. AARP, *Employment Discrimination Against Midlife and Older Women*, vol. 2 (Washington, D.C.: AARP), 6, fn. 11.

4. *Gastineau v. Austin Nichols & Co.*, 73 FEP Cases 1409 (N.D. Ill. 1997).

5. *Thelen v. Marc's Big Boy Corp.*, 64 F.3d 264 (7th Cir. 1995).

6. Webb, "How Old Is Too Old?" 66, referring to the research findings of Dorothea Braginsky of Fairfield University in Connecticut.

7. AARP, *Employment Discrimination against Women*, vol. 1.

8. Howard C. Eglit, *Age Discrimination*, vol. 2 (Deerfield, Ill.: Clark Boardman Callaghan, 2000), 7–268.

9. *Reeves v. Sanderson Plumbing Products, Inc.*, No. 99–536 (June 12, 2000), 2000 WL 743663.

10. Eglit, "Age Discrimination in Employment Act," 702.

11. Dan Stormer and Anne Richardson, "The Graying of America: Age Discrimination in the Nineties," *University of West Los Angeles Law Review* 26 (1995): 189, 191.

12. Friedman, *Your Time Will Come*, 51.

13. *Moses v. Falstaff Brewing Co.*, 550 F.2d. 1113 (8th Cir. 1977).

274 NOTES TO PAGES 263–264

Conclusion

1. Julie Flaherty, "A Company Where Retirement Is a Dirty Word," *New York Times*, December 28, 1997, business sec.,1.
2. Norman Matloff, "Now Hiring! If You're Young," *New York Times*, January 26, 1998, op-ed page.
3. *Graefenhain v. Pabst Brewing Co.,* 827 F.2d 13 (7th Cir. 1987).

Index

AARP, 25, 255

Acme Cleveland Corporation, 60

ADEA. *See* Age Discrimination in Employment Act (1967)

age: discrimination (*see* discrimination, age); status and, 27; stereotypes, 1, 5, 16–30

Age Discrimination in Employment Act (ADEA) (1967): arbitration and, 226–234; business concerns of employers and, 207, 208; class actions and, 249–250; disparate impact and, 158–162; early retirement and, 49–62; employee assessment and, 26; enforcement of, 191–204; gaps in coverage, 19, 20, 249–253; hiring older workers and, 75–86, 248–249; intent of, 4, 6; liquidated damages and, 171–177; as litigation source, 21; negative court attitudes toward, 191–204, 258; protections from

retaliation in, 103–113; recommendations for changes in, 247–259; statute of limitations and, 251–253; strengths/weaknesses of, 7, 29, 75, 76, 86, 247–259; waivers of claims and, 64–74

Allied Van Lines, 69–70

AMA. *See* American Medical Association

American Cast Iron Pipe Company, 90

American Home Products, 100–101, 185–187

American Medical Association (AMA), 91–92

arbitration, 220–234; as condition of employment, 223, 254; development of law and, 227; discovery and, 225; employer bias in, 224, 227, 234; judicial review of, 225, 226; lack of benefits and protections of courts in, 224–226; lack of

About the Author

Raymond F. Gregory is an attorney who has been engaged in the practice of employment discrimination law for more than thirty-five years. He lives with his wife in South Salem, New York.